TRIBUTE TO WILLIAM WIL

Thy country, Wilberforce, with just disdain,

Hears thee, by cruel men and impious, call'd

Fanatic, for thy zeal to loose th' enthrall'd

From exile, public sale, and slav'ry's chain.

Friend of the poor, the wrong'd, the fetter-gall'd,

Fear not lest labour such as thine be vain!

Thou hast achiev'd a part; hast gain'd the ear

Of Britain's senate to thy glorious cause;

Hope smiles, joy springs, and tho' cold caution pause

And weave delay, the better hour is near,

That shall remunerate thy toils severe

By peace for Afric, fenc'd with British laws.

Enjoy what thou hast won, esteem and love

From all the just on earth, and all the blest above!

—William Cowper (1731–1800)
SONNET TO WILLIAM WILBERFORCE, ESQ.

"It is my sincere hope that our next generation will be able to build on the example of William Wilberforce and the many modern-day Wilberforces as they work to right wrong and build better communities. Really working together as communities has largely eluded humans throughout history. Yet, we have a moment in time today where we can do just that."

—*Floyd Flake, President of Wilberforce University, former Congressman and Senior Pastor, Greater Allen Cathedral, New York*

"Leadership and character are essential for engaging the culture and making a better world. It is at the core of our college curriculum for the next generation. William Wilberforce and his Clapham colleagues show the way to the essentials of leadership and character, engaging and working with others, while never compromising principle."

—*J. Stanley Oakes, President, The King's College, New York*

"William Wilberforce led the great moral struggle against the slave trade with passion born of conviction. He was a man of profound faith, but also a man of reason. His convictions were the fruit of prayer and reflection. In this, he was true to the insight that faith must seek understanding if it is to be efficacious in the lives of men, women, and societies. Today, as in Wilberforce's time, we are faced with the need for social reform and moral renewal. So, we must urgently be about the business of training faithful young people to engage the culture in thoughtful ways. This volume draws inspiring lessons from Wilberforce and his modern-day successors, and challenges readers to 'go and do likewise.' "

—*Robert P. George, McCormick Professor of Jurisprudence and Director of the James Madison Program in American Ideals and Institutions, Princeton University*

"This book will be of great benefit to your church community. It is an effective vehicle for 'transforming conversation'—the kind that leads people to actively engage the culture. Wilberforce's character, faith, courage, and leadership are a wonderfully relevant example for today's world. This book is no ordinary Bible study. It makes an irresistible call to action for building a better world."

—*Dr. Geoff Tunnicliffe, International Director of the World Evangelical Alliance*

"Wilberforce's commitment to the 'reformation of manners,' what we would call the 'transformation of culture,' was accomplished by his steadfast determination and ability to be a networker and encourager as a politician with the ethical principles that derived from his deep faith. This book outlines a way that we can all use our time and talents to the same end."

—*Jean Bethke Elshtain, Laura Spelman Rockefeller Professor of Social and Political Ethics, University of Chicago Divinity School*

BETTER HOUR
CREATING THE

LESSONS FROM WILLIAM WILBERFORCE

Edited by Chuck Stetson

STROUD&HALL
PUBLISHERS

Research and editorial development by Kevin Belmonte
Edited by Cullen W. Schippe
Cover and interior design by Lynda Hodge, Monotype, LLC, Baltimore, MD
Cover illustration by Clint Hansen
Composition by Monotype, LLC, Baltimore, MD

Stroud & Hall Publishers
P.O. Box 27210
Macon, GA 31221

www.stroudhall.com

Library of Congress Cataloging-in-Publication Data
  Creating the better hour : lessons from William Wilberforce / edited by Chuck Stetson ;
foreword by Rick Warren.
    p. cm.
  1. Christian life—Textbooks.   2. Church and social problems—Textbooks.
3. Wilberforce, William, 1759–1833.   I. Stetson, Chuck.
  BV4501.3.C737 2007
  283.092—dc22
  [B]
                        2007035433

ISBN-13: 978-0-9796462-1-8

1 2 3 4 5   11 10 09 08 07

contents

PART III
Wilberforce as a Model for Effecting Change

PART IV

Foreword

◉ Although he lived two hundred years before my time, William Wilberforce has been one of the greatest influences on my life. Both his character and his mission are worthy of deep consideration.

Wilberforce was a man of great purpose. He understood that the purpose for having influence is to speak up for those who have no influence, and he used his God-given talents, position, relationships, and fortune to make a difference in the world. On October 28, 1787, he wrote down in his journal this personal mission statement: "God Almighty has set before me two great objects: the suppression of the Slave Trade and the reformation of manners."

Wilberforce's life and mission show how God's power is unleashed whenever we answer God's call to live out the Gospel. That power can accomplish the impossible and bring about, in the words of the poet, a "better hour."

When Wilberforce set out to rid the British Empire of slavery, most people thought it was impossible. The economics of the slave trade were deeply rooted in England's way of life. Yet he saw slaves as fellow creatures precious in the sight of God—as brothers and sisters—and he knew he could not fail them. Despite years of struggle and personal suffering, Wilberforce refused to give up—he knew that he was on God's side in the struggle and that with God all things are possible!

Another of Wilberforce's great examples of "faith in action" is how he and his friends drew together people from diverse viewpoints and organizations—government, business, and churches—to fight against slavery. He understood that all sectors of society—public, private, and the faith community—must work together in order to defeat major social problems such as the slave trade. This fight took years of hard work and persistence in spite of disappointments. In the end, Wilberforce and his friends succeeded.

We still have unfinished work today when it comes to slavery. More than a century after Wilberforce's death, bonded labor, human trafficking (much of it sex trafficking), and other forms of human degradation and enslavement still exist. The "global giants" of spiritual emptiness, extreme poverty, pandemic disease, rampant illiteracy, and corruption in leadership oppress billions of people on our planet today.

I hope that as you read and study CREATING THE BETTER HOUR, you'll be inspired to walk in the footsteps of William Wilberforce. I hope his example will compel you to work together with others to defeat the evil giants that loom over the twenty-first century.

Wilberforce made no excuses. He was a frail man who was sick most of his adult life, yet he never gave up. Drawing strength from prayer, his daily study of the Bible, and the support of his close friends, he worked tirelessly in order to fulfill his great mission.

Today our world needs a new generation of people like Wilberforce. I pray this book spurs you on to make a difference just as he did.

—*Dr. Rick Warren*
THE PURPOSE DRIVEN LIFE
Saddleback Church, Lake Forest, CA

Preface

The year 2007 is the 200th anniversary of the abolition of the British and the U.S. slave trade. One man in British Parliament, William Wilberforce, led the British effort to abolish the slave trade and was highly influential on the American effort. Before his death, Wilberforce achieved the emancipation of all slaves in the British Empire at a huge financial and economic cost to England. The emancipation cost 20 million pounds. Historian Seymour Drescher documented that Britain additionally paid for the much higher costs of sugar and food from the West Indies and effectively committed econocide—the British killed their economy for over a generation so that they could rid themselves of barbaric treatment of human beings in slavery.

During this time period, Wilberforce was also a prime catalyst for reshaping English society. He was a leader in changing the world around him from an oppressive society in which the rich in London gambled and womanized while seventy-five percent of children died before adulthood. The children of the poor often worked eighteen-hour days as chimney sweeps or workers in unsafe textile mills. Wilberforce lifted up the poor and the oppressed in society, instituting the first child labor laws and so much more. And he did it all through the power and persuasion of his character.

France, in the early days of the Industrial Revolution, had similar conditions: the rich did well and the poor barely had bread to eat. But the rich chose not to do anything about the poor and the oppressed. The people became violent, and France got a revolution. During the bloodiest period of the French Revolution, the Reign of Terror, thousands were sent to the guillotine, including the King and the Queen.

England, facing the same conditions, was able to avoid revolution because of the efforts of Wilberforce and the Clapham Circle, wealthy men who saw that what was going on in the world around them was wrong and decided to engage what was wrong and change it for the better. As a consequence, England got reformation.

William Wilberforce, despite at times being disorganized and a "muddler," as biographer John Pollock notes, was at the heart of change and a driving force with his colleagues in Clapham. He is truly a remarkable, unsung hero of the humanities and a giant in his own time—a commoner in England who was buried in Westminster Abbey in the company of kings and queens. Sitting in his library on Sunday, October 28, 1787, he wrote in his diary that "God Almighty has set before me two great objects, the suppression of the Slave Trade and the reformation of manners," the latter being the reform of contemporary society.

Wilberforce was at one time well known not only in England, but also in the United States, the Caribbean, and around the world. In 1856, Wilberforce was acknowledged by Abraham Lincoln as a person that "every school boy" in America knew. The emancipation leader Frederick Douglass saluted the energy of Wilberforce and his co-workers who "finally thawed the British heart into sympathy for the slave, and moved the strong arm of government in mercy to put an end to this bondage. Let no American, especially no colored American, withhold generous recognition of this stupendous achievement—a triumph of right over wrong, of good over evil and a victory for the whole human race."

Why don't we know more about Wilberforce today? One of the answers is that recognizing the unselfish concern for others that Wilberforce demonstrated has gone out of fashion. Eric Williams, an Oxford-educated historian who later became the Prime Minister of Trinidad and Tobago, wrote his doctoral thesis on this subject. His thesis, THE ECONOMIC ASPECT OF THE WEST INDIAN SLAVE TRADE AND SLAVERY, was considered an important contribution to research on the subject and was published in 1944 in Williams' CAPITALISM AND SLAVERY. His theory of history was that people are motivated by their economic self-interest. According to a leading historian today, most historians have adopted this approach to history. Wilberforce and the Clapham Circle are a contradiction to this theory of history because they fought for changes that were not in their economic self-interest. Their fight against economic self-interest leads many to downplay the incredible accomplishments of Wilberforce and the Clapham Circle.

A second answer is the misunderstanding today of how the Christian faith has grown and changed society. The faith has stayed involved with seeking after the least, the last, and the lost as Jesus did and pointed out in Matthew 25:31–45. Scholars are beginning to again recognize that the phenomenal growth of Christianity during the Roman Empire had its seeds in this focus. The people who took care of the sick during the two plagues of the third century were the Christians; the pagans fled the cities. In A.D. 364 the Emperor Julian the Apostate wrote an angry letter to a pagan priest in Galatia in Turkey complaining that the Greeks took care of the Greeks, the Romans took care of the Romans, but the Christians took care of everyone.

After his "great change," his conversion to a deep faith in Jesus Christ, Wilberforce devoted his whole life to improving the conditions of the least, the last, and the lost. This belief was at the heart of his two great objects, which he pursued unrelentingly all of his life. As Wilberforce lay dying on July 26, 1833, he was able to know that the emancipation of slavery in the British Empire had finally been achieved. He had also witnessed many other improvements in England, such as better living conditions for the poor, particularly children who had become better protected from work at an early age through the first child labor laws. If Wilberforce had lived longer, he would have seen the birth of the YMCA in England, the Salvation Army, the Boys and Girls Scouts, and the many other nonprofits founded as Christian organizations in response to the Christian focus on serving others: a direct result of Wilberforce's second objective in life.

This book, a tribute to William Wilberforce, is a collection of short articles by leading scholars and luminaries. The articles will illuminate how Wilberforce and his friends—who were living in Clapham, England, in conditions of extreme wealth—reformed the depraved and self-indulgent world around them and thus can be an inspiration to us today.

These reforms changed the known world for the better, abolishing the world slave trade (where Britain had more than fifty percent of the slave ships) and eventually achieving emancipation for all slaves in the British Empire. Reforms also included implementation of the first child labor laws, prison reform, Parliamentary reform, and the creation of societies (today called nonprofits) to improve the conditions of the poor. Wilberforce himself either started or was involved in sixty-nine such British societies in addition to his duties as a prominent member of Parliament and close colleague and friend of the Prime Minister.

The British approach diametrically opposed the French approach under the same corrupt conditions in Paris. It is also interesting to note that five other nations in Europe—Spain, Portugal, Sweden, Denmark and Holland—had slave colonies. Yet, like France, none of these five had an antislavery crusade of which to speak. The absence of a popular movement in Sweden, Denmark, and Holland is particularly striking in light of the fact that these nations had higher literacy rates than England.

In today's world, there are many similarities to these early days of the Industrial Revolution, when the great accumulation of wealth by a few people left many others behind. There is a similar dark side to Globalization.

This book will examine conditions in England in the eighteenth century and the transatlantic slave trade. Part I will focus on how William Wilberforce and his Clapham colleagues planned and organized the improvement of the world around them in England. We will look at the passion and character of Wilberforce and specifically his motivation and persistence in achieving his two great objectives in life, "the suppression of the Slave Trade and the reformation of manners."

Part II will examine the unfinished business of slavery today, both narrowly and broadly defined: How does the dark side of the Industrial Revolution compare to the dark side of

Globalization? Part III will look at how cultures are changed today, and individuals that have been engaged today in removing forms of slavery will tell how they have been following in the steps of Wilberforce. Part IV will explore a life commitment to work on behalf of others.

William Wilberforce and the Clapham Circle were truly extraordinary Christian reformers. They changed their times for the better. Our goal in creating this book is to recognize them for their great work and continuing influence on leaders today engaged in the same tradition and tasks.

—Chuck Stetson
October 2007

Introduction: Your
Biblical Faith in Action

There is a widely circulated and most likely spurious account concerning President Calvin Coolidge—a man of very few words. When he returned from Church one Sunday morning, his wife asked him the topic of the preacher's sermon. "Sin," replied the president. "What did he have to say about it?" she pressed. "He was against it!"

It is very easy to be against evil. We are all guided by our faith and God's grace to avoid evil in all its forms and manifestations. But Biblical believers are not defined by what they are against. They are defined by what they are *for*! If William Wilberforce had simply been against slavery and against the evils of his day, he might have a small footnote in history as a member of the British Parliament. He may even have garnered a larger historical role as a Lord or as Prime Minister.

William Wilberforce was driven by his faith to be *for* something. He was for the complete cessation of the slave trade. He was for total abolition of slavery and the emancipation of all those held in bondage. He was for education, for better conditions for prisoners, for full rights for Catholics, for prevention of cruelty to animals, and for a whole host of other causes that in their aggregate effected a reform of the manners and morals of British society.

In short, William Wilberforce was for creating a better hour for humankind—an hour in which goodness is more fashionable than evil, in which generosity is more fashionable than greed, and in which freedom is more fashionable than slavery. This positive approach was based on persuasion, not demagoguery. That persuasion was shared at dinner tables across England. It used symbols and public relations. It worked to gain for goodness a positive press. Perhaps most importantly the approach was rooted in communal action. Wilberforce understood that one person can make a powerful difference, yet he knew the power of people joined together in one spirit to act decisively and effectively.

This book is meant to be so much more than a few essays on the life and legacy of William Wilberforce. It is designed to engage you in the lessons from the life of this great Christian citizen. Although Wilberforce did indeed proclaim the Reign of God with his words and in his writing, his primary proclamation was his activity in society. Every Christian and the whole Body of Christ are called to put Biblical Faith into action. All are called to recognize Jesus in the hungry, the thirsty, the naked, the enslaved, the imprisoned, and the sick, and to work tirelessly to improve their lot. Surprisingly enough God's own judgment is based on just such recognition and the actions that flow from that recognition.

Transforming Conversation

One of the best tools to ensure that recognition of Christ in those least brothers and sisters is something as simple as conversation. Wilberforce was a master of conversation. He was broadly read. He had charm and poise. He was very witty indeed. Within his circle of friends, however, conversation was so much more than a way to amuse or to pass the time or to gossip. The conversation Wilberforce had with Rev. John Newton transformed William from a bon vivant to a passionate public advocate. Conversation is a way to share ideas, certainly, but it is also a way to explore issues, generate passion and zeal, effect personal change, and support one another in action.

Think of some of the great conversations in the Bible. The conversation between King David and the Prophet Nathan brought about the king's repentance. The conversation between Jesus and Nicodemus revealed the need to be born again of water and the Spirit. The conversation with the Samaritan woman at the well led to the announcement of Jesus as a Savior—not just for the Jews, but also for other nations. The conversation of the two disciples on the road to Emmaus explained why the Messiah had to suffer and that he was alive and in their midst. The conversation Peter had at the house of Cornelius opened membership in Christ's Body to all tribes and nations. The conversation between Philip and the Ethiopian eunuch sped the Good News into Northern Africa.

In the spirit of these transforming conversations, each chapter in this book has an Extended Observation—a guide to reflection and conversation. The study process is based on four observable approaches on the part of William Wilberforce.

1. He did not simply read the Word of God—he *attended* to it. He let it have its way with him, and he took seriously the messages revealed.

2. Wilberforce *engaged* that Word in his life and in society. For him the Word was a treasure to be shared and to be revealed to others—always in action.

3. Wilberforce *moved* constantly *forward*. Despite setbacks, personal trials, slander, hostility, and even threats, he moved relentlessly toward his goal.

4. He *prayed*. His spirit of prayer and devotion held him together and propelled him back to the Word, to engagement, and to moving ever onward until his goals were accomplished.

So each Reflection & Conversation section is based on those four action terms:

Attend to the Word

Engage

Move Forward

Pray

In This Together

Although the lessons from William Wilberforce provide a great source of individual inspiration and reflection, the ideal way to put one's Biblical faith into action is to work in a community of friends. Christianity is not the faith of loners. Of its very nature it is the Body of Christ—the community of believers. In this Body, people can set aside squabbles and differences to work for the greater glory of God, for freedom, for justice, and for a reform of society. And so, if at all possible, go through these lessons with a trusted group of friends. Be open to one another. Challenge one another. Encourage one another.

There is no prize for going through this book at breakneck speed. Take your time; for though the need for justice, freedom, and peace is great, God is not holding a stopwatch.

Remember that perhaps the greatest lesson from William Wilberforce is perseverance. Welcome to the lessons in this book. Strengthened by what you learn and share, you can more effectively put your biblical faith into action. You can help make goodness fashionable and create the better hour for people in need and for the world in which you live.

PART I

WILLIAM WILBERFORCE
& THE CLAPHAM CIRCLE
CREATED THE BETTER HOUR

William Wilberforce

By John Pollock

John Pollock is one of today's leading scholars on William Wilberforce. He is a celebrated contemporary author with over 1.2 million books in print. He has authored the full biographies of William Wilberforce as well as of Billy Graham and of General Gordon of Khartoum, among others. In researching the biography of Wilberforce, Mr. Pollock was able to access a number of letters and correspondence from the decedents of Wilberforce and those that knew Wilberforce that has significantly advanced the scholarship on Wilberforce and his Clapham Circle friends. The following essay by John Pollock, a celebrated contemporary biographer, is a slightly expanded version of an acclaimed lecture he delivered in February 1996 at the National Portrait Gallery in London.

One evening in 1787, a young English Member of Parliament pored over papers by candlelight in his home beside the Houses of Parliament. William Wilberforce had been asked to propose the abolition of the slave trade, although almost all Englishmen thought the trade necessary, if nasty, and that economic ruin would follow if it stopped. Only very few thought the slave trade wrong, evil.

Wilberforce studied first the state of slaves in the West Indies. What he found disturbed him greatly. Then he looked at the harm done in Africa from the slave trade and this disturbed him more. Then he examined the conditions for the wretched men, women, and children as they were shipped—like bales, a black cargo—across the Atlantic. And he was appalled.

The death rate on this "Middle Passage" was dreadful. Every dead slave meant loss to a slave ship's owner, yet hundreds were allowed to die every year at terrible humanitarian cost. Wilberforce hesitated no longer. "So enormous, so dreadful," he told the House of Commons later, "so irremediable did the trade's wickedness appear that my own mind was completely made up for Abolition. . . . Let the consequences be what they would, I from this time determined that I would never rest until I had effected its abolition."

That was a key moment in British and world history. For a few months later, on Sunday October 28, 1787, he wrote in his Journal the words that have become famous: "God Almighty has set before me two great objects, the suppression of the Slave Trade and the Reformation of Manners"—in modern terms, "habits, attitudes, morals." By achieving his first object—after a long battle—he made possible the second.

Let's look at William Wilberforce in his prime. As contemporary accounts make plain, he was an ugly little man with too long a nose. Yet he was a man of great charm. He had a marvelous smile and laughed a lot; he was a man of wit. His voice made you long to hear him more. Underneath lay a deep penitence, but his overriding quality was a sunshine of spirit. His contemporary, the poet Robert Southey, wrote: "there is such a constant hilarity in every look and motion, such a sweetness in all his tones, such a benignity in all his thoughts, words, and actions, that . . . you can feel nothing but love and admiration for a creature of so happy and blessed a nature."

Significantly, he was a stirring speaker with extraordinary debating powers. Prime Minister William Pitt said that he possessed "the greatest natural eloquence of all the men I ever knew." In fact Pitt valued his oratory so much that he once offered to postpone the meeting of Parliament for ten days rather than face the session without him. Such an estimate from a renowned orator in an age of renowned orators that included Edmund Burke and Charles James Fox was widely shared. Wilberforce's speeches, one Parliamentary reporter wrote, "are so distinct and melodious, that the most hostile ear hangs on them delighted."

William Wilberforce was born in 1759, the same year as his great contemporary, William Pitt the Younger, and a decade before his other eminent contemporaries Napoleon Bonaparte and the Duke of Wellington. His father was a rich merchant of Hull, which made his success in politics the more surprising, as a mercantile origin was despised in that era of aristocrats and landed gentry.

Wilberforce's father died young, and his mother was grateful when her Wimbledon brother-in-law and his childless wife,

William and Hannah Wilberforce, had little William to stay for long periods.

These relatives were despised evangelicals, friends of the preacher George Whitefield, a leader in the first Great Awakening, and John Newton, best known today as the author of "Amazing Grace." Newton, an old seadog, ex-naval deserter, ex-lecher, and ex-slave-trader who had been converted slowly in and after a storm at sea, fascinated the boy with his yarns. Newton showed little William "How sweet the Name of Jesus sounds" until his mother, horrified that he was turning "Methodist," took him away.

Later, when Wilberforce had graduated from Cambridge and was a young MP and "man about town," Newton said sadly that nothing seemed left of his faith except a more moral outlook than was usual among men of fashion.

Wilberforce had entered the House of Commons as Member for Hull at the age of twenty-one. Then, at a crisis in the political fortunes of William Pitt, his great friend and the youngest Prime Minister in British history, Wilberforce brilliantly won the important seat of Yorkshire. He became one of the two "knights of the Shire" and an immense help to Pitt. In fact it was Yorkshire that made Wilberforce a man of power and significance in politics; many thought he might one day be Prime Minister. Thus, in his early twenties, Wilberforce had reached a position of considerable power and eminence. Welcome in the highest circles, privy to Cabinet secrets, the closest friend of the Prime Minister, Wilberforce had a future that was bright with opportunities.

But that winter and spring of 1784–1785, Wilberforce, aged twenty-five, underwent a deep, long, drawn-out experience of conversion or, rather, a rededication or rediscovery of Christ. He described it as the "great change." Humanly speaking, it came about when he invited his former schoolmaster Isaac Milner, a don at Cambridge, to be his companion on a journey by carriage in the south of France. Wilberforce had not realized that Milner was an evangelical and ridiculed evangelicals mercilessly. But as a result of their conversations and reading, Wilberforce was forced to think. He returned to England in turmoil of soul, deeply conscious of his need for Christ yet loath to abandon his political ambitions or carefree social life. In his distress he turned to John Newton.

Newton led Wilberforce to peace. Equally importantly, Newton stopped him throwing up politics for the church: "It is hoped and believed that the Lord has raised you up for the good of His church and the good of the nation." But what was to be his new purpose? "The first years I was in Parliament," Wilberforce wrote later, "I did nothing—nothing to any purpose. My own distinction was my darling object." But that changed forever as he came to believe that God was calling him to champion the liberty of the oppressed—as a parliamentarian. "My walk," he concluded, "is a public one. My business is in the world; and I must mix in the assemblies of men, or quit the post which Providence seems to have assigned me."

Soon after his conversion Wilberforce was approached with a suggestion that he take up the cause of Abolition. He later marked his entry into the battle to a day in May 1787 when, lolling beneath an oak tree, Pitt said to him, "Wilberforce, why don't you give notice of a motion on the subject of the slave trade?" But the principal agents in securing Wilberforce were Captain Sir Charles Middleton of the Royal Navy and his artist wife.

Middleton was the father-in-law of one of Wilberforce's easygoing Cambridge friends and one of the only two open evangelicals in the House. He was Comptroller of the navy and was chiefly responsible for its high state of preparation when the French Revolutionary War came. At the end of his life, as Lord Barham, he was first Lord of the Admiralty and the mastermind of the celebrated Trafalgar campaign. As a young man he had won fame in the West Indies; the surgeon on his ship, James Ramsay, had become a rector in St. Kitts until his care and love for the slaves caused the white planters to force him out. Ramsay was now the Middleton's rector in Kent, longing to see the abolition of the slave trade—and of slavery. Both men knew that a trade considered so vital to the interests of the British Empire could be suppressed only by costly, radical reform and parliamentary action.

Abolition of the Slave Trade

Abolition of the slave trade, the first of Wilberforce's "two great objects," was perhaps the greatest moral achievement of the British people, putting right a horrible wrong. For Britain two hundred years ago was the world's leading slave-trading nation; uprooting the vile practice threatened the annual trade of hundreds of ships, thousands of sailors, and hundreds of millions of pounds sterling. It took Wilberforce and his colleagues twenty years, and the abolition of slavery itself nearly thirty more.

At first Wilberforce had "no doubt of our success," but his early optimism was tempered by a warning from John Wesley. Written just the day before the great evangelist lapsed into a coma and died, the letter was marked by Wilberforce as "Wesley's last words." "Dear Sir," Wesley wrote, "Unless the divine power has raised you to be as Athanasius *contra mundum* [Athanasius against the world], I see not how you can go through your glorious enterprise in opposing that execrable villainy, which is the scandal of religion, of England, and of human nature. Unless God has raised you up for this very thing, you will be worn out by the opposition of men and devils. But if God be for you, who can be against you?"

The fight was indeed costly and long. Twice Wilberforce was waylaid and physically assaulted. Certainly he became the most vilified man in England. Many people denied outright that there were problems with slavery. A group of admirals even claimed that the happiest days of an African's life was when he was shipped away from the barbarities of his home life. And most people, including most members of Parliament, feared change. Such radicalism, critics said, would threaten sacred rights, property, and liberties, not only in the colonies but at home. After all, the horrifying events of the French Revolution were soon on everybody's minds and news of the slave revolts in the West Indies sent shudders down many spines.

To make matters worse, Wilberforce was opposed by some of England's greatest heroes and most powerful forces, including the Royal Family, most of the Cabinet, and powerful vested interests. Admiral Lord Nelson wrote from his flagship, Victory, that he would not allow the rights of the plantation owners to be infringed "while I have an arm to fight in their defense or a tongue to launch my voice against the damnable doctrine of Wilberforce and his hypocritical allies."

Wilberforce's initial strategy was to secure abolition by international convention, since obviously the British traders were not going to agree to abolition if other nations simply seized their share of the market. But his early hopes were dashed.

The strain of preparing the massive case led to exhaustion, fever, and a breakdown in Wilberforce's health. Many thought he was dying. "That little fellow," his doctors declared, had "not the stamina to last a fortnight." Pitt had to introduce the first moves, which led to a Privy Council inquiry. The doctors treated Wilberforce with opium. At that time, it was considered to be a pure drug with no moral question involved. He never became an addict but the prescribed doses, for the rest of his life, must have made him more muddled at times and certainly worsened his eyesight.

Recovered, Wilberforce introduced a motion on May 10, 1788, to consider the Privy Council report (which was a damning indictment of the slave trade). Though feeling unwell, he spoke for three and a half hours and was supported wholeheartedly by Pitt, Burke, and Fox who followed him. His conclusion was stirring:

> *Sir, the nature and all the circumstances of the trade are now laid open to us. We can no longer plead ignorance. We cannot evade it. We may spurn it. We may kick it out of the way. But we cannot turn aside so as to avoid seeing it. For it is brought now so directly before our eyes that this House must decide and must justify to all the world and to its own conscience, the rectitude of the grounds of its decision . . ..*
> *Let not Parliament be the only body that is insensible to the principles of natural justice. Let us make reparation to Africa, as far as we can, by establishing trade upon true commercial principles, and we shall soon find the rectitude of our conduct rewarded by the benefits of a regular and growing commerce.*

Swayed by the facts, yet worried by their implications, the House was uneasy. Wilberforce had to make the trade so insufferably odious that the House would vote for outright abolition. But—and this was possibly a mistake—he ended by proposing twelve resolutions instead of a single, clear-cut decision, and the Commons turned aside.

As the campaign gathered momentum over the next years Wilberforce faced tremendous opposition—from planters, merchants, ship owners, the Royal Family, and the powerful ports of Bristol and Liverpool. One of Wilberforce's friends wrote to him cheerfully, "I shall expect to read of you being carbonadoed by West Indian planters, barbecued by African merchants and eaten by Guinea captains, but do not be daunted, for—I will write your epitaph!"

To face the onslaught Wilberforce needed all his parliamentary skill, his patience, his sense of humor, his faith, and prayer. "Surely," wrote the slave owners' agent in Antigua, "the Enthusiastic rage of Mr. Wilberforce and his friends cannot prevail in a matter of such consequence to the Colonies and the Mother Country." But others of his opponents were not so sanguine. The agent for Jamaica and its slave owners complained, "It is necessary to watch him as he is blessed with a very sufficient quantity of that Enthusiastic Spirit, which is so far from yielding that it grows more vigorous from blows."

When war broke out with revolutionary France in 1793, Pitt, once hot for abolition, cooled off, putting national interests first. Friends tried to make Wilber—as his friends called him—cool off too, but he replied that while in politics it is sometimes expedient to push and sometimes to slacken, as regards the slave trade, "when the actual commission of guilt is in question, a man who fears God is not at liberty" to stop pushing. He, Wilberforce, would never sacrifice the great cause to political convenience or personal feeling.

In the end it was the war that brought victory at last. Pitt died in 1806. An ingenious discovery by James Stephen, the maritime lawyer, showed that abolition would actually help the war effort. The opposition was outflanked, the waverers won over. The new Prime Minister, Lord Grenville, himself introduced the Abolition Bill into the House of Lords.

On February 23, 1807, after twenty years of tireless campaigning by Wilberforce, the House of Commons debated the bill and it was obvious it would pass this time. There was a most dramatic moment when Attorney General Samuel Romilly, in his speech, contrasted Napoleon and Wilberforce retiring to rest that night—Napoleon in pomp and power, yet his sleep tormented by the blood he had spilled and Wilberforce returning after the vote to the bosom of his delighted family (actually Mrs. Wilberforce was a most tiresome woman and friends said you wouldn't know the definition of an angel unless you had watched Wilber with his wife), lying down in pure happiness knowing he had "preserved so many millions of his fellow creatures."

Before Romilly could finish, the House rose as one man and turned toward Wilberforce with Parliamentary cheers, "Hear, Hear! Hear, Hear!" Then somebody gave a most un-parliamentary "Hurrah!" And the House erupted in hurrahs. Wilberforce was scarcely aware of it. He sat, head bowed, tears streaming down his face. The bill was carried by 283 votes to 16. The odious slave trade was ended.

The Reformation of Manners

When Wilberforce and his great friend Henry Thornton went back after the vote in the small hours of the morning to Wilberforce's house nearby, Wilberforce said gaily, "Well, Henry, what shall we abolish next?" And Thornton, who had no sense of humor, replied gravely, "The lottery, I think." And indeed the lottery was abolished nine years later.

Actually, the struggle for the full abolition of slavery had only just begun. But Wilberforce's momentous victory in the abolition of the slave trade gave him unrivaled moral prestige to help forward his second great object—the reformation of manners, his campaign to remake England. This, which in some ways is the harder and less known of the two projects, is also the most interesting and relevant thing about him. It had been going in tandem with his abolition campaign since 1787.

The campaign had arisen from Wilberforce's compassion. Too many men and women were hanged. Venality, drunkenness, and the high crime rate arose from the general decadence— especially the corruption and irreligion of the trendsetters—not in those days pop stars and media moguls, but the nobility and landed gentry. The "high civilization" of eighteenth-century England was built on the slave trade, mass poverty, child labor, and political corruption in high places. As one historian wrote, there was little to choose between the morals of the English and French aristocracies in the century before the French Revolution.

Knowing that many aristocrats pretended to be worse than they were because it was fashionable to be loose in morals and skeptical in religion, Wilberforce set out to change the country by changing the moral climate, making goodness fashionable, and restoring respect for the law in all classes. He hit on an ingenious scheme. It is important to realize that the eighteenth century was a hierarchical age, and so changing the leaders meant changing society. And in those days the Crown did not normally prosecute; it was left to the victim or to the local authorities, which often left the big fish alone.

Wilberforce knew that the first proclamation of a new monarch's reign was a ceremonial one on behalf of "the

Encouragement of Piety and Virtue and for the Preventing of Vice, Profaneness and Immorality." Such proclamations had always been a rather formal and useless exercise except once, in the reign of William and Mary when a society had been formed to promote its aims and had considerable effect for some years: a Society for the Reformation of Manners.

Wilberforce decided to revive the society. Covering his tracks by "an amiable confusion" he managed to get King George III to reissue his proclamation in June 1787 and then persuade many bishops, dukes, and other notables to join the newly founded "Proclamation Society" and do their best to fulfill its aims. Few realized that the young member from Yorkshire had anything to do with it. Thus he began to give the trendsetters of society a strong social conscience and eagerness to help the poor. The movement caught on.

Interestingly, the campaign was never specifically religious. Wilberforce never tried to enlist the religious or even the professedly moral. Some of the grandees whose support he gained were in fact notoriously dissolute. But Wilberforce believed strongly that the destinies of a nation could best be influenced by deeply committed followers of Christ, and that conversion to Christ was a person's most important political action as well as religious.

But vibrant faith was out of fashion when he started, most of all among the upper classes. John Wesley had hardly touched the nobility and gentry. George Whitefield had done so, but his influence had been limited. As Wilberforce's friend and fellow-reformer Hannah More wrote, "To expect to reform the poor while the opulent are corrupt, is to throw odors into the stream while the springs are poisoned." Soon, wrote Wilberforce about his own class, "to believe will be deemed the indication of a feeble mind and a contracted understanding."

Wilberforce set out to change that too. He wrote a big book with an immense title, generally contracted to A PRACTICAL VIEW (of true faith as contrasted with its contemporary imitation). This became a best seller. He also thought out "launchers," phrases or gambits to use at dinner parties to turn the talk to deeper directions. Perhaps most important of all was his own vibrant personality.

A circle of friends and fellow followers of Christ grew around Wilberforce's informal leadership. It included a royal prince, George III's first cousin the Second Duke of Gloucester whom the Prince Regent hated for his moral stand and nicknamed (unfairly) "Silly Billy." He was a great help as a royal patron. Another friend was Lord Belgrave, later First Marquess of Westminster. Yet another friend was Josiah Wedgwood, the now internationally famous potter, with whom Wilberforce designed his celebrated "tract": a Wedgwood piece with the profile of a negro slave at the center and the question inscribed around it, "Am I not a Man and Brother?"

Wilberforce taught too, to the fury of the radicals of the day, that social reform must have a spiritual base, that reformers and educators who reject God will flaw their programs and end by hurting the poor.

There is little doubt that Wilberforce changed the moral outlook of Great Britain, and this at a time when the British Empire was growing and Britain was the world's leading society. The reformation of manners grew into Victorian virtues and Wilberforce touched the world when he made goodness fashionable. Contrast the late eighteenth century (you must allow a broad brush in a brief essay like this) with its loose morals and corrupt public life, with the mid-nineteenth century. Whatever its faults, nineteenth-century British public life became famous for its emphasis on character, morals, and justice and the British business world famous for integrity. Most of those who ruled India and the colonies had a strong sense of mission, to do good for those they ruled—a far cry from the original colonizers.

The half-century after Wilberforce saw a marvelous flowering of the Christian faith and a myriad of applications in countless constructive enterprises. In the process the Bible became the best-loved book of the newly literate. Christian attitudes molded the British character, a Christian social conscience attacked abuses left by the more pagan age that coincided with the early Industrial Revolution, and Christian compassion relieved its victims.

William Wilberforce is proof that a man can change his times, though he cannot do it alone. Wilberforce's own philanthropies were legion and he impoverished himself in the process. He was described as a "Prime Minister of a cabinet of philanthropists." But importantly, he allowed no bulkhead between faith and philanthropy. His "good works" included prisons and prisoners of war, hospitals and the poor, reforms in India and around the world, as well as in Africa.

It was a contemporary libel, painful to Wilberforce and quite untrue, that he cared for black slaves but nothing for white "wage slaves." William Cobbett, the radical journalist, in the hope of preventing emancipation, put about the accusation that he believed would harm the English working class. The libel had little effect on Wilberforce's contemporaries who regarded him as always on the side of the poor, but it was repeated as if proven in a celebrated book of 1917 and was widely accepted for sixty years. You can fault Wilberforce's judgment over this or that issue, but never his concern for human beings in need.

Wilberforce was also a great lover of animals and a founder of the Royal Society for the Prevention of Cruelty to Animals, which led me to a lovely story. His last surviving great-grandson, who was then over a hundred and blind, told me how his father, as a small boy, was walking with Wilberforce on a hill near Bath when they saw a poor carthorse being cruelly whipped by the carter as he struggled to pull a load of stone up the hill. The little liberator expostulated with the carter who began to swear at him and tell him to mind his own business, and so forth. Suddenly the carter stopped and said, "Are you Mr. Wilberforce? . . . Then I will never beat my horse again!"

But for all Wilberforce's myriad philanthropies—at one stage he was active in sixty-nine different initiatives—the call of the slaves always came first. Full emancipation had always been his ultimate aim. When the planters failed to turn their slaves into a free peasantry as he had hoped once abolition of the slave trade dried up the supply, Wilberforce knew he had to "go to war again." His failure depressed him, and when a friend suggested that the condition of the climbing boys (sent naked up chimneys to clean them) was as bad as that of the slaves, he was "a little scandalized." His reaction showed how much Wilberforce understood the real enormity of slavery. It was not so much the occasions of cruelty but the "habitual immorality and degradation and often grinding suffering of the poor victims of this wicked system." The evil of slavery was the "systematic misery of their situation."

Wilberforce said that in 1827. By then he felt he was too old to finish the task of the complete abolition of slavery. Many of the original abolitionists and his closest friends had died. And Wilberforce, now in his late sixties, was in constant ill health. His head had fallen forward on his chest. He even wore a steel frame to remedy the condition (this would not have been known by posterity had he not left his spare one behind, "decently clad in a towel," and wrote to his host to send it on!).

In 1821 Wilberforce had brought in Thomas Fowell Buxton to lead the final campaign. Frail though he was, he cheered from the sidelines. Just three months before his death he was persuaded to propose a last petition against slavery at Maidstone. "I had never thought to appear in public again," he began, "but it shall never be said that William Wilberforce is silent while the slaves require his help."

Wilberforce was on his deathbed when he heard that the Emancipation Bill had passed the House of Commons on July 26, 1833. All the slaves in the British Empire were to be freed in one year's time and their masters were to be given £20 million compensation. Wilberforce rejoiced and three days later he died. "It is a singular fact," Buxton wrote later, "that on the very night on which we were successfully engaged in the House of Commons, in passing the clause of the Act of Emancipation— one of the most important clauses ever enacted . . . the spirit of our friend left the world. The day which was the termination of his labors was the termination of his life."

By his last years, Wilberforce's name was said to be the greatest name in the land. An Italian diplomat remarked at an opening of Parliament that "every one contemplates this little old man, worn with age, and his head sunk upon his shoulders . . . as the Washington of humanity." Historian G. M. Trevelyan described abolition as "one of the turning events in the history of the world." But this is only the beginning of Wilberforce's incalculable legacy—to Britain, the United States, Africa, India—and countless other places, concerns, and people touched by his life and influence.

William Wilberforce lies buried in Westminster Abbey. In a red manuscript book in a country house I found an MP's description of the funeral—two royal dukes, the Lord Chancellor, the Speaker of the House of Commons, and four peers were the pallbearers as his coffin entered the Abbey. Behind, most MPs and many peers walked in procession.

The MP wrote in his diary that night: "The attendance was very great. The funeral itself with the exception of the choir of the Abbey was perfectly plain. The noblest and most fitting testimony to the estimation of the man."

Extended Observation

Reflection & Conversation

If this is your first serious contact with William Wilberforce, reflect on your initial impressions of the man and of his mission. How do you respond to this profile of him? If you are quite familiar with Wilberforce, what new insight or new facts did you glean from the Pollock article? If you are using this book in a group, begin your conversation by reviewing everyone's reactions and impressions.

Attend to the Word

Read Hebrews 11:8–10. Have someone in the group read the verses aloud. As the words are read, link this message with the life of William Wilberforce. How does this passage reflect the mission Wilberforce had. How did he look for the better hour for Britain? How did he look "forward to the city that has foundations, whose architect and builder is God?" After the reading, spend some time in silent reflection.

Engage

People want to know who they are and what their purpose is. When Wilberforce found his purpose, everything changed for him. Even though Wilberforce had serious health issues that at times led to exhaustion, fever, and near breakdown, God was able to use Wilberforce and his frailty to stand up for what was right. Focus this conversation on the need for a sense of purpose and mission.

1. What do you see as your purpose in life? Be as specific as you can.

2. Do you see this purpose as a God-given mission? Explain why or why not.
3. What role does your faith play in working out your purpose in life?
4. Express your life's purpose in a simple mission statement.

Move Forward

Wilberforce pressed forward with the bill to abolish the slave trade even though he kept on receiving opposition and was vilified. He persisted because it was part of his personal mission statement. Look at each of the three questions below. Discuss how each of them can propel you forward in a sense of mission and purpose. Keep in mind the verses from Hebrews as well.

1. What do you see as your biggest obstacle to a faith-filled sense of mission?
2. What do you see as your greatest help in living with a sense of mission?
3. What would you like to have accomplished in this mission one year from now?

Pray

> *Lord and Father of all, help us set out for a place unseen. Help us learn a great lesson from the life and legacy of William Wilberforce. Each of us has been created in your image. Each of us has a purpose. Each of us can help to bring about a better hour for the society in which we live. Help us work together to build and create a world of justice, love, and peace. And we ask this in the name of Jesus your Son. Amen.*

Wilberforce & the
Clapham Circle

By Clifford Hill

The Rev. Dr. Clifford Hill is a theologian and sociologist. In 2004, he published THE WILBERFORCE CONNECTION, *from which this essay is adapted.*

In 1919, a table was built into the south wall of Clapham Parish Church in London bearing the following inscription:

LET US PRAISE GOD

*For the memory and example of all the faithful departed who have worshipped in this church, and especially for the under named Servants of Christ sometimes called "*THE CLAPHAM SECT*" who in the latter part of the 18th and early part of the 19th centuries labored so abundantly for the increase of national righteousness and the conversion of the heathen and rested not until the curse of slavery was swept away from all parts of the British dominions—Charles Grant, Zachary Macaulay, Granville Sharp, John Shaw (Lord Teignmouth), James Stephen, Henry Thornton, John Thornton, Henry Venn, John Venn, William Wilberforce.*

"O God, we have heard with our ears, and our fathers have declared unto us, the noble works that thou didst in their days, and in the times before them."

In his efforts to abolish first the slave trade, and then slavery, from the British Empire, William Wilberforce was aided by a number of people, principally a group of men and women who lived in Clapham, England, then a suburb of London five miles from its center, and now part of London itself.

Although a number of the Clapham Circle lived in the village of Clapham, others did not, including some who were in the core leadership group. It was, however, a community in the strict sociological connotation of the term. It was a community of interest with its core in a geographical community. Its members shared a strong Christian commitment with a personal faith in God and an experience of Jesus as Lord and Savior. They also possessed a shared set of social values derived from the biblical basis of their faith and a shared commitment to the application of the Gospel to the great social issues of their day. They saw this in terms of a commitment to a moral, spiritual, and social transformation, with a particular focus on what they saw as the evils of slavery in the British Empire and the miseries of the poor in Britain.

In the 1780s, when a number of wealthy people moved there, Clapham was a pleasant village of some 2,000 inhabitants who wanted to live outside of London, but near enough to it to work there.

The Growth & Development of the Community

The community did not come together at Clapham and subsequently begin to discover its identity. Members gravitated to Clapham in order to be near to those who were like-minded. They each had a different story in regard to their Christian faith and what God had done in their lives. They usually found each other through the discovery of a shared commitment to social change and the embracing of a particular cause, such as the abolition of slavery. It was this, for example, that brought Granville Sharp and Zachary Macaulay into the community. Some, such as Lord Teignmouth, who were drawn to the community through a common commitment to India, moved to live around Clapham Common in order to be near to Wilberforce and Thornton. Others, such as Hannah More of Somerset and

Charles Simeon of Cambridge, remained in their places of work but were regular visitors to Clapham or met with the Clapham leadership at other venues.

On the plaque in the church in Clapham, the group is referred to as the "Clapham Sect." Strictly speaking, they did not constitute a sect in the contemporary usage of the term. While there is some dispute over the origin of the term, it is generally agreed that the name first appeared in the EDINBURGH REVIEW long after the death of Wilberforce. It was either coined by James Stephen, or by Sydney Smith as a term of disparagement. Since it is not a sect and to avoid misunderstanding, we have chosen to use the term Clapham Circle, mindful of the fact that during the lives of these men and women they would never have known or heard the term.

The abolition of slavery is the issue for which the Clapham Circle is best known, but it would be quite wrong to assume that this was the major focus of the entire group. It was much more than one issue that drew this group of friends together. They had a shared faith in God, a shared commitment to the application of their Christian faith to the reformation of society, to improving the living and working conditions of the poor, and above all, to Christian education both at home and overseas. Their shared passion was to see the Gospel and teachings of Jesus acknowledged throughout the world.

It was John Newton who advised Wilberforce, soon after his "great change," to spend time with John Thornton and his family. Thornton, who had secured a pastorate in London from Newton, financially supported him. It was through Newton that Wilberforce met John Thornton's son Henry, a meeting which began a friendship that would last a lifetime. The two men were also related by marriage as Wilberforce's uncle, also a William Wilberforce, was married to Hannah Thornton, John Thornton's sister. Henry Thornton invited Wilberforce to live in his newly acquired home in Clapham and the two men stayed there until Henry's marriage.

It was Henry Thornton, with his characteristic precision, who was responsible for establishing the Clapham Circle, first by inviting Wilberforce to share his home and then by encouraging other like-minded Christians to come to live in the village.

Battersea Rise (Thornton's home) proved an ideal center for such a community of friends, some of whom lived there, others who came for short or long stays. Thornton added several wings to the house until it eventually had thirty-four bedrooms as well as a magnificent oval library designed by Pitt, which was, until Thornton's death in 1815, the "cabinet room" and general center of the community. He also built two smaller houses on the extensive grounds, Broomfield Lodge, which was rented by Edward Eliot and, after his death, by Wilberforce, and Glenelg, which was bought by Charles Grant.

Many years later Henry Thornton wrote in his diary:

> *Few men have been blessed with worthier and better friends than it has been my lot to be. Mr. Wilberforce stands at the head of these, for he was the friend of my youth. It is chiefly through him that I have been introduced to a variety of other most valuable associates, to my friends Babington and Gisborne and their worthy families, to Lord Teignmouth and his family, to Mrs. Hannah More and her sisters; to Mr. Stephen and to not a few respectable Members of Parliament. Second only to Mr. Wilberforce in my esteem is now the family of Mr. Grant.*

Thornton and Wilberforce were also close friends with John Venn, the pastor at the Clapham Parish Church. Together with Grant, Eliot, Stephen, Teignmouth, Macaulay, Smith, Gisborne, Babington, and Hannah More, they formed the core of the Clapham Circle. In Viscountess Knutsford's Life and Letters of Zachary Macaulay she speaks of them as:

> *Regarding every member as forming part of a large united family, behaving towards each other as members of such a family. They treated each other's homes as their own, taking with them as a matter of course their wives and children; they kept together for their holidays and while in London arranged to meet for breakfast or dinner to discuss their many common concerns. The weight of continual business was lightened and cheered by sharing it with congenial companions.*

As a result of a conversation with James Ramsey shortly before the publication of his abolitionist Essay on the Treatment of Slaves in the British Sugar Colonies, Wilberforce began to take an interest in the abolition of the slave trade. In the autumn of 1786, Sir Charles Middleton had urged Wilberforce to take up the subject of the slave trade and Wilberforce had promised to give it serious consideration. Early in 1787, he began his collaboration with Thomas Clarkson, a young man who was to become one of the main proponents of abolition. Clarkson had begun his interest in the slave trade when, as a Cambridge student, he had written an essay on the subject in Latin and received a prize.

Parliament

The work of the Clapham Circle in Parliament, often derisively referred to by their opponents as the "Saints," began in the 1780s and brought about a sea change in both the social and religious situation in Britain. Their political activities took place against the international background of the French Revolution and the War of Independence with America. Fear of a bloody revolution spreading across the Channel caused them to be cautious in the steps they took toward political and social reform. This caused some of their detractors to underestimate their passion for the reform of society. This commitment to reform stemmed from their Christian convictions rather than from political philosophy, and it is largely this fact that has resulted in twentieth-century British historians being generally unkind to the Clapham Saints and often presenting Wilberforce and the Clapham Circle in a derogatory light.

The Clapham Circle concentrated their energies intensely on the abolition of the slave trade. They also had a broad interest in a variety of issues, particularly the poor in England. In 1796, fellow Claphamite Thomas Gisborne, with the support of Wilberforce, focused attention on the fearful conditions endured by children working in the factories, declaring that the case "cried loudly for the interference of the legislature." It was The Society for Bettering the Condition of the Poor, founded in Wilberforce's house and usually called The Bettering Society, that first called for definite legislation to limit the hours worked by children in the cotton mills, regulate the age and conditions of apprenticeship, and provide for regular inspections. In 1802, with strong backing from Wilberforce, one of its Vice Presidents, Sir Robert Peel, carried through a bill ending forced apprenticeship and forbidding night work for children in the Lancashire cotton mills.

The prime consideration of the Clapham Circle was the application of biblical principles to work in Parliament and in the country. They believed that they had been called by God to become members of Parliament and to use their position of privilege in society for the good of the nation. They believed that they were accountable to God, not only for their words and actions, but also for the use of their time and money.

Many of them were men of wealth, but their generosity and philanthropy is well documented and beyond dispute. Henry Thornton consistently gave away as much as six-sevenths of his entire income each year. Generosity on this scale was characteristic of all the Clapham Circle. This is quite remarkable at a time when most wealthy men spent money on gambling, womanizing in London, and themselves.

Granville Sharp, who was too poor for a parliamentary career in which Members of Parliament had to support themselves, nevertheless lavished his time, talents, and money on the cause of setting Africans free from the evils of slavery. Zachary Macaulay faced fever and hardship on an immense scale in the freed-slaves' colony of Sierra Leone. Later, he gave years of unstinting service without pay as editor of the magazine, THE CHRISTIAN OBSERVER. It was this level of selfless service and generosity, characteristic of the Clapham Circle, that was unrivaled with regard to their contribution to the political reform movement of their generation. The personal generosity of their lifestyles was also unmatched by their political opponents or their social detractors.

In the giving of their substance, as in the use of their time, the dominant motive was their Christian faith and belief in accountability. This was a prime purpose, which directed their political objectives.

It was this sense of accountability to God which gave the Clapham Circle an integrity which acted as salt and leaven in the House of Commons; it was this sense of accountability to God that enabled the anti-slave trade team to persevere with its campaign during a major European war and in the face of twenty years of defeat, disappointment, and disillusionment. Pitt once asked Henry Thornton why he voted against him on one occasion. Thornton replied, "I voted today so that if my Master had come again at that moment I might have been able to give an account of my stewardship."

The Influence of the Circle

The group of Members of Parliament who looked to
Wilberforce for leadership was considerably larger than some
historians have recorded. Over the forty years of his political
career there were no fewer than 112 Members who either
regularly or occasionally voted with Wilberforce. There was
an inner core of thirty Members who formed the Clapham
Circle of Members of Parliament and followed Wilberforce
into the lobbies. It was this inner core, which became known as
the "Saints," who asserted their primary allegiance to biblical
principles rather than to party affiliations. They shared the type
of reformism of the Clapham Circle. All were personal friends
or associates of William Wilberforce and usually voted with
him when he opposed the government. Although most of this
parliamentary group carried party labels, they formed a distinct
group within the House of Commons and as such were an
influential force that could not be ignored by any government.
They regularly met to discuss their political objectives, either in
the Clapham home of Henry Thornton, or in one of the country
houses of their associates such as Tothey Temple, the home of
Thomas Babington, or Moggerhanger Park, the house of Godfrey
and Stephen Thornton. Their meetings were not like those of any
other political group or party. Rather they centered on worship
and prayer, seeking to know the mind of God on the issues that
confronted them.

John Venn, the Rector of Clapham Parish Church, and
Charles Simeon of Cambridge were the theologians and chaplains
to the Circle and exercised a considerable influence upon the
spiritual life, not only of each of the members, but also of their
families. The diaries kept by John Venn and Henry Thornton
show that Venn often attended family prayer in Thornton home
and preached sermons addressed to the family. These prayer times
included not only close family members, but also domestic servants
and visitors.

Another non-parliamentary member of the Clapham Circle
was Granville Sharp, who played an important role in gathering
empirical evidence on the cruelty and inhumanity of the slave
trade and the treatment of slaves in the West Indian colonies.
His cooperation with Thomas Clarkson was an important factor
in the gathering of evidence for the campaign. Together they not

only amassed statistics, but also published many pamphlets to put their evidence in the public domain. They collected specimens of the instruments of torture, such as thumbscrews and manacles, that were used in the notorious "middle passage" from Africa to the West Indies. They supplied these to Wilberforce who used them with considerable effect in his lengthy speeches in the House of Commons as part of the abolition debates. Wilberforce was able to use this evidence to expose the ruthless horrors of the journey across the Atlantic during which up to half of the slaves lost their lives.

Zachary Macaulay also played an important role in the gathering of evidence. As a sensitive young man he had gone to Jamaica seeking a career in bookkeeping but instead found himself in a management role that required him to administer floggings to a slave or lose his job. This, together with the terrible scenes of cruelty he witnessed, made an indelible impression upon him, and upon returning to England and converting to "vital Christianity" he used his experiences of life in the colonies to propel all his energies into the movement for the abolition of slavery. He even traveled on a slave ship to the West Indies to experience firsthand the indescribable suffering inflicted upon Africans during their transport to the Caribbean.

Macaulay was an indefatigable and meticulous researcher with an incredible memory for details. He had an encyclopedic mind that was recognized by members of the Clapham Saints in Parliament. When facts were needed for a debate in the House, it was often said, "Go and consult Macaulay!" It is said of Macaulay that on one occasion, when he was looking for a firsthand witness among sailors, he spent many months visiting scores of ships in order to locate the seaman he needed to procure the evidence.

One of the remarkable things about the Clapham Circle is the balance of professional skills and experience within the group. They were lawyers, bankers, churchmen, researchers, politicians, and businessmen. Most of them were laymen, but they were all deeply committed Christians who were not content with merely having a personal faith in God but rather needed to express their faith in action. The kind of evangelical Christianity developed at Clapham impelled them, not only to seek the salvation of others in the spiritual sense, but also to devote their energies to the welfare of humanity. For them, this meant using the talents and experiences that God had given them in service of others. It was difficult for those who had never had such a faith in God to understand their motivation. The reaction of skeptics was not simply to dismiss the faith that motivated them while giving a just assessment of their achievements. Instead, they became bitter opponents and used any means of personal abuse to try to discredit those whose faith and motivation they could not understand.

Although not specifically committed to socio-political reform as part of a political philosophy agenda, the Clapham Saints undoubtedly paved the way for the movement of social reform that grew during the Victorian era. They also laid the socio-cultural foundations of Victorian society as well as the period of peace and prosperity that lasted into the twentieth century. Their political activity, in addition to their work outside Parliament, was influential in changing the moral values of the nation, reducing the crime rate, stabilizing family life, reducing illegitimacy, drunkenness and violence, tackling poverty, and improving social conditions for the poor.

Strategies & Dynamics of Social Change

The Clapham Saints introduced a dynamic of social change based upon a strategy of research, publicity, parliamentary lobbying, national campaigning, public meetings, and legislation into the situation. They made good use of the media, which in those days consisted largely of newspapers and tracts. Their objective was to change the mindset of the nation in order to prepare the way for successful legislation that would tackle some of the major issues of the day: slavery and religious ignorance in the British Empire, the exploitation of workers, and the reformation of personal and social morality in Britain. Wilberforce claimed this latter objective was one of "making goodness fashionable" among the upper ranks of society, which would have been a reversal of the existing fashion that both flaunted and admired bawdiness and immorality.

The strategy of the Clapham Circle in social reform was based on undertaking field research to produce empirical facts that were then presented in a form that would touch the conscience of the nation and build up a groundswell of support forcing the ruling classes, who were the only ones with seats in Parliament, to pass reforms. An outstanding example of the success of this method of political activity was the way in which they mobilized and used public opinion to generate support for their campaign to get missionaries into India. When the renewal of the East India Company's charter came before Parliament in 1793, Wilberforce and his colleagues had lost the "missionary clause." When the charter came up for renewal again in 1813, they were determined to be better organized. In fact, their campaign was so well-organized that it resulted in what has gone down in history as the greatest evangelical vote on any single issue ever recorded in the House of Commons.

The Clapham Circle used THE CHRISTIAN OBSERVER, pamphlets, and the Church Missionary Society in a nationwide campaign to mobilize public opinion to back up their painstaking lobbying of Members both in the House of Commons and the House of Lords. All the churchmen in both Houses were actively involved in this lobbying and in extra-parliamentary campaigning. Numerous public meetings were held throughout the country that brought a groundswell of support for the parliamentary Clapham Circle, which became regarded as the representative of Christianity in Parliament. All church groups combined to support a national petition. This resulted in 837 petitions with more than half a million signatures being presented in the House of Commons to support the religious clause of the charter. Half a million signatures in a total population of only nine million is an impressive proportion!

The rousing of public opinion across the nation was undoubtedly a major factor in swaying the vote in Parliament, both in the House of Lords and in the House of Commons. Wilberforce's speech lasted three hours. The Commons vote on the first reading of the bill produced a majority of eighty-nine votes to thirty-six votes. Although the majority was reduced in the second and third readings, the religious clauses were retained, and the East India charter received Royal Assent on July 21, 1813, a major triumph for the Clapham Circle.

Their use of research, publicity, parliamentary lobbying, and the mobilizing of public opinion was unique in their day, but has since become a model for much political activity. It may have been carried to a level of excess in the twenty-first century that was beyond the wildest dreams of politicians in the eighteenth century. The modern use of "spin" would undoubtedly be deeply offensive to the Clapham Saints whose commitment to truth and integrity were recognized by all, if only grudgingly by their detractors and political opponents.

Their method of campaigning was directed at rousing the conscience of a nation. The objective was not to further political ambition or seek power for selfish ends but to serve a humanitarian purpose. In order to achieve the abolition of slavery, they actually had to change the mindset of the majority of the members of Parliament who had a vested interest in the colonies and who feared that the loss of cheap labor would ruin them.

The slave owners and those who benefited from slave labor were a powerful body in Parliament and they argued that the institution of slavery was good for the Africans. They actually presented the case for slavery in humanitarian terms, saying that the slaves were saved from brutal tribal wars, given free transport across the Atlantic to the Caribbean, provided with free clothing, food and housing, and given work.

Conclusion

It took forty years to change the mindset of Parliament, but the Clapham Circle achieved this through the Saints in Parliament and through the tireless campaigning of the Circle in the country where they succeeded in rousing the conscience of the nation, especially in the growing middle classes. In so doing, they set a precedent of campaigning for social change that has lasting relevance for the great social and moral issues that face each generation.

Extended Observation

Reflection & Conversation

There is often plenty of public acclaim for heroic individual effort. Yet, most lasting campaigns for good demonstrate the work of a community of dedicated people. In many respects, the Clapham Circle is a prototype for a modern activist community. Its members harnessed their talents and their intellectual gifts. Their strategy and approach to reform may have actually spared Britain the bloody revolution experienced in France. Talk about the qualities of the Clapham Circle that struck you as most important. What attracts you to such community action? What might you find intimidating or difficult about such an intense and active Christianity?

Attend to the Word

Read Ephesians 4:15–16, 5:1–2, 15–20. Feel free to extend the reading to include some of the verses that have been skipped. Although it may be better if the reading is done aloud for the group, it is quite all right for each person to read from his or her own Bible. After the reading is complete, spend some time in silence with the following phrases: "Speak the truth in love;" "promotes the body's growth in building itself up in love;" "be imitators of God;" and "live not as unwise people but as wise."

Engage

The Clapham Circle lived and worked together to support and encourage one another. They often had large family dinners together. They discussed the great issues of the day. They worshipped together at the same church—Holy Trinity Clapham. They sang songs and hymns of praise. They encouraged one another. They looked after each other. They understood themselves as Christians united together in their love for Jesus and in the need to serve others.

1. How do you periodically set aside time to get together with friends to talk about common concerns? Does your group socialize and pray together as well?
2. If you are not currently a member of such a group, how might you go about forming one or joining one?
3. Using the experience of the Clapham Circle as a model, how can biblical principles guide the discussion of common concerns?

Move Forward

Wilberforce and his circle used organizations (they called them societies) to work for social change. The strength of these organizations was the effectiveness of a communal and well-focused effort.

1. What kind of organization would suit your mission—your desire "to build up the body in love?"
2. What are the issues of today where you find oppression, slavery, or other forms of injustice? Create a plan to study up on these issues.
3. Create a simple plan that keeps you involved with a circle of concerned people who apply biblical principals to "create the better hour."

Pray

Behold, how good and how pleasant it is
for brethren to dwell together in unity!

It is like the precious ointment upon the head,
that ran down upon the beard,
even Aaron's beard:
that went down to the skirts of his garments;

As the dew of Hermon,
and as the dew that descended upon the mountains of Zion:
for there the LORD commanded the blessing,
even life for evermore.

Psalm 133 (King James Version)

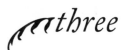

three

A Man of Character

By Kevin Belmonte & Chuck Stetson

Kevin Belmonte is the author of several books on William Wilberforce, including Travel with William Wilberforce: The Friend of Humanity *and* Hero for Humanity: A Biography of William Wilberforce. *Belmonte is the editor of Wilberforce's* A Practical View of Christianity. *Belmonte has also served as a script consultant for the BBC and for the last five years as the lead historical consultant for Walden Media's motion picture,* Amazing Grace. *Most recently he has served as script consultant for a documentary on Wilberforce and the Clapham Circle. Belmonte is a Visiting Author at Gordon College where he has been the director of the Wilberforce Project, an initiative that fosters scholarship relating to all aspects of Wilberforce's legacy. Belmonte holds a BA in English Literature from Gordon College and an MA in church history from Gordon-Conwell Theological Seminary, and is author of the recently released* A Journey Through the Life of William Wilberforce.

William Wilberforce, the great English statesman, was a man of extraordinary character. Because of his character, he was able to influence those around him to change the world.

Wilberforce wrote one of the greatest personal mission statements ever written. On Sunday, October 28, 1787, he penned in his journal "God Almighty has set before me two great objects, the suppression of the Slave Trade and the reformation of manners." (1) Largely through his own leadership, Wilberforce saw the realization of his mission statement. In his lifetime, Wilberforce helped to bring about the end of the British slave trade and the emancipation of slaves in the British Empire. To a large degree, Wilberforce influenced the reformation of manners—restoring goodness, integrity, and modesty as civic virtues. In both these objects, it was Wilberforce's character and determination that led the British Parliament and the British people to change the world around them from the horrid and depraved cultural conditions of the late eighteenth century to a much more caring world that lifted up the least, the last, and the lost of society. England became a nation that held high, seeking after "the better hour," as the English poet William Cowper said in his tribute poem to Wilberforce.

In order to understand Wilberforce and his achievements, it is necessary to answer the following questions: Why is Wilberforce important today? What were the character traits of Wilberforce? How did these character traits stand out at the time? What gave Wilberforce the inner power to possess these character traits that enabled him to influence others to change the world?

Character Traits of Wilberforce

William Wilberforce's greatest accomplishments grew out of his study of the Bible. Wilberforce began reading it virtually every day during the roughly two-year period that he always referred to afterwards as his "great change"—his embrace of Christianity, a process completed by Easter 1786. His reading of the Bible redirected the course of his life. Seven character traits in the *Letter to the Colossians* define Wilberforce's character and, in turn, helped him define the world around him.

1. Compassion

Wilberforce could in many ways identify with the sorrow of others. He was sick most of his life. He nearly died of what appears to have been ulcerative colitis in 1788. And it was at this time that he suffered what appears to have been the first of two nervous breakdowns. His health was only restored through the sparing use of opium, considered a proper medication in his day. As he grew older, he suffered from severe curvature of the spine and had to wear a metal back brace to provide support and help him remain erect. A dangerous inflammation of his lungs forced his retirement from Parliament in 1825.

A narrow defeat of Wilberforce's Slave Trade Abolition Bill in 1796 by only four votes was particularly hard on him.

Opponents used a gift of must-see opera tickets to lure away supporters of the bill and ultimately snatch victory from Wilberforce. Devastated, he became dangerously ill and had to be confined to his house for several weeks. It was, however, anguish of the mind and spirit that caused him the most pain, for it was at this time that he suffered what appears to have been a second nervous breakdown. "I am permanently hurt," he says about the Slave Trade. He wrote in his diary. (2) His own heart was sickened to see his great cause sacrificed to the carelessness of lukewarm friends and the intrigues of interested enemies. (3)

Wilberforce also had suffered a number of deaths in his immediate family—his father when he was eight, his two sisters while growing up, his daughter Barbara, a grandson, and, finally, his daughter Elizabeth. For many people today, death of one's children would be utter devastation. Wilberforce, nevertheless, wrote about the death of his daughter Barbara, "I humbly trust to a better world. Praise the Lord, O my soul. [This is] my dear, and I trust imparadised, child's birthday." (4)

Thus it is not surprising that compassion, born of his own experience, was at the heart of Wilberforce. He cared for others, particularly for the oppressed and the poor. He took on seemingly impossible situations such as abolition of slavery, a highly economic and well-organized industry that today would be equivalent in size to the U.S. defense industry. The economics of slavery were deeply and widely ingrained in the economy. The idea of taking on such a large industry was laughable to many— inconceivable to others.

Yet Wilberforce and his friends in the village of Clapham (known as the Clapham Circle) dedicated their lives from 1789 onward to improving the lives of others and eliminating the slave trade. They worked as a community because they were determined that it was the right thing to do.

It was a "concert of benevolence," Wilberforce wrote to President Thomas Jefferson when asked to describe the Clapham Circle. This concert of benevolence is best illustrated by the way in which Wilberforce and Thomas Clarkson worked together. (5) Clarkson, a recently ordained young graduate from Cambridge University, collected much of the research and organized many of the abolitionist meetings around the country. Clarkson also collected many of the signatures for petitions to end the slave trade. Wilberforce, with his great gift for parliamentary oratory, presented to Parliament in graphic detail accounts of the cruel and inhumane treatment of black men enslaved in Africa and transported to the Americas. He made the stories understandable, documenting them with data. Often Wilberforce concluded by presenting before the House of Commons the many petitions that Clarkson had collected. Filled with hundreds of thousands of signatures, the petitions made a deep impression on the House.

On the night of February 23, 1807, the House of Commons was in the midst of the final debate on the British slave trade. In order to help convince the House to end the slave trade, Solicitor General Sir Samuel Romilly spoke of Wilberforce's compassion. Contrasting Wilberforce with Napoleon, Sir Samuel's speech painted a picture of each man returning home. Napoleon would arrive in pomp and power, a man who knew the height of earthly ambition, yet one tormented by bloodshed and oppression of war. Wilberforce would come home to "the bosom of his happy and delighted family," able to lie down in peace because he had "preserved so many millions of his fellow creatures."

Today many historians have developed theories of history based on self-interest. Wilberforce and the Clapham Circle are particularly perplexing to historians since no one has ever been able to see evidence that any of these men profited in any way from their philanthropic undertakings. On the contrary, these men put their money and their lives on the line for what they believed from their reading of the Bible—that it was "the true duty of every man to promote the happiness of his fellow creatures to the utmost of his power." (6) Collectively, they worked to make a "better hour." Along the way, they were attacked, receiving death threats and huge vilification. Yet in the end, they were vindicated. (7)

Sir James Stephen, in his classic biographical essay, stated that Wilberforce's character was distinguished by an "instinct of philanthropy." Stephen continued: "The basis of the natural . . . character of Mr. Wilberforce was laid in [his] quick fellow-feeling with other men." (8) Wilberforce was responsive to those immediately around him as well as those far away. But although ready to weep with those who wept, he was still more prompt to rejoice with those who rejoiced.

2. Kindness

Wilberforce's kindness is perhaps best explained by what he did for others. Wilberforce was constantly giving to others. He either started or gave to sixty-nine societies (today called nonprofits). These societies addressed aspects of specific cruelty, oppression, and injustice of the day. They comprised a strikingly diverse set of projects designed to better society: founding the Royal Society for the Prevention of Cruelty to Animals, establishing Britain's National Portrait Gallery, conducting scientific research designed to improve the lives of the poor, and making more humane working conditions in factories.

Beyond his involvement with these societies, he gave generously. Before his marriage in 1797, he was able to give at least one-fourth of his annual income to charitable organizations—far above the one-tenth tithe that is often held up as a Christian ideal and the actual charitable giving today (about two percent of annual income for Americans). Using incomplete records for the years between 1785 and 1797, Wilberforce's sons report that he gave away two thousand pounds, the equivalent of eighty thousand dollars today, to nearly every charitable institution in London and Yorkshire.

Wilberforce liked to assist young people. "Assistance to young men of promise had always been with him a favorite charity," wrote Wilberforce's sons:

> [H]e gave more than merely money; he made his house the home of one or two youths, the expense of whose education he defrayed; all their holidays were spent with him; and hours of his own time were profusely given to training and furnishing their minds. Nor were the poor forgotten; they were invited to join in his family worship on the Sunday evening, and sought out often in their cottages for instruction and [financial] relief. (9)

Wilberforce often gave anonymously. One such group that received his anonymous aid was the Elland Society. He donated the equivalent of several thousand dollars a year with the proviso that "my name must not be mentioned." (10) This society, run by his friend William Hey, was devoted to identifying poor but promising students and educating them for ministry, or as Wilberforce phrased it, "catching the colts running wild on Halifax Moor, and cutting their manes and tails and sending them to college." (11) He often welcomed these young men to his home to arrange for their employment.

Wilberforce was highly sought after at parties in London. He was called "a most amusable" man, a person whom people loved to have around. He could sing and entertain others. Wilberforce, furthermore, was a joy to be with. He has been described as a Calvinist with joy. Sir James Mackintosh said, "I never saw anyone who touched life at so many points." (12)

3. Humility

Despite being at the center of power of the British Empire, humility was a key character trait of Wilberforce. Even though he provided leadership in the House of Parliament, Wilberforce worked constantly with and sought out the opinions of others. His conduct encouraged teamwork. Wilberforce liked to work behind the scenes, as he did in getting the King to make a Royal Proclamation. The issues were not about Wilberforce, but about the issues. He believed that he was only a vehicle for getting things done. His own words capture this approach succinctly: "I wish to give my vote not with a view to men, but measures." (13)

In A PRACTICAL VIEW OF CHRISTIANITY, Wilberforce wrote about his view on virtues and his focus on humility and self-denial:

> The virtues most strongly and repeatedly and by our progress, in which, we may best measure our advancement in holiness, are the fear and love of God and of Christ: love, kindness, and meekness towards our fellow-creatures: indifference to the possessions and events of this life, in comparison with our concern about eternal things; self-denial and humility.
>
> The chief causes of enmity among men are pride and self-importance, the high opinion which men entertain of themselves and the consequent deference which they exact from others, the over-valuation of worldly possessions and of worldly honors, and in consequence, a too eager competition for them. The rough edges of one man rub against those of another, if the expression may be allowed. . . . (14)

Wilberforce also acted on his views of humility. As he was retiring from Parliament in 1824, Sir John Sinclair suggested an arrangement to Wilberforce to award him peerage, a title of Lord, so that he could continue public life in the House of Lords. Wilberforce refused it, noting:

> *I will not deny that there have been periods in my life,*
> *when on worldly principles that attainment of a permanent,*
> *easy and quiet seat in the legislature, would have been a*
> *pretty strong temptation to me. But, I thank God; I was*
> *strengthened against yielding to it. For [understand me*
> *rightly] as I had done nothing to make it naturally come to*
> *me, I must have endeavored to go to it; and this would have*
> *been carving for myself, if I may use the expression, much*
> *more than a Christian ought to do.* (15)

In rejecting the offer of peerage, Wilberforce also kept to a promise that he had made early in his political career when he joined a group called the Independents. A club of about forty members of the House of Commons, the group's principle of union was a resolution not to accept a plum appointment to political office, a government pension, or an offer of hereditary peerage. Over time only two members of the original group of Independents held to their resolution: Henry Bankes and Wilberforce. In his lifetime, Wilberforce was the only Member of Parliament who represented a county who was not raised to peerage.

Humility also characterized Wilberforce's relationship with his children. As an older man, he listened to his sons quietly and patiently. When they were grown, he "courted their advice and deferred to their judgments with the same kindly confidence with which he stayed his feeble steps by leaning on their more vigorous arms." (16) James Stephens noted that Wilberforce rejoiced "to gather . . . the harvest of seeds which, in earlier days, he had himself sowed in their minds." (17) He often accompanied his sons on their pastoral visits and joined in the prayers they offered by the beds of the sick or dying parishioners.

4. Gentleness

Those who knew Wilberforce in his early life knew he had a quick temper and a sharp tongue. Prior to the completion of his "great change" in 1786, he often showed a disdain for the judgment of others—and when he did, he didn't try to hide his dissatisfaction. At such times, his temper could flare and his gift for eloquence could be transformed into cutting sarcasm and bitter invective. Political opponents in particular knew first hand that he had a rhetorical rapier. In 1784, he attacked his friend Pitt's great political rival, Charles Fox, so bitterly that Fox hated him for a time. At this time Pitt charged him to "tear the enemy to pieces," and he had not hesitated to do so.

Yet in the years immediately after 1786, Wilberforce resolved to "show respect" for other people's judgment and to "manifest humility in myself rather than dissatisfaction concerning others." He also strove to show the "forbearance of a temper naturally quick." In their biography of their father, Wilberforce's sons noted that these restraints now became a primary concern. Gradually, Wilberforce became a different man. He genuinely repented his earlier conduct, taking time—years in fact—and care to mend broken relationships with Fox and others whom he had offended. By the end of his life, few remembered how Wilberforce had once been. They knew a man who greatly valued "removing or lessening prejudices [and] conciliating good-will." (18) His life had become one distinguished by humility and gentleness.

5. Patience

Wilberforce had enormous patience and never quit. After his announcement in 1787 of his intention to abolish the slave trade, Wilberforce introduced a bill year after year to do so. Each year, despite opposition, personal vilification, and even death threats, Wilberforce proceeded onward with his mission. It took nineteen years of "no"s to get a "yes" on the abolition of the slave trade. It took another twenty-six years to achieve emancipation for all of the slaves in the British Empire.

Wilberforce and the Clapham Circle believed that slavery was wrong. Once engaged, Wilberforce was patient and persistent. Wilberforce's character was in sharp contrast to that of Thomas Jefferson. Jefferson made three accusations of the oppression of the slave trade against the King of England in one of the original drafts of the Declaration of Independence. Yet when Jefferson received a setback, he didn't pursue it. Wilberforce, in contrast, tirelessly pursued the issue of the abolition of the slave trade although he was rejected for nineteen years. He kept at it. He persevered until the goal was achieved.

Once he had penned his mission statement, there was no turning back on the abolition of slavery or the reformation of manners. He had to be involved. He could not back down, no matter the cost.

Wilberforce's friend Isaac Milner, a Fellow of the Royal Society and President of Queen's College Cambridge, wrote in 1792 to Wilberforce: "I had no expectation of success respecting the Slave Trade; then you seemed to be carrying every thing and now we are down in the mouth again . . . However, you have great reason to be thankful, for God seems to bless your labors; and I remember I told you long ago, if you carry this point in your whole life, that life will be far better spent than in being Prime Minister many years." (19) Indeed, many people had expected that Wilberforce, with his talents and position, would have been Pitt's successor as Prime Minister "if he had preferred party to mankind. His sacrifice of one kind of fame and power gave him another and a nobler title to remembrance." (20)

6. Forbearance & Forgiveness

Because the moral issues that Wilberforce took on were often against the economic interests of so many, Wilberforce was attacked in the press, often viciously. Yet, William Jay, a minister in Bath, remembers how Wilberforce chose to respond to such attacks: "Mr. Wilberforce gave me an admonition never to notice anything concerning one's self in the public prints. 'If you do,' said he, 'you must notice everything, or what passes unnoticed will pass for truth which cannot be refuted.'" Wilberforce added, "Our character and conduct must be both our defenders and advocates." (21)

One person who attacked Wilberforce was William Corbett. Corbett published his opposition to Wilberforce's desire to abolish bear baiting, his advocating smallpox inoculations, and his campaign to encourage the growth of potatoes. Yet Wilberforce found a way to be charitable to him. In a letter to a friend, Wilberforce wrote:

> *I have not seen 'Corbett' for some time. My chief reason for ever taking his paper [the* POLITICAL REGISTER*] was, that*

I could not otherwise see it; and I thought it right to know
what were the lessons of a very able and influential political
teacher on the passing events of the day. But when I heard
his paper circulation has much declined, I declined also. (22)

Wilberforce proactively sought to heal wounds that he had
created. One such wound he healed was that with Charles Fox,
the opposition leader whom he had contested with in the early
1780s. Their relationship so improved that Fox paid this tribute
to Wilberforce while he was recovering from a life-threatening
illness: "It is better," Fox said, "that the cause [of abolition] should
be in his hands than in mine; from him, I honestly believe that it
will come with more weight, more authority and more probability
of success."

It is ironic that Charles Fox, not William Pitt, proved in
the end indispensable to the abolition of the slave trade. After
the death of Pitt in 1806, Fox came into office as part of the
administration of Lord Grenville. Now the fruit of Wilberforce's
relationship mending with Fox paid lasting dividends. The two
consulted with one another about legislative strategies to end the
slave trade—strategies that were ultimately successful.

7. *Love*

Wilberforce loved others. It was his view of the world. His
actions reflected the parable of the Good Samaritan. In that
parable, there were three people who had very different views
of life. The robber, a person much like the slave traders of
Wilberforce's day, robbed a man on his way from Jerusalem to
Jericho. The robber's view of life was, in effect, "what is yours
is mine, and I will take it." The priest and the Levite, whose
view could represent that of the wealthy and the Members of
Parliament, held the view that, in effect, "what is mine is mine,
and I will keep it." Lastly, the Samaritan, a person hated by the
Jews at the time of Jesus, could be compared to Wilberforce, who
was also vilified by many. The Samaritan's view was, in effect,
"what is mine is yours, and I will give it to you." Wilberforce
acted on that view—even though it cost him both his time
and his money. Though Wilberforce had been very wealthy
throughout his life, he died a poor man in large part because of
all the money he donated to make a better world.

Wilberforce loved his wife and his family. Wilberforce was devoted to his wife even though a number of his friends found her difficult to get along with. Wilberforce wrote at one point: "A more tender, excellent wife, no man ever received [as a] gift from the Lord." They had six children—four boys and two girls. Wilberforce wrote a friend: "I delight in little children. I could spend hours in watching them." (23) One of the great legacies to the Victorian era was Wilberforce's family life, which was emulated by many households of every class throughout Britain. Children were not only seen and heard around the house, but parents spent more time with their children, educating them, praying with them, reading to them, and playing with them.

Wilberforce knew how to be a friend to others. To James Stephen, father of Sir James Stephen and grandfather of the writer Virginia Woolf, he wrote: "You appeared to me to look unhappy last night, as if something was giving you pain—either in body or mind. It will be a pleasure to me to hear that this was not so; or if it was, and I can help to remove it, let me try." (24)

Other Character Traits

Besides the character traits in the *Letter to the Colossians*, Wilberforce focused on other traits found in the Bible. Wilberforce wrote at length about what he called "moderation in political attachments":

> *Let Christians espouse that party in political life whose measures appear to them best adapted to produce public happiness; but let them be moderate in their political attachments. Let them love their fellow-citizens with 'a pure heart, fervently;' considering their obligations to love and friendly sympathy, which are not to be dissolved by differences as to the characters of public men, or the issue of public measures . . . (25)*

Wilberforce continually sought to form wise judgments about people and events. "The events of the past," he asserted, "teach a lesson of moderation and sobriety in our judgments and feelings on human affairs and character." (26)

At the same time, he acknowledged the "difficulty of judging right in complicated cases, which should teach those who think differently on political subjects, mutual moderation, forbearance, and candor." Moderation, forbearance, and candor—three words which can do much to foster a more civil society and political discourse.

"Walk charitably," Wilberforce admonished himself on another occasion in his diary. "Wherever you are, remember that your conduct and conversation may have some effect on the minds of those with whom you are." (27)

The clergyman and Methodist founder John Wesley, just days before his death in 1791, wrote his last letter to Wilberforce during a particularly dark and dangerous patch in Wilberforce's efforts: "Unless God has raised you up for this very thing," Wesley wrote, "you will be worn out by the opposition of men and devils; but if God be for you who can be against you? *Oh be not weary of well-doing.* Go on in the name of God, and in the power of his might, till even American slavery, the vilest that ever saw the sun, shall vanish away before it." (28)

The moral high ground established by Wilberforce echoed across America for the better part of the nineteenth century. Fifty years later, Abraham Lincoln said he could remember Wilberforce as the man who ended the slave trade, but Lincoln said that he could not name one man who tried to keep it alive. Frederick Douglass noted in his tribute to Wilberforce: "It was the faithful, persistent and enduring enthusiasm of . . . William Wilberforce . . . and [his] noble co-workers, who finally thawed the British heart into sympathy for the slave, and moved the strong arm of government in mercy to put an end to this bondage. Let no American, especially no colored American, withhold generous recognition of this stupendous achievement— a triumph of right over wrong, of good over evil and victory for the whole human race." (29)

Yet the abolition of slavery, though his primary cause, was only one of his many interests. Wilberforce, as we have seen, was engaged in many issues.

The Impact of These Character Traits

In the second half of the eighteenth century, as William Wilberforce grew up, the world around him had become dissolute and venal. In the opening paragraph of A TALE OF TWO CITIES, Charles Dickens described the situation of Wilberforce's time as being both "the best of times" and "the worst of times." Dickens' words described how the Industrial Revolution made the rich much richer while making the situation worse for those who were poor.

Like the wealthy described by Dickens, Wilberforce had enjoyed himself at Cambridge University as well as afterwards when he won election as a Member of Parliament. Writing some years later, Wilberforce described that period: "The first years that I was in Parliament, I did nothing—nothing I mean to any good purpose; my own distinction was my darling object." (30) Ambition, advancement, and the use of a rapier wit to savage those who might cross swords with himself or with Pitt—these were the things that had distinguished Wilberforce's life prior Easter 1786, when his "great change" was complete.

In the course of his "great change," Wilberforce changed from a person of the world to a deeply believing Christian through his reading of the Bible. Today his "great change" would be described as "a conversion experience." In the *Letter to the Colossians*, Paul urges the believer in Jesus Christ to "put off, therefore, whatever belongs to your earthly nature," after which he lists a number of items: "sexual immorality, impurity, lust, evil desires, greed, which is idolatry" as well as "anger, rage, malice, slander and filthy language from your lips." Many of these character traits were found in those in politics and in business in London in the 1780s. A number of these people went each nigh to private clubs where they gambled and womanized. While Wilberforce was not fully caught up in all of the aforementioned traits of those around him, it would have been hard to resist all of them.

Yet following through on the guiding principles of Christianity was not something easily or quickly done by Wilberforce—he had a strong temper and fought to curb it, as we have seen.

Nevertheless, after his great change, Wilberforce gradually became a different man—one who repented his earlier conduct, taking time—years in fact—and care to mend broken relationships with Fox and others whom he had offended.

But why would Wilberforce have come to care so deeply about so markedly altering his life and conduct? Why would he have cared so much about the place of character?

The answer lies in how he saw himself after his embrace of Christianity. In 1795, he described his great change and the results that flowed from it in terms that are at once eloquent and philosophical:

*... I seem to myself to have awakened about nine or ten years
ago from a dream, to have recovered, as it were, the use of
my reason after a delirium. In fact till then I wanted first
principles; those principles at least which alone deserve the
character of wisdom, or bear the impress of truth. Emulation,
and a desire of distinction, were my governing motives; and
ardent after the applause of my fellow-creatures, I quite
forgot that I was an accountable being; that I was hereafter
to appear at the bar of God; that if Christianity were not a
fable, it was infinitely important to study its precepts, and
when known to obey them ... I know but too well that I
am not now what I ought to be; yet ... I hope, through the
help of that gracious Being who has promised to assist our
weak endeavors, to become more worthy of the name of
Christian. ... (31)*

Wilberforce's lifelong goal was truly to become worthy of
the name of a Christian. In 1797, Wilberforce wrote the book A
PRACTICAL VIEW OF THE PREVAILING RELIGIOUS SYSTEM OF PROFESSED
CHRISTIANS IN THE HIGHER AND MIDDLE CLASSES IN THIS COUNTRY
CONTRASTED WITH REAL CHRISTIANITY—a best seller in the United
Kingdom and in the United States for fifty years.

While he did not always succeed in curbing his temper (he
even sparred with Pitt on one notable occasion over proposed
legislation on assessed taxes), and often had other reasons to
reproach himself, Wilberforce worked on his character. Over
time his colleagues in Parliament took note of the changes in
his character. Increasingly his new beliefs came to be seen as a
good faith, not least because he now strove to act in good faith
with many with whom he had previously disagreed or viewed as
political enemies.

Without question Wilberforce's spiritual life was
transformed as a result of his great change, but so too was his
public philosophy—that set of principles that he now strove to
act upon in political life. Sir James Stephen described this aspect
of Wilberforce's life succinctly: "God was in all his thoughts."

Sources of Strength

Wilberforce found the strength to maintain his strong character
through a combination of his reading of the Bible and his

friends—who provided both a community and an earthly accountability. Regarding his reading of the Bible, Wilberforce's biographer sons tell us:

> *The entrance of God's word into his heart [which] gave light to his intellectual as well as to his moral nature. A keen remembrance of wasted time and a sense of his deficiency in the power of steady application, led him to set about educating himself. Various and accurate were now his studies, but the book which he studied most carefully, and by which perhaps above all others, his mental faculties were perfected, was the Holy Scripture. This he read and weighed and pondered over, studying its connection and details, and mastering especially, in their own tongue, the apostolical epistles. . . . It was now his daily care to instruct his undemanding and discipline his heart.* (32)

Within the Bible, Wilberforce drew upon six key principles:

1. Divine Stewardship. As a political philosophy, Wilberforce in 1784 (after his "great change") adopted the principle of divine stewardship to guide his work. "When summoned to give an account of our stewardship, we shall be called upon to answer for the use we have made of the means of relieving the wants and necessities of our fellow creatures." With a notion of divine accountability, Wilberforce maintained a sharp focus on his personal mission statement of abolition and reformation of manners. Divine stewardship became a guiding principle for Wilberforce.

Wilberforce's understanding of stewardship was also a central tenet of his public philosophy. "High rank is not a property," he wrote, "but a trust. Power always implies responsibility." (33)

In other places, Wilberforce wrote at greater length about stewardship: "We shall be called upon to answer for our employment of all the instruments and opportunities of diligent application, and serious reflection, and honest decision." (34) Elsewhere he stated even more forcefully: "In such a situation as mine *every moment* may be made useful to the happiness of my fellow-creatures." (35)

Wilberforce wrote about his motivation, a consuming desire to exhibit "a disposition honorable to God and useful to man; a temper composed of reverence, humility, gratitude and delighting to be . . . employed in the benevolent service of the universal Benefactor." (36) Wilberforce had discovered God to be his "patron and benefactor and friend 'who loved us and gave himself for us.'" (37) The "labors of a whole life," Wilberforce wrote, are "but an imperfect expression of [. . .] thankfulness." (38)

2. Faith. His faith was central for Wilberforce, and it trumped everything. Before the "great change," Wilberforce was a consummate politician. He voted the party line. He took the opposition party. When Prime Minister Pitt asked Wilberforce to attack the opposition, that is what Wilberforce did.

After his "great change," Wilberforce changed from politician to statesman. He voted his Christian conscience. In the instance of the war with France, Wilberforce ended up opposing his very good friend Prime Minister Pitt because of faithfulness to God. But as soon as he could, Wilberforce made up with Pitt because of their long-term friendship. Wilberforce was steadfast in his faithfulness to God and unswerving dedication to serving others.

3. Justice. The virtue of justice in God's name was particularly important to Wilberforce and a common theme in his speeches in Parliament. In a speech in 1789, Wilberforce said to Parliament:

. . . the nature and all the circumstances of this (slave) trade are now laid open to us; we can no longer plead ignorance [. . .] it is brought now so directly before our eyes, that this House must decide, and must justify to all the world, and to their own conscience, the rectitude of the grounds and principles of their decisions. A society has been established for the abolition of this trade, in which dissenters, Quakers, churchmen have all united. Let not Parliament be the only body that is insensible to the principles of national justice. (39)

Later, in 1791, Wilberforce told Parliament:

Never, never will we desist till we have wiped away this scandal from the Christian name, released ourselves from the load of guilt, under which we at present labour, and extinguished every trace of this bloody traffic, of which our posterity, looking back to the history of these enlightened times, will scarce believe that it has been suffered to exist so long a disgrace and dishonor to this country. (40)

James Stephens, a Clapham colleague of Wilberforce, noted that Wilberforce's "determination [was] fearless to pursue the right, into whatever consequences it might conduct him." Wilberforce himself affirmed this most strong view when he wrote "The author of all moral obligation has enjoined us to renounce certain actions, without an inquiry as to reasons or consequence." (41)

4. Happiness. Promoting the happiness of others was central to Wilberforce. The notion of happiness was much discussed in Wilberforce's day. Thomas Jefferson included the notion of happiness in the Declaration of Independence. Yet Wilberforce's notion of happiness went far beyond Jefferson's "pursuit of happiness." Wilberforce believed that when individual citizens promote the happiness of others, they are truly promoting their own happiness. In this sense, every individual becomes a powerful agent of social change, and the power for positive social change is multiplied to the extent that more people pursue, or properly promote, the happiness of others. Wilberforce drew upon the golden rule: "Let everyone regulate his conduct by the golden rule of doing to others as in similar circumstances we would have them do to us." (42) This tenet was the basis of his abolitionist efforts and of every other human rights and philanthropic issue with which he was involved in public life.

5. Bible Study & Prayer. Wilberforce reinforced these character traits every day by both his study of the Bible and by his prayers. His daily routine was largely the same from 1784 onward. He would get up and spend the first hour and a half of his day closeted for personal prayer and devotions. For prayer he used the *Book of Common Prayer* as well as prayers that he wrote. These first hours of the day were important to Wilberforce; he once remarked that "I always find that I have the most time for business and it is best done, when I have most properly observed my private devotions." (43)

After devotions, Wilberforce dressed and read a book (or in later years had a book read to him) for three quarters of an hour. Then Wilberforce would gather his household for family worship, reading a portion of the Bible, generally the New Testament, "with a natural and glowing eloquence, always with affectionate earnestness and an extraordinary knowledge of God's word," as his sons later described. He would then have breakfast with his family and, often times, friends.

Wilberforce's routine during the day varied over the years, but generally included a walk where he often saw, as he wrote in his diary, "a nature pour fourth, as it were, its songs of praise to the great Creator and Preserver of all things. I love to repeat Psalms 104, 103, 145 at such a season." (44)

Even though Wilberforce was personally attacked and vilified by his opponents (and frequently in the press), Wilberforce was at peace with himself. Study and prayer encompassed much of his daily routine; perhaps the third chapter of the *Letter to the Colossians* was helpful to him:

Let the peace of Christ rule in your hearts, since as members of one body you were called to peace. And be thankful. Let the word of Christ dwell in you richly as you teach and admonish one another with all wisdom, and as you sing psalms, hymns and spiritual songs with gratitude in your hearts to God. And whatever you do, whether in word or deed, do it all in the name of the Lord Jesus, giving thanks to God the Father through him.

Colossians 3:15–17

President George Washington had a similar approach in his public speeches. Typically in the first line, President Washington gave thanks to the Almighty for some recent event.

6. Accountability. Being held accountable by his friendships was an important source of stability in Wilberforce's life. In addition to the Bible that he read and revered, it was Wilberforce's friends who helped to keep him accountable. Friends were central to his life. He treasured the gift of friends, and he had much to say about them in his diary. One of the chief benefits of life, he wrote, "results from having a friend to whom we open our hearts, one of the most valuable of all possessions."

Wilberforce knew loneliness and despondency, and needed understanding. His Christian friends among the Clapham Circle came alongside him, steadying him in his course through advice and encouragement. Through long walks or rides on horseback with them, Wilberforce could find solace and recharge his batteries.

Friends provided Wilberforce with accountability, which he valued no less than companionship and understanding. "The best prerogative, the most sacred and indispensable duty of friendship," he wrote, was "a friend who will frankly tell me of my faults in private." Wilberforce knew only too well that pride, temptation, and other pitfalls were a part of his pilgrim's progress. Friends could help him keep to the right path.

Wilberforce once described his famous group of friends, the Clapham Circle, to Thomas Jefferson as "concerts of benevolence," but it is well worth considering what Wilberforce said to his son Samuel about such gatherings of friends:

A principle on which I have acted for many years and which I recommend to you early in life, is that of bringing together all men who are like-minded, and may one day combine and concert for the public good. Never omit any opportunity, my dear Samuel, of getting acquainted with any good or useful man. (45)

Summary

Speaking to the Massachusetts Legislature on January 9, 1961, President John F. Kennedy asked four questions of how to measure the success of a person:

For of those to whom much is given, much is required. And when at some future date the high court of history sits in judgment on each one of us—recording whether in our brief span of service we fulfilled our responsibilities to the state— our success or failure, in whatever office we may hold, will be measured by the answers to four questions:

*First, were we truly men of courage—with the courage to
stand up to one's enemies—and the courage to stand up, when
necessary, to one's associates—the courage to resist public
pressure, as well as private greed?*

*Secondly, were we truly men of judgment—with perceptive
judgment of the future as well as of the past—of our own
mistakes as well as the mistakes of others—with enough
wisdom to know what we did not know, and enough candor
to admit it?*

*Third, were we truly men of integrity—men who never ran
out on either the principles in which they believed or the
people who believed in them—men whom neither financial
gain nor political ambition could ever divert from the
fulfillment of our sacred trust?*

*Finally, were we truly men of dedication—with an honor
mortgaged to no single individual or group, and compromised
by no private obligation or aim, but devoted solely to serving
the public good and the national interest.* (46)

Wilberforce and the Clapham Circle could answer "yes" to
each of these questions. Samuel Morse, a gifted American painter
whose achievements included the invention of the telegraph,
wrote:

*Mr. Wilberforce is an excellent man; his whole soul is bent
on doing well for his fellow man. Not a moment of his time
is lost. He is always planning [some] benevolent scheme or
other and not only planning [them] but executing [them];
he is made up altogether of affectionate feeling. What I saw
of him in private gave me the most exalted opinion of him
as a Christian. Oh, that such men as Mr. Wilberforce were
more common in this world. So much human blood would
not be shed to gratify the malice and revenge of a few wicked,
interested men.* (47)

As historian G.M. Trevelyan has written, Wilberforce "could
not have done what he did if he had desired [high] office. With
his talents and position he would probably have been Pitt's
successor as Prime Minister if he had preferred party to mankind.

His sacrifice of one kind of fame and power gave him another and a nobler title to remembrance."

Following Wilberforce's death, at the request of politicians of all parties, he was interred in Westminster Abbey. This tribute attests the power of principled politics.

Wilberforce had also been willing to be thought a fool for his "perennial resolution" during the twenty-year fight to abolish the slave trade. He had been willing to sacrifice his "sacred honor," inasmuch as it referred to a choice between reputation and one's duty to his fellow man.

Indeed, he showed most powerfully that he did not consider his reputation as something his work created. His reputation was a byproduct of his faithfulness to the path he felt called to follow. His love for his "fellow-creatures," informed by the golden rule, was the sacred guiding principle of his life.

Extended Observation

Reflection & Conversation

This is a particularly long and rich chapter in the book. It also provides many of the key habits of life that fired Wilberforce's passion to create a better hour. These lessons are building blocks that will help you be an effective witness and advocate for what is good and right and true. If you are using this book in a group, it would be most helpful for you to spread your conversations on this chapter over two sessions.

Attend to the Word

Read Colossians 2:12–17. Have someone read the words aloud— slowly with meaning. As you hear the words, receive them as if the Apostle Paul were speaking them just to you in this moment. When the reading is finished, remain in silence for several moments to let the message of Colossians and what you have learned about the character and passion of Wilberforce nourish your spirit.

Engage

Wilberforce was a politician. The public platform of Parliament was his pulpit. His Gospel message was discovered in his powerful speeches and his actions on behalf of others.

1. Spend some time talking in general about your own reactions to what you learned about Wilberforce in this chapter. Share one or two things that stood out for you.
2. Many of the key traits of his character reflected exactly what Paul wrote as key elements in the Christian personality. Look at each of these characteristics and talk about how it would make a difference to you as you put your faith into action in your life. Be sure to discuss exactly *why* each of these characteristics is important in the life of a Christian—especially in a Christian who strives to transform society to create a better hour.

   a. Compassion

   b. Kindness

   c. Humility

   d. Gentleness

   e. Patience

   f. Forbearance and Forgiveness

   g. Love

Move Forward

Beyond the character traits, the passion, and the zeal, William Wilberforce had his own system of checks and balances to keep him on the Gospel path. Talk about each of these through the viewpoint of how each can help you move forward as Christians who, together, can be transformers.

1. ***Divine Stewardship:*** Do our actions pass the test of Jesus' prayer, "Not my will, but thine be done?"

2. ***Faith:*** Are we guided by our faith in Jesus Christ more powerfully than any other motive?

3. ***Justice:*** Do we strive to work for the rights of others— even for those who may not share our faith and vision?

4. ***Happiness:*** Do we reflect joy in our actions and do we rejoice in the happiness of others?

5. ***Bible Study & Prayer:*** Is there time in our days to read the Word of God and to spend time in God's presence in prayer and reflection?

6. ***Accountability:*** Are we willing to work together with others and to let our friends shine the light of truth on our actions?

Pray

Lord, fill our hearts with your peace and love. As members of one body you have called us to bring peace and justice to our world. Let your Word dwell in us as we teach one another and admonish one another. Give us wisdom. Let us sing songs of praise to you with awe and gratitude in our hearts. Let us do all that we do—consistent words and consistent deeds—be in your name, Lord Jesus, as we give thanks to God the Father through you.

four

The Zeal of Hannah More

By Anne Stott

Anne Stott is an Associate Lecturer at Open University and a Lecturer at Birbeck College in London. She has written the first substantial biography of Hannah More in more than fifty years and is the first to validate her unpublished correspondence. The new material shows More as having a more lively and attractive character than previous stereotypes have suggested. It also reinforces the growing perception that she was a complex and contradictory figure: a conservative who was accused of political and religious subversion and an ostensible antifeminist who opened up new opportunities for female activism. Understanding More's influence on William Wilberforce and on her society is a key to understanding the creation of "the better hour."

In the tumultuous times of the late eighteenth century at the dawn of the Industrial Revolution, Hannah More (1745–1833) was a well-known writer, a key participant in the abolition of the slave trade, an educator of the poor, and a person concerned with the development of literacy and education for women. In her time, More was better known than Mary Wollstonecraft, and her books outsold Jane Austen's many times over. Her now forgotten play, Percy, was the most successful tragedy of the day. Her tracts had a wider circulation than Thomas Paine's Rights of Man. More set up Sunday schools to teach the poor and was an early and influential part of the Sunday School Movement. She campaigned against the slave trade. She wrote books on conducts, political pamphlets, and a best-selling novel.

She was an early feminist who has been misunderstood as an anti-feminist, a well-known writer and one of the most influential female philanthropists of her day. Active, enterprising, and generous, More was born into obscurity, but died leaving nearly 30,000 pounds to charity, an unprecedented sum for a woman writer.

More was an invaluable role model for women who came after her. Her fame did not die with her, and for a generation or so after her death she figured in a biographical series with imposing titles, such as WOMEN OF WORTH and LIVES OF EMINENT AND ILLUSTRIOUS ENGLISHWOMEN. These biographies established her as a high achiever who had done much to widen the range of activities available to women. Her career demonstrates the possibilities for a woman, in the late eighteenth and early nineteenth centuries, who was neither wellborn nor wealthy and did not owe her advancement to becoming the mistress of a prominent man.

An Educator at an Early Age

Born in 1745 in Fishponds, a village near Bristol, More grew up as the daughter of a headmaster of a school in Stapleton. At an early age, she, along with her four sisters, was trained by her father to be a teacher. The three older More sisters decided to open a boarding school for "young ladies" and set about establishing it. They were only nineteen, seventeen, and fourteen at the time. Opening in 1758 in Bristol and funded initially by subscriptions, the school was a success from the start, and its reputation spread. Within a short time, Hannah and her younger sister Martha joined the staff. One aspect of the success of the school was the sisters' ability to make and develop contacts and friendships, particularly with prominent people of the day. Charles and John Wesley were friends with Hannah's older sister Mary. James Ferguson, the astronomer, and Thomas Sheridan both lectured at the school, and the British statesman Edmund Burke was a frequent visitor.

A Writer of Note

After a failed engagement, More received an annuity from her suitor that allowed her to be independent and become a "woman of letters." She had been writing poetry for some time and had written a play for the young women at the school that she started with her sisters. More now turned to the professional stage and her first effort, THE INFLEXIBLE CAPTIVE (later known as REGULUS), opened at the Theatre Royal, Bath in 1776. More plays followed, including PERCY in 1777 (produced at Garden Theater) and THE FATAL FALSEHOOD. She turned to religious writings, beginning with her SACRED DRAMAS in 1782, which rapidly ran through nineteen editions. These were followed by her THOUGHTS ON THE IMPORTANCE OF THE MANNERS OF THE GREAT TO GENERAL SOCIETY (1788) and AN ESTIMATE OF THE RELIGION OF THE FASHIONABLE WORLD (1788). More wrote many ethical books and tracts: STRICTURES ON FEMALE EDUCATION (1799), HINTS TOWARDS FORMING THE CHARACTER OF A YOUNG PRINCESS (1805), PRACTICAL PIETY (1811), CHRISTIAN MORALS (1813), CHARACTER OF ST. PAUL (1815) and MORAL SKETCHES (1819).

More had a gift for writing rapidly and with a freshness of storytelling that became extraordinarily popular.

More and her sisters were introduced to London society by Sir Joshua Reynolds and his sister Frances, both of whom were accomplished painters. More met many important political and societal figures, including Samuel Johnson and Edmund Burke. As her interests changed, More soon began to turn away from the stage. She began to rewrite stories from the Bible in dialogue form. She also started to lose interest in the social relationships that she had established in London. Over time, she became close friends with a group of men from Clapham, a few miles south of the center of London.

Engaged in the Abolition Movement

In the 1780s, More widened her circle in London to include many religious and philanthropic figures including John Newton, the slave trader, Evangelical clergyman, and hymn-writer, Beilby Porteus, the Bishop of London, and William Wilberforce, with whom she would develop a deep and lasting friendship. In 1786, More also met James Ramsay and a young Thomas Clarkson, both of whom were central to the early abolition campaign.

More made a significant contribution to the movement to abolish the slave trade. She was the most influential female member of the Society of Effecting the Abolition of the African Slave Trade. She assisted in running the society and in February 1788, her publication of SLAVERY, a poem, was recognized as one of the more important poems of the abolition era. Her relationship with the Clapham Circle was close, particularly with William Wilberforce. In fact, she spent the summer of 1789 with Wilberforce planning for the abolition campaign.

In the mid-1790s, More wrote several tracts opposing slavery and the slave trade, as well as THE SORROWS OF YAMBA and THE NEGRO WOMAN'S LAMENTATION, which was co-authored with Eaglesfield Smith and appeared in November 1795. She continued to oppose slavery throughout her life. Yet, at the time of the Abolition Bill of 1807, she was in poor health and unable to take an active role in the abolition movement.

The passionate involvement of women in the antislavery movement would eventually culminate in the publication of Harriet Beecher Stowe's UNCLE TOM'S CABIN in 1852.

The Sunday School Movement

One of the Clapham men More met who had a significant influence on her life was William Wilberforce. They first met in Bath in 1786. He became a regular visitor to her cottage at Cowslip Green. During one of these visits, in 1787, Wilberforce told More that something had to be done for Cheddar, a nearby village. Wilberforce had spent some time in this village and came away with a resolve that action needed to be taken to improve conditions for the people there.

Sunday schools had begun emerging in the seventeenth century, particularly after 1780 when Robert Raikes began the establishment of his schools. Their orientation and methodology were popular, especially within evangelical groups. Both Wilberforce and More, not surprisingly, saw it as a way forward. In Cheddar in 1791, More wrote:

> *We found more than 2,000 people in the parish, almost all very poor—no gentry, a dozen wealthy farmers, bard, brutal and ignorant. . . . We went to every house in the place, and found every house a scene of the greatest vice and ignorance. We saw but one Bible in all the parish, and that was used to prop up a flower-pot. No clergyman had resided in it for forty years. One rode over from Wells to preach once each Sunday. No sick were visited and children were often buried without any funeral service.* (1)

Besides the level of poverty, Wilberforce was upset at the lack of spiritual comfort. Out of the discussions that followed, the idea emerged that the establishment of a Sunday school where the poor could be taught on their day off from work was the necessary first step. In 1789 Hannah and Martha More opened a school in Cheddar.

The historical context of More's advocacy for the poor was the pervasive tumult of the French Revolution, which started in 1789 and by 1792 had morphed into the Reign of Terror. The attitudes of the wealthy in England were very much shaped by these developments and accordingly, there was great concern for stability in society. In the climate of alarm in England over the French Revolution, More's fresh and forceful defense of traditional values was met with strong approval.

At the same time the Industrial Revolution, which began around 1765, was in its early stages and children were working 16- to 18-hour days from the age of seven upward. Education would have been impossible for children of the lower and even middle class, except for Sunday school. Thus, it is not surprising that More's goal for children was "not to teach dogmas and opinions, but to form the lower classes to habits of industry and virtue." The framework for this activity was clear. More wrote: "I know of no way of teaching morals but by teaching principles, or of inculcating Christian principles without imparting a good knowledge of Scripture."

Sunday School activities were aimed at both children and adults. Sunday was the main teaching day because it was a time when students and teachers were free from work. However, some classes were held during the weekday evenings, particularly for young mothers. Reading, knitting, and sewing were the main activities. More did not teach writing, believing that this could cause sedition and give the lower classes ideas that were above their position in society. It should also be noted that local farmers were already opposed to teaching, in that they thought this would ruin the agricultural industry.

In preparation of starting a school in Cheddar, Hannah and Martha went around seeking support for the venture and gathering students. They found a house for the schoolmistress and a barn for the classroom and opened the school in October 1789.

At first More's lessons featured the reading of the Scripture only, though later she began to write stories, homilies, and poems with a moral purpose for use in instruction. She believed, as

John Wesley did, that it was no use to teach people reading if all there was to read was the "seditious or pornographic literature of commercialism." The object of the schools was also to cultivate honest and virtuous citizens, and this objective was furthered by her various savings societies. At each meeting all the members, especially the women, were encouraged to deposit a little, even a penny a week, against a rainy day. This was used as a kind of insurance fund from which a sick contributor was able to draw out 3 schillings per week. Maternity grants of 7 shillings, 6 pence were also available. She also hoped to raise the moral standard of the village by refusing membership to her schools to the non-virtuous. Girls found indulging in "gross living" were to be shunned and excluded.

What was particularly significant about the More sisters' activities with regard to Sunday schools was the pedagogy that they developed, the range of activities they provided, and the publicity they generated.

More's teaching method is outlined in HINTS ON HOW TO RUN A SUNDAY SCHOOL. (2) Besides aiming programs at the level of the students, More recommended variety in the programs and as entertaining a curriculum as possible. If energy should wane, the sisters recommended singing. Kindness was promoted as a method to elicit the best out of students. Philosophically, More urged that it was a "fundamental error to consider children as innocent beings" rather than as beings of a "corrupt nature and evil dispositions." (3) More allowed for paying students to learn:

> "Those who attend four Sundays without intermission, and come in time for morning prayer, receive a penny every fourth Sunday; but if they fail once, the other three Sundays go for nothing, and they must begin again. Once in every six or eight weeks I give a little gingerbread. Once a year I distribute little books according to merit—those who deserve most get a Bible—second-rate merit gets a prayer book—the rest, Cheap Repositor Tracts." (4)

Alongside these schooling activities, Hannah and Martha More also developed programs for the community. For example, the More sisters encouraged use of a village oven for baking bread and puddings, thus saving fuel.

When all of this was combined with the efforts of Robert Raikes, the Sunday School Society, which had been founded in

1785, led the effort to coordinate and develop the phenomenal growth of the Sunday School Movement in the nineteenth century.

Cheap Repository Tracts

More became alarmed at the growing influence of Thomas Paine's RIGHTS OF MAN. At the prompting of the Bishop of London, More wrote something that would open people's eyes to the folly of notions such as liberty and equality. The result was her first tract published under a pseudonym: VILLAGE POLITICS, by Will Chip, A Country Carpenter.

The book employed four basic arguments:

1. The gentry should look after the worthy poor.
2. No relation exists between government and want.
3. Government is no concern of the common man.
4. God knows what is best for his people. (5)

The success of VILLAGE POLITICS encouraged More and other of her Clapham friends to produce the CHEAP REPOSITORY TRACTS. These were a series of readable moral tales, uplifting ballads, and collections of readings, prayers, and sermons. More was to write and edit many of the tracts, while other Claphamites raised the money for printing and distribution (the tracts were sold at a little under cost).

The first tract was published in March 1795 and the last some three years later. The tracts were published monthly and overall sold over two million copies in one year, teaching the poor to rely on the virtues of contentment, sobriety, humility, industry, reverence for the British Constitution, and trust in God and in the kindness of gentry. The most famous and popular tract was THE SHEPHERD OF SALISBURY PLAIN describing a family of phenomenal frugality and contentment. More than one hundred were produced, fifty of them by More.

More later explained her involvement in writing the tracts:

And, as an appetite for reading had, from a variety of causes,
been increasing among the inferior ranks in this country,
it was judged expedient, at this critical period, to supply
such wholesome aliment as might give a new direction

to their taste, and abate their relish for those corrupt and
inflammatory publications which the consequences of the
French Revolution have been so fatally pouring upon us. (6)

Books on Education

As well as the tracts, More also wrote a number of more
substantial didactic works. Three particular works look to
education:

- STRICTURES ON THE MODERN SYSTEM OF FEMALE EDUCATION
  (1799)—which went through thirteen editions and sold
  more than nineteen thousand copies
- HINTS FOR FORMING THE CHARACTER OF A PRINCESS (1805)—a
  far less popular book that was basically designed as a
  course of study for Princes Charlotte, daughter of the
  Prince of Wales
- COLEBS IN SEARCH OF A WIFE (1809)—More's only novel. The
  book proved to be very popular, selling more than thirty
  thousand copies in the United Sates before More's death.

It is these books that have been a source of considerable
debate as to More's view of women and their role. On the one
hand, her view of women's education was more progressive than
many others in the middle classes at the time. For example,
More pointed out that it was unjust to keep women ignorant
and scorn them for it. More believed that education should be
a preparation for life rather than for adornment. She would
have the average girl trained in whatever "inculcates principles,
polishes taste, regulates temper, subdues passion, directs the
feelings, habituates to reflection, trains to self-denial and more
especially, that which refers to all actions, feelings and tastes and
passions to the love and fear of God." She would have history
taught to show the wickedness of mankind and the guiding hand
of God and geography to indicate how Providence has graciously
consulted man's comfort in suiting vegetation and climate to
his needs. (7)

More and her contemporary, Mary Wollstonecraft, both
believed that the education of women was deficient and in need
of reform. Wollstonecraft proposed universal literacy that placed
"importance on the cultivation of reason, without prescribing

functional use of education." For Wollstonecraft, education was meant to enlighten individuals without restricting them to particular skills or reading materials, as More sought to do.

Controversy

More's views and activities became the focus of the struggle in two areas: one between the farmers, who thought that education, even to the limited extent of learning to read, would be fatal to agriculture, and the clergy, who accused her of Methodist tendencies. She was also in the middle of the struggle between the evangelical wing of the Church of England, which saw Sunday schools and similar activities as a way forward, and a more conservative wing, which viewed such "Methodist" activities as dangerous. As the Sunday School Movement developed and the Methodists became more involved, the reaction grew stronger. One Monday night at a meeting for adults associated with Hannah and Martha More, a controversy known as the "Blagdon Controversy" erupted. The local pastor accused More of being a Methodist. The situation became the subject of various letters to the press and more than twenty pamphlets over a period of four years (1800–1804). The temper of the debate rose, with More being represented as the founder of a sect. In the end, More closed the Blagdon school as the controversy affected her health and she collapsed.

As "Victorian values" later came under attack, so did More, the epitome of these values. She became a hate object to the iconoclasts of later generations. The essayist and politician Augustine Birrell, who thought her "one of the most detestable writers that ever held a pen," gleefully buried a nineteen-volume edition of her works for garden compost. More, an enthusiastic gardener, might have smiled.

Philanthropy

More was one of the best-known philanthropists of the day. Not only did she donate her money, she dedicated her time to improving the conditions of children in the mining districts of the Mendip Hills near her home at Cowslip Green and Barley Wood. She developed Sunday schools with her sister Martha. She wrote popular tracts and her broader literary efforts marked her as an important figure.

> *(More's Christian) faith, hope, and charity to national purpose ... Though narrow in its theology and often conservative in its politics, evangelicalism was wide in its sympathies. This "vital religion" was intensely emotional and left its adherents obsessed with human depravity and the ideal of Christian perfection, whose very elusiveness animated conduct.* (8)

More believed that philanthropy was a woman's profession. Her argument had its weaknesses as well as its strengths. While it validated female activism and subtly undermined the ideology that sought to confine women to the purely domestic sphere, it remained a one-size-fits-all model that could never do justice to the diversity of women's needs and abilities.

At the time of her death, she left more than £30,000 to charities and religious societies—an amount probably worth millions in today's economy.

Conclusion

Hannah More, while she did not embrace universal literacy, did much to recognize the importance of "popular functional literacy." She also believed in a role for women as contributing members of society. Although her works were somewhat restrictive, she did ascribe importance to the education of women. More taught and practiced education with an informal air and a range of methods. More sought to find the right atmosphere for learning. She was also a leading advocate of lifelong education and learning. She cultivated the virtues of sobriety and industry as well as trust in God and in the kindness of the gentry.

More was a key person in advancing the role of women. One commentator noted:

> *Without in the least intending to do so, she was marking out a new sphere for the young women of the middle classes, and their revolt against their own narrow and futile lives followed as a matter of course."* (9)

Another commentator said:

"Her truly valuable legacy was not only the example of what one woman could be, and could do, but a real influence on the tone of education in all classes of English women. (10)

For a person that never left Britain, except for a brief trip over the border to Wales, More's influence extended far beyond her own country. This is symbolized by the founding of the Barley Wood School in Ceylon (known today as Sri Lanka) and by the policy of the Church Missionary Society to name orphaned African girls after her. She rejoiced in Britain's imperial mission, seeing it as, among other things, a liberating force in the lives of women. Already, the movement for women's education in the Indian subcontinent had begun with the Society for Promoting Female Education in the East, and it was to be continued in the work of the Zenana missions. With the abolition of the slave trade and the expansion of missionary work, the way was open for More and those who thought like her to argue that the British Empire was part of a divine plan to spread Christian truth and civilization throughout the world.

A commentator summarized More's achievements: "The woman who, for many years, educated at her own expense a thousand children annually, and whose munificent charities were not maintained by any inherited wealth or rank, but by the product of her own talents, is one of whom England may be justly proud." (11)

Extended Observation

Reflection & Conversation

Hannah More, in addition to her tireless work for the abolition of slavery, was really one of the first feminists. In a man's world, she was an accomplished playwright and writer. Because of her concern for the instruction of young people who were deprived of an education, she wrote tracts with stories that were quite popular and illustrated moral values to follow. She was one of the most influential female philanthropists of her day. In this reflection and conversation, concentrate on how she used her great gifts in the service of others. Concentrate as well on More as a model of Christian feminism.

Attend to the Word

Read 1 Samuel 2:1, 7–8 aloud. This is a selection from the Canticle of Hannah. As you listen to the words, relate their sentiments to what you have just learned about More. Think about and discuss how the Lord used More to "lift the needy from the ash heap."

Engage

More used education as a source of growth, change, and freedom. She had a heart for education. She also had a heart for young people who were being deprived of an education. Her CHEAP REPOSITORY TRACTS displayed that heart. More was also an early abolitionist. She stood out from the very beginning because there were very few women who were members of the abolitionist movement. More used her position as a prominent writer to publish SLAVERY, a poem that was one of the most important poems of the abolition period.

1. What was Hannah More's particular talent?
2. How did Hannah More reflect her biblical namesake?
3. How did Hannah More give of her time, her talent, and her treasure?
4. What were the results of her writing, her work, and her example?

Move Forward

Most children and adults worked six days a week. Sunday was their only day off. It was on Sunday that More would teach both young people and adults to read and provide them with a basic education. This instruction eventually became the Sunday School Movement, which was based on this basic education the church imparted to the children of poor families. As she moved forward in her life, More pressed for women to be contributing members of society.

1. What are your particular talents?
2. How can you use your talents to "raise the poor from the dust and the needy from the ash heap"?
3. How can you really give of your time, talents, and treasure using More or William Wilberforce as examples?
4. What would be the result of your using More or Wilberforce as examples?

Pray

Mary's song of praise recorded in Luke 1:46–55 echoes the words of Hannah in the Old Testament. They can also easily be applied to Hannah More. Use these words as a source for your prayer.

And Mary said:

"My soul glorifies the Lord
and my spirit rejoices in God my Savior,

for he has been mindful
of the humble state of his servant.

From now on all generations will call me blessed,
for the Mighty One has done great things for me—
holy is his name.

His mercy extends to those who fear him,
from generation to generation.

He has performed mighty deeds with his arm;
he has scattered those who are proud in their inmost
thoughts.

He has brought down rulers from their thrones
but has lifted up the humble.

He has filled the hungry with good things
but has sent the rich away empty.

He has helped his servant Israel,
remembering to be merciful

to Abraham and his descendants forever,
just as he promised our ancestors."

Luke 1: 46–55 (TNIV)

*five*

Wilberforce's Principles

By J. Douglas Holladay

*J. Douglas Holladay is a General Partner with Park Avenue Equity
Partners, LP and The Thornton Group, LLC. He is a former trustee and
frequent moderator of the Trinity Forum. Prior to his involvement in
Park Avenue Equity Partners, Holladay was a senior officer with the
international investment-banking firm, Goldman Sachs. He also served
as founding president of the One to One Mentoring Partnership, an
initiative by the New York financial community to bring imaginative
solutions to some of our nation's most pressing urban youth challenges.
Prior to joining Goldman Sachs, Holladay held senior positions in the
U.S. State Department and the White House. He was appointed to the
rank of ambassador and charged with coordinating the U.S. response to
South Africa's apartheid policy.*

*Holladay has written numerous articles that have been published
in* The New York Times, The Washington Post, USA Today,
Leaders Magazine, *and other major journals. He has also made several
appearances on national television. Holiday holds degrees from the
University of North Carolina Chapel Hill, Princeton University, and
Oxford University, and has been an adjunct professor at the University
of Virginia. He sits on numerous boards and presidential commissions
for various institutions and organizations, including Morehouse
College, United Way International, and Oxford Analytica, Ltd.*

Several times recently I've
come across a rather curious exercise: People in a group are
asked to put pen to paper and write their own obituaries. To be
included in their musings is how they hope to be remembered by
family, friends, colleagues, and communities. Projecting forward
like this, far from striking a morbid chord, actually provides some
needed perspective on what truly matters.

All of us seek to live lives that count. The big question that gnaws at us is: "How can our lives truly make a difference?" As one business executive said to a close friend of mine, "It's easy to make a fortune, but harder to make a difference."

Making a difference, finding true meaning, exercising real significance, contributing decisively to our children, our society, and our generation—whether expressed or not, such aspirations are widespread. As a boy, I remember being stirred by President Kennedy's challenge: "Ask not what your country can do for you, but ask what you can do for your country." We long for lives that count.

For me, that deeply personal desire for meaning and significance is closely tied to a very public question that stalks many discussions and debates in the United States and the West as a whole: Once a nation or society shows signs of drift or decline from its original ideals and vision, can that process be reversed? Can a culture genuinely be won back? Or is the attempt forlorn, a futile gesture destined to end in reactionary hardness and failure?

A mere ten years ago the question itself would have sounded absurd. But the mid-eighties' "morning in America," for example, has given way to a widespread sense of deep cultural and social crisis. American conservatives lament the social indicators of "American pathologies" while liberals rue the perils of "cynicism and mistrust" in public life. One widely quoted 1995 study showed that whereas three out of four Americans trusted the federal government and other institutions thirty years ago, only one in four does today. (1) A front-page story expressing our dilemma stated it this way: "Cure for Nation's Cynicism Eludes its Leaders." (2) Similar trends and responses are also evident elsewhere.

But the fashionable pessimism is premature. So too is the failure of nerve of the sophisticated, cynical, and jaded. At least two great periods in history stand as shining examples of the triumph of truth and reform over pessimism and decline. Complex modern problems may not be resolved by political, legal, and economic means alone. Precedents show that profound, history-changing restoration of culture is possible through the vision and enterprise of people motivated by a vital faith. Russian poet Boris Pasternak expressed it well: "It is not revolutions and upheavals that clear the road to new and better days but someone's soul, inspired and ablaze." (3)

One example of such vision and enterprise, though more remote from our own time, is the salvage of Western civilization by the Irish in the sixth century. It was a saving by "the skin of our teeth," as art historian Kenneth Clark famously said. The books, learning, scholarship, and culture saved by the tireless Irish missionaries who streamed out across Europe were almost erased by the marauding barbarians after the fall of "invincible Rome."

Another example, much closer in terms of time and approach, is the extraordinary story of the lives of a band of men and women led by a little known figure of the English speaking world: William Wilberforce. An indefatigable reformer and supreme abolisher of Britain's odious slave trade, Wilberforce arguably led the single most effective stand against evil and injustice in all of history. Perhaps the life and deeds of this remarkable individual, although of a simpler age, will offer a measure of hope to many resigned to our present situation.

Born in comfortable circumstances, young Wilberforce began a political career at the age of twenty-one with dazzling prospects. As a Member of Parliament, the closest friend and confidant of the young Prime Minister William Pitt, and one with access to high society circles, Wilberforce might well have succeeded Pitt as Prime Minister if (in one historian's words) he had "preferred party to mankind." But by age twenty-five, Wilberforce was ablaze with a mission for his life—one that, although daunting in light of the deeply entrenched opposing interests, would change the world.

Historians have detailed the achievements of Wilberforce and his colleagues regarding his "two great objects" (abolishing slavery and the reform of manners) as one of the significant turning points in history. England, in the early nineteenth century, was fueled by the economic benefits derived from slave trading. This heinous practice generated millions of pounds sterling and reached to the fashionable country homes of the landed aristocracy. If the reformers had not succeeded in the task of abolition, Africa would have been transformed into a slave-trading enterprise of monstrous proportions. The combination of slavery in nations such as the United States and the worldwide slave trade carried on by Britain and other European nations could have created the single greatest moral evil in history. More than any other person, Wilberforce blocked the course of that terrible possibility.

Success in this endeavor concerned only the first of Wilberforce's "two great objects." His success in the second, which is less measurable but perhaps even more daunting, was equally historic. He helped transform the civil and moral climate of his time. No wonder that when Wilberforce died, his own distinctive tradition of faith was described as the single most decisive force in Britain and the rock on which the nineteenth-century English character was formed.

Although biographers have attempted to describe William Wilberforce, it is understandably impossible to capture the encyclopedic range of his accomplishments in a brief essay. Nonetheless, we should stand back and reflect on some of the defining features of Wilberforce's life. Remarkable in themselves, they offer at least seven principles that illuminate what it means to live a life of significance today.

1. Faith

Wilberforce's entire life was animated by a deeply held, personal faith in Jesus Christ. Rather than ascribing to lifeless dogma or dull, conventional religious thinking, Wilberforce and his colleagues were motivated by a robust personal belief in a living God who is concerned with individual human lives, justice, and the transformation of societies. At their core was a profound sense of the presence and power of God, giving them vision, courage, and the necessary perspective to choose their issues and stand against the powerful interests aligned against them. Wilberforce, along with his friends, viewed himself as a pilgrim on a mission of mercy, never defining his identity or purposes by the flawed values of his age. This transcendent perspective made him the freest of men, and therefore the most threatening force against the status quo.

2. A Sense of Vocation

Wilberforce had a deep sense of a calling, which grew into the conviction that he was to exercise his spiritual purpose in the realm of his secular responsibility. Too often people of faith draw a dichotomy between the spiritual and the secular. Religious activities are considered a lofty calling while secular involvements are viewed with disdain and believed to have little to do with true spirituality. As Wilberforce came to see, such thinking is flawed at its core and frequently results in a two-tiered religious caste system. Those with spiritual sensitivities are urged to pursue "religious" affairs, such as the ministry, rather than face the tough, complex struggles inherent in the swirl of business or politics.

Fortunately, both Prime Minister Pitt and John Newton, the former slave-trader and composer of the well-known hymn "Amazing Grace," strongly urged young Wilberforce to remain in Parliament to pursue his calling. These friends helped Wilberforce appreciate the unique opportunity to launch a host of important initiatives and reforms that his position provided. Wilberforce's life forcefully demonstrates that a person of conviction can make a real difference in a secular environment.

3. Common Effort

Wilberforce was committed to the strategic importance of a band of like-minded friends, devoted to working together in chosen ventures. History bears testimony to the influence of individuals combining energies and skills to achieve a shared objective. As the Old Testament states, "How could one have routed a thousand, and two put a myriad to the flight?" (4) In his pursuit of reform, Wilberforce embodied this approach, which enables a small group to achieve enormous results. His particular band of associates was tagged "the Saints" by their contemporaries in Parliament—uttered by some with contempt and by others with deep admiration.

At certain points these friends even resided in adjoining homes in a suburb of London called Clapham Common, functioning as one. In fact, their esprit de corps was so evident and contagious that, together or apart, they operated like "a meeting that never adjourned." The achievement of Wilberforce's vision is largely due to the value he and his colleagues placed on harnessing their diverse skills while suppressing their egos for the greater public good.

4. The Power of Ideas

Wilberforce believed deeply in the power of ideas and moral beliefs to change culture through a campaign of sustained public persuasion. As historians point out, he and his associates actually pioneered many of the familiar modern forms of political organization and lobbying through their campaigns to change the attitudes of their nation. This was no small task, particularly in an age that pre-dated modern media and technology.

In one campaign, for example, Wilberforce and his friends presented a petition to Parliament signed by ten percent of the British people. He persuaded the famous potter Josiah Wedgwood to create a special medallion, at the center of which was a kneeling slave in shackles. Inscribed around the edge was the question: "Am I not a Man and a Brother?" This ceramic tract was designed to provoke a discussion of the moral status and human dignity of slaves. Wilberforce called such thought-provoking inventions "launchers," as they were designed to launch a most serious discussion concerning an issue of the times.

Public opinion changed as people became sensitive to the plight, not only of slaves, but of children and animals as well. Numerous organizations for bettering the lot of such groups had roots with the Clapham friends; they also published books, periodicals, and tracts to win hearts and minds. Wilberforce's own book went into five editions within its first six months of publication and remained a bestseller for forty years.

5. Personal Endurance

Wilberforce was willing to pay a steep cost for his courageous public stands and was remarkably persistent in pursuing his life task. As one who pursued ideals that endure, Wilberforce stands in dramatic contrast to both the "headline grabbing" of our age and the "bottom-line" mentality concerned only with swift results, regardless of long-term consequences.

For forty-seven years Wilberforce labored for a goal some thought unachievable—the total eradication of slavery in the British Empire. Suffering defeat after defeat, he would not be denied. Only three days before his death in July 1833, Parliament made one of the greatest moral decisions by a legislative body in history, a decision counter to its own economic advantage. Wilberforce and his commitment to enduring virtues had prevailed, despite the cost to his health, reputation, and political ambitions.

6. Genuine Humanity

Wilberforce's labors and faith were grounded in a genuine humanity rather than a blind fanaticism. Throughout his life, Wilberforce portrayed disarming wit and unassuming modesty, possessing a contagious joy even in the midst of the most serious personal and professional crises. Marianne Thornton, the daughter of Wilberforce's close colleague, banker Henry Thornton, portrayed the authentic quality of this remarkable man in her remembrance from childhood: "He was as restless and as volatile as a child himself, and during the grave discussions that went on between him and my father and others, he was most thankful to refresh himself by throwing a ball or a bunch of flowers at me, or opening the glass door and going off with me for a race on the lawn 'to warm his feet.'" (5) No dour piety for Mr. Wilberforce.

It was characteristic of Wilberforce that he worked comfortably, not only with friends, but also with those opposed to his views on faith and society. His character remained the same. Without being defensive or sanctimonious, he expressed his beliefs in a natural and straightforward manner. Another description of Wilberforce comes from the Scotsman Sir James Mackintosh, a Radical and free-thinker who observed the breadth and charms of this extraordinary person:

> *If I were called upon to describe Wilberforce in one word, I should say that he was the most "amusable" man I ever met in my life. Instead of having to think of what subjects will interest him it is perfectly impossible to hit one that does not. I never saw anyone who touched life at so many points and this is the more remarkable in a man who is supposed to live absorbed in the contemplation of a future state. When he was in the House of Commons he seemed to have the freshest mind of any man there. There was all the charm of youth about him.* (6)

Wilberforce, while committed to deeply passionate causes, had his identity and contentment anchored elsewhere. He was a man at peace in the storms of his time, one who integrated every facet of his life and thought within the borders of his faith. It could truly be said of him that he lived sub specie aeternitatis, in the light of eternity.

7. Strategic Partnerships

Wilberforce forged strategic partnerships for the common good irrespective of differences over methods, ideology, or religious beliefs. He attacked evils vigorously but worked with a spirit of respect and tolerance for people of very diverse allegiances. What mattered to him was real change, not rhetorical posturing. In a letter to Speaker Addington, Wilberforce explained his desire "to promote the cordial and vigorous and systematical exertions of all, . . . softening prejudices, healing divisions and striving to substitute a rational and an honest zeal for fundamentals, in place of a hot party spirit." (7) For example, when learning of the plight of a widow of an influential leader with whom Wilberforce and his friends had battled, he and two friends arranged for a lifetime annuity for her comfort and security.

Wilberforce is a powerful example of the old Anglican principle: "In things essential, unity, in things nonessential, diversity, and in all things, charity." Compromise on principle was unthinkable, but compromise on tactics was never a problem. Wilberforce resisted the tendency of narrow partisanship, instead seeking common ground where possible, and sharing credit for success with his various allies.

Lessons for Our Times

The life and work of William Wilberforce directly counters the cynical pessimism of our day and the pervasive belief that an individual is powerless to affect real change. We often think that contemporary problems are simply too complex and overwhelming to address, so we typically respond, either by escaping into a private world far from the challenges of the big issues, or by exaggerating the role of politics as the engine for social transformation. Both approaches are a dead end.

Wilberforce was born in an age when the privileged classes stood to gain little by reforming their conditions. In fact, they had much to lose. Yet armed with a vital faith, accompanied by a band of committed and gifted colleagues, and inspired by a burning vision to fight evil, Wilberforce decisively influenced this very class and transformed his times. As his biographer John Pollock emphasizes, "Wilberforce proved that a man can change his times, but that he cannot do it alone." (8)

Are there issues to be tackled in our time? Is there a role today that only a vital faith can play? Are we each prepared to find our part and work with others? Are you conceivably a man or woman in your own sphere of influence on whom God has placed his finger and said, "This is your time, your cause, your calling"?

Tiny in stature but towering in significance, William Wilberforce stands before us as an inspiration and a challenge.

Extended Observation

Reflection & Conversation

J. Douglas Holladay gives a clear and compelling picture of the principles that propelled William Wilberforce into action. His principles were easily turned into strategies. There is no reason to speculate about Wilberforce's motives. He kept a diary. His addresses to Parliament have been carefully preserved. He even wrote a bestselling book early on in his career. Focus this conversation and reflection on the values behind the man. Use the seven principles outlined in this chapter to advance your understanding of Wilberforce and to assess what principles guide your life.

Attend to the Word

Read aloud Hebrews 12: 1–6, 12–14. These verses—especially verses one through three—were of particular importance to William Wilberforce. As you heed these words, consider what practical impact they can have on your life and actions. Spend at least a few moments in silence after the reading. It is always helpful to share your thoughts as well.

Engage

Review the seven principles outlined in this chapter summarized below.

- Faith
- A Sense of Vocation
- Common Effort
- The Power of Ideas
- Personal Endurance
- Genuine Humanity
- Strategic Partnerships

Discuss each one briefly and then reflect on or discuss the following:

1. How did Wilberforce's principles provide him with the motivation he needed?
2. How did his principles provide him with a significant life?
3. In your opinion, what is the legacy of William Wilberforce?

Move Forward

This chapter begins with an observation about people writing their own obituaries. As you move forward from the principles that drove Wilberforce, consider your own principles, significance, and legacy.

1. What are one or two principles that you live by?
2. How do these principles provide your life with significance?
3. What legacy do you want to leave behind? Try to be as specific as possible with your responses.

Pray

The power of the Wilberforce legacy and the message of this chapter are discovered in the words of Issiah below. Use them as the source for your prayer.

> *Before I was born, the Lord appointed me,*
> *he made me his servent to bring back his people,*
> *to bring back the scattered people of Israel.*
>
> *The Lord give me honor;*
> *he is the source of my strength.*
>
> *The Lord said to me,*
>
> *"I have a greater task for you, my servant,*
> *not only will you restore to greatness the people of Israel*
> *who have survived,*
>
> *but, I will also make you a light to the nations—*
> *so that all the world may be saved.*

Isaiah 49:51–6 (GNT)

six

The Birth of Issue Campaigning

By Chuck Stetson

Today when one wants to make a point nationally on an issue and convince others across the nation, how does one go about it? Lance Armstrong got people's attention with a yellow bracelet—Live Strong—for his cancer foundation. Bono, a celebrity and a rock star, meets regularly with the heads of government wanting to "make poverty history." But what can the average person do?

William Wilberforce and Thomas Clarkson pioneered what we would recognize today as issue campaigning and lobbying methods in the fight for the abolition of slavery. These two men were innovative in organizing pressure groups and developing techniques to mobilize public opinion to effect change in government. (1) Wilberforce himself applied many of these techniques to the many other causes he espoused. Amazingly, these techniques are still applicable today.

Wilberforce and a small group of wealthy men lived in what was then the village of Clapham, a few miles south of the center of London. And it was from Clapham, now a part of greater London, that they were able to take on and prevail against the economic interests of slavery so deeply engrained in the British economy.

The task was a formidable one. More than half of the ships in the transatlantic slave trade were British. The major ports in Britain depended on the slave trade for employment. Sugar and rum from the West Indies were produced at low cost with the labor of slaves, and many Members of Parliament were landowners in the West Indies who profited from slave labor.

Wilberforce and his Clapham colleagues were people of great influence who saw the need to exercise stewardship and principled leadership in public life. In that spirit, they came to the decision to engage in the important issues of the day, especially slavery. They also worked with a number of individuals throughout Britain who were able to play key roles in the abolitionist movement. Both people of influence and people from the grass roots of society proved instrumental in making change happen.

In the late 1780s, Thomas Clarkson, a recently ordained graduate of Cambridge University, encouraged Wilberforce to go public with the strong beliefs that he already had on the abolition of slavery. Clarkson played a leading role in researching the evils of the slave trade. He was indispensable as well in the mobilization of public opinion against slavery, in establishing boycotts of products produced by slave labor, and in organizing petition drives, all of which had a deep influence upon Parliament. Such an all-out campaign was without precedent.

There was also the consideration of friendship and co-belligerence. (2) When Wilberforce took on the challenge of leading the parliamentary fight to end the slave trade, he had been for many years a close friend of William Pitt, the youngest Prime Minister in British history. Through Wilberforce, Clarkson's great contributions to the abolitionist cause were brought to Pitt's attention. Through Wilberforce, Clarkson was able to meet Pitt. Wilberforce and Clarkson's friendship was something they both valued in its own right. But they also recognized that as individuals, they and the members of the Clapham Circle were less effective than they were as a unified force. (3) As an individual, each might well have made his or her mark upon British society. Because they all worked together, combining resources, talents, and opportunities for usefulness, they exercised an influence out of proportion to their numbers. (4) It was only because they worked in concert that the British slave trade was ended in 1807, as was slavery itself throughout the British Empire in 1833.

Methods & Strategies

Because Wilberforce and his associates were pioneers in many forms of political organization and lobbying familiar to us today, their campaigns changed the attitudes of a nation. This is no small task, particularly in an age without modern media and technology. An analysis of their issue campaigning reveals ten basic methods or strategies.

1. The Long View

It took forty-six years for Wilberforce and his colleagues to achieve the unachievable: the total eradication of slavery from the British Empire. Despite incredible resolve, they suffered many defeats along the way. The key to eventual success was the strategic decision to "divide and conquer": to focus first on eliminating the slave trade (the transport of slaves to the West Indies), then on ending slavery itself throughout the British Empire (i.e. freeing those already enslaved and resident in the West Indies).

When it came to ending the slave trade, the initial focus in the late 1780s was international. Wilberforce and those who sided with him in Parliament aimed at a multilateral abolition of the trade by Britain and the major European powers, most notably France. Wilberforce and Clarkson worked closely with the Amis des Noirs—the most prominent French abolitionist organization—of which a leading member was the Marquis de Lafayette, hero of the American Revolution. During this period, Clarkson told Wilberforce: "Monsieur LaFayette has absolutely a greater respect for you than for any other person in the English nation." (5)

These early hopes for a multilateral, international abolition were dashed by the fall of the Bastille, the subsequent Reign of Terror under Robespierre, and the eventual world war against Napoleon's France that embroiled Europe. From start to finish, these events convulsed Europe for more than twenty-five years (1789–1815).

In the early 1790s, Wilberforce and his colleagues had to change tactics. They now sought to focus solely on putting the slave trade on the national agenda in Britain and trying to end it there first. A capacity for adaptation generally, but particularly in the face of sobering international unrest was, again, crucial to eventual success. So too was an organizational willingness to reassess goals and learn from setbacks. Wilberforce and his colleagues consistently kept a long view. How they kept up that struggle over time ensured their eventual victory.

2. The Development of a Team

Wilberforce's natural capacity for forming friendships and the value he and his friends placed upon combining their efforts served them well. Wilberforce had been the close friend of Prime Minister William Pitt for years when the fight to end the slave trade began, but Wilberforce also realized he needed to build bridges. In so doing he began to form a unique kind of political coalition. Recognizing the need "to conciliate good will" in pursuit of goals that would serve the good of the country as well as the good of all humankind, he reached across the aisle to Charles Fox, leader of the opposition party. This was a fruit of Wilberforce's so-called "great change" or embrace of Christianity. Only a few years before, in the heat of a general election, Wilberforce had sought to tear Fox and other perceived political enemies to pieces.

After his spiritual transformation, Wilberforce's conduct in political life underwent a thorough change. Because he came to believe that the golden rule was binding over all of life, he took great care to mend his broken relationship with Fox. Wide differences in their political views would remain, but they became unlikely friends and co-workers in the fight to end the slave trade. "I quite love Fox for his generous and warm fidelity to the Slave Trade cause," Wilberforce wrote in 1806, one year before the slave trade was abolished. (6) Some years before, Fox, who had himself thought of seeking to lead a push to end the slave trade, wrote: "It is better that the cause should be in [Wilberforce's] hands than in mine; from him I honestly believe that it will come with more weight, more authority, and more probability of success." (7)

Aside from building bridges across the political aisle with men like Charles Fox, Wilberforce had a group of friends such as few men have had in the Clapham Circle. They spent significant time with each other and with each other's families. They provided each other with moral support and encouragement. Jointly, they provided financial support for the scores of philanthropic societies they formed. We would call them nonprofits today.

The list of Clapham Circle members and their non-resident co-belligerents reads like a Who's Who of late eighteenth- and early nineteenth-century England. Among this number were Granville Sharpe, John Wesley, Edmund Burke, Hannah More, James Stephen, Thomas Clarkson, Thomas Fowell Buxton, and

Elizabeth Fry. What Wilberforce understood and valued was the need to harness the diverse and complementary skills of his friends. Their egos and individual ambitions were also subservient to larger goals. Wilberforce and his colleagues resisted the tendency of narrow partisanship. Instead they sought common ground where possible and shared credit for successes with their allies.

3. Impeccable Research

Research is an essential tool in constructing arguments that will change minds on an issue. Volunteer organizations bent on getting out their message often overlook the need for solid research. The kind of market research done by highly successful companies in today's global economy is foreshadowed by the research of the Clapham Circle.

The group gathered raw data, both qualitative and quantitative. Thomas Clarkson worked with Richard Phillips, who was a young lawyer with a clear knowledge of the workings of government and who had connections to many of the politicians and officials able to provide records of custom houses and other important sources of statistics. This effort yielded vital information about, for example, the mortality rate of seamen involved in the slave trade. From the data, Clarkson was able to demonstrate that twenty percent of the sailors on board slave ships died at sea. Another thirty percent never returned to England. Two trips to Africa for slave commerce, Clarkson learned, would kill more sailors than eighty-three trips to Newfoundland.

Clarkson haunted the key slave ports of England. He boarded slave ships berthed in Bristol, Liverpool, Birmingham, and London. He personally interviewed hundreds of people connected with the slave trade. At one point, he boarded 317 ships to relocate a vital witness whose name he had misplaced. All told, in the years that he conducted his investigations, Clarkson traveled an estimated 1,600 miles on horseback around England. (8)

Ultimately research on the slave trade (both for and against) was collected in an 850-page report published by the Privy Council of Parliament. The report included much of the testimony Clarkson had obtained. When the report came out, Clarkson provided Wilberforce with extracts and summaries he could use effectively in Parliament.

In Wilberforce's hands this research yielded vivid word pictures that made an indelible impression on the Members of Parliament. He graphically described the horrors of the Middle Passage, the route most commonly taken by slave ships to the New World. He described the factors that gave rise to a devastating mortality rate for those enslaved. One hundred fifty-five might die on a ship with 650 persons, 200 on another ship with 405 persons. At other times, Wilberforce spoke of the netting that had to be put in place to restrain slaves from jumping overboard and the ways in which slaves were forced to eat to avoid having them die from self-imposed starvation. The power of the research allowed him to communicate to the House of Commons his indefatigable resolve to "demand justice for millions who could not ask it for themselves." (9)

Based upon a drawing Clarkson had rendered to demonstrate how slaves were packed into the decks of the slave ship Brookes, Wilberforce commissioned a wooden model of the ship. In an age long before multimedia presentations and video clips, Wilberforce helped his colleagues graphically experience what it meant for human beings to be subjected to the Middle Passage.

4. Cogent Arguments & Active Networks

The reformers developed simple and cogent arguments that they disseminated through their personal and professional networks. Few within the ruling elite of the British Empire could have seen much wrong with their society. Most would have seen their economy as the most robust and secure in the world, their political process as the most democratic, and their culture among the most noble and elegant.

The Christian worldview of Wilberforce and the Clapham Circle afforded them the moral imperatives needed to stand against the slave trade and slavery. However, they possessed a capacity for framing arguments that could be powerful and persuasive to people who did not share their faith commitment. Clarkson's research about mortality rates—for British seamen and slaves alike—was gleaned from official government records and painstaking interviews. To spread the cogent arguments against the trade, Wilberforce, Clarkson, and the other abolitionists relied on the strength that comes from a union of talents and insights: they forged networks. They united their energies and exploited any and all of their relationships to raise public consciousness of the evils of the trade and of slavery.

5. Maximizing Influence

When Wilberforce wanted to get something done, he worked directly with society's gatekeepers. Throughout the twenty-year fight to abolish the slave trade, he worked closely with his friend Prime Minister William Pitt. He also worked with Charles Fox, the leader of the opposition party.

Wilberforce also engaged the services of popular, widely read literary figures such as Hannah More and William Cowper. Their poems against slavery had a wide impact among all classes of people in Britain. Cowper's poem, "The Negro's Complaint," was printed on expensive paper and circulated among tens of thousands in Britain and America. In Britain, it was set to music and became an abolition anthem. In America, it was beloved by African-Americans like Benjamin Hughes, who quoted from it in his celebrated Eulogium on the Life of William Wilberforce, a funeral oration given at "the request of the people of color" in New York City. Hughes's eulogy is now regarded as a classic of African-American literature.

6. Mobilizing Nationwide Support

Wilberforce's colleague Thomas Clarkson traveled extensively around England arranging public meetings, distributing pamphlets, obtaining petitions, and organizing the boycott of sugar made with slave labor. Because of his status as a clergyman, he was also a frequent speaker in churches.

One tactic to garner nationwide support was the petition. Petitioning had never before been done on such an extensive scale in Britain. In 1792, a record total of 519 petitions came in before one of Wilberforce's speeches in Parliament. Twenty thousand men had signed the petition in the city of Manchester alone. Glasgow and Edinburgh sent in petitions with 22,000 signatures. At one point in the summer of 1814, in thirty-four days, eight hundred petitions with nearly one million signatures— approximately ten percent of the English people—were sent to the House of Commons. This would be the equivalent of getting

30 million signatures on a petition in the United States today. The great nationwide support as evidenced by the petitions got the full attention of Parliament.

7. Symbols

Because they understood the need to develop a symbol or icon that would focus people's attention on the plight of the slave, the abolitionists engaged the famous Josiah Wedgwood, the Potter to the Queen, to create a special cameo. At the center of the cameo was a kneeling slave in shackles. Inscribed around the edge was the question: "Am I Not a Man and a Brother?"

The "Wedgwood cameo" became the powerful symbol of the human dignity of the sons and daughters of Africa that Wilberforce and the entire abolitionist group hoped it would be. For example, even though women could not vote at the time, they could wear the anti-slavery cameo on their dress or on their jewelry to show their support of abolition. This image from the cameo appeared on everything from plates to snuff boxes. Thomas Clarkson himself gave out five hundred of the medallions to people he met. (10) Over time, the cameo enjoyed the kind of success marked today by the End Poverty Now and Live Strong bracelets.

In the United States, the cameo image was later changed to the figure of a woman, and the question became "Am I not a Woman and a Sister?" Women throughout the United States wore this image as a message of solidarity.

8. Launchers

Dinner conversations were important elements in the strategies of the abolitionists. The Wedgwood cameo, the drawings of slave ships, and even actual shackles from slave ships served as "dinner launchers," or conversation starters. Carried into polite and influential company as these cameos were, they often generated compelling discussions. For example, because the cameo's legend was framed as a question, not a condemnation, it stimulated constructive debate and conversations that extended beyond dinner or other social events.

Poems like those of Hannah More and William Cowper also generated conversation. The cumulative effect of all these dinner launchers was such that in 1789, Samuel Romilly, a prominent Member of Parliament, wrote to a friend about a dinner party he attended: "The abolition of the slave trade was the subject of conversation, as it is indeed of almost all conversations."

9. Mass Communication

In this era, mass communications were effected by a storm of books and pamphlets. Clarkson and Wilberforce each wrote books and pamphlets that were widely distributed. Clarkson began with an essay written in Latin that had won first prize at Cambridge: "Anne Liceat invitos in servitutem dare?" or, "Is it right to enslave men against their will?" This essay was published in 1786 in the 256-page book AN ESSAY ON THE SLAVERY AND COMMERCE OF THE HUMAN SPECIES, PARTICULARLY THE AFRICAN.

In the first year of the Committee for Effecting the Abolition of the Slave Trade, 51,432 books and pamphlets and 25,636 copies of reports and other papers had been distributed. After the first parliamentary debate on the slave trade in 1788, the committee distributed 10,000 copies of the debate to the public.

In 1807, Clarkson's book HISTORY OF THE RISE, PROGRESS AND ACCOMPLISHMENT OF THE ABOLITION OF THE AFRICAN SLAVE TRADE BY THE BRITISH PARLIAMENT was published. To finance the publication, Clarkson encouraged about 4,000 people to purchase copies before it was published. Later, in 1822, Clarkson wrote THOUGHTS ON THE NECESSITY OF IMPROVING THE CONDITIONS OF SLAVES IN THE BRITISH COLONIES, WITH A VIEW TO THEIR ULTIMATE EMANCIPATION, AND THE PRACTICALITY, SAFETY AND ADVANTAGES OF THE LATTER MEASURES.

Wilberforce and the Clapham Circle circulated a significant amount of abolitionist literature and then started their own magazine, THE CHRISTIAN OBSERVER, which carried articles on issues of the day. Zachary Macaulay, the editor of THE CHRISTIAN OBSERVER, founded the ANTI-SLAVERY MONTHLY REPORTER, a small paper that published 113 issues from June 1825 to July 1836.

10. Infrastructure of Volunteers

Wilberforce and the abolitionists would never have reached their goal without building an infrastructure of individual volunteers and voluntary societies. The volunteers were a key to getting broad public involvement. While today we take for granted the idea of volunteer organizations that take up a cause and work to change public opinion, there was very little of that at the time of Wilberforce. Yet volunteers became a crucial organization tool, particularly since the issues undertaken, such as slavery, were difficult issues that required dedication and a long-term approach.

Having an infrastructure, therefore, that could pursue a particular issue was critical. The Committee on Effecting the Abolition of the Slave Trade was an important organizing entity for initially developing strategy for abolition and distributing pamphlets. Later, in 1822, the Society for Mitigating and Gradually Abolishing the State of Slavery throughout the British Dominions was formed to carry on emancipation once the slave trade had been abolished, and it built on the success of the earlier committee.

Wilberforce was active in numerous volunteer societies. These societies included the Society for the Betterment of the Poor, The British and Foreign Bible Society, the Society for the Relief of Persons Imprisoned for Small Debts, the Society for the Reformation of Prison Discipline, and the Royal Society for the Prevention of Cruelty to Animals. The work of such societies as these set the standard for social actions for decades to come.

The Result of the Abolition Campaign

On February 23, 1807, after twenty years of tireless campaigning by Wilberforce, the House of Commons debated the Bill for Abolition, and it was obvious it would pass this time. It was a most dramatic moment. Cheers—robust cheers—marked the vote in the House. The years of issue campaigning, dinner launchers, research, and the tide of public opinion finally stopped the trade. A small incident underscores how issue campaigning became an essential tool for those who would work with Wilberforce to reform the country's manners. After the vote on abolition and all the accompanying celebration were over, Wilberforce and his great friend Henry Thornton were walking back to Wilberforce's house in the small hours of the morning. Wilberforce said, "Well Henry, what shall we abolish next?" Thornton, who had no sense of humor, replied gravely, "The Lottery I think."

The campaign to abolish slavery had arisen from
Wilberforce's love for others and his compassion. Those same
emotions drove his work for social reform. Too many men and
women were hanged and their executions were public spectacles.
Public drunkenness and a high crime rate had their source in a
general decadence and corruption that crossed all segments of
society. The "high civilization" of eighteenth-century England
had been built on the slave trade, mass poverty, child labor, and
political corruption.

Wilberforce and the Clapham Circle had gained moral
authority during the drive to abolish the slave trade. Everyone
could see that they were working for the well being of fellow
human beings, to alleviate oppression, and *not* for any economic
self-interest. Wilberforce and the Clapham Circle were able to
extend their moral authority from the slave trade to other areas
of their concern, including the horrible working conditions
of children and women, conditions in prisons, and cruelty to
animals.

From this moral high ground, Wilberforce and his friends
used similar campaign strategies to remake England, to make
goodness fashionable, and to restore respect for the law in all
classes. Wilberforce hit upon an ingenious idea. In a hierarchical
age, if he changed the leaders, he would change society.
Accordingly, Wilberforce formed the Society for the Reformation
of Manners, engaging King George III to reissue a proclamation
on manners and persuading many bishops, dukes, and other
notables to join his newly founded society.

The Legacy of Clarkson & Wilberforce

Clarkson and Wilberforce were an incredible team. In 1830
at a large meeting in London, they paid tribute to each other.
Clarkson moved that Wilberforce chair the meeting "as the
great leader in our cause." Wilberforce, in his last public speech,
acknowledged that no one was dearer to him than Clarkson, "my
valued friend and fellow-laborer."

Wilberforce, in particular, had an important impact on
philanthropy and social reform and how to go about it. Today,
the United Nations estimates that there may be one million
non-governmental organizations working to alleviate ignorance,
oppression, poverty, disease, cruelty, or injustice. Wilberforce may

not have invented the volunteer sector, but no single individual did more to advance its currency or impact. Anyone working today to "build the good society" shares a debt of gratitude to Wilberforce.

The power of ideas and moral beliefs can change the world. Wilberforce's life makes that point! Any reflection on his life and the impact of his campaigning begs the question: Were Wilberforce alive today and working in Parliament or in Congress, what would his "great object" be?

Extended Observation

Reflection & Conversation

William Wilberforce was an accomplished campaigner. He and his colleagues were also creative in the methods they used to change a society that was dissolute and corrupt. Focus your reflection on how you can bring faith to contemporary campaigning to accomplish changes in the world in which you live.

Attend to the Word

Read Romans 12:1–18. This passage should be engraved on the heart of every person who would live a life of significance or who would work to make changes in society. Spend some time in silence after the reading. Let Paul's powerful exhortation fill your thoughts and imagination. Think about how these words were manifest in the campaigning of Wilberforce, Clarkson, and the Clapham Circle. (Note: If you are working in a group and are pressed for time, be sure to read at the very least verses 3–8.)

Engage

This chapter articulates ten basic methods or strategies that Wilberforce, Clarkson, and the rest effectively used to gain passage of the bill to abolish the slave trade. Pick two or three of these strategies and reflect on how they can be a part of any social action you engage in. Review some issue campaigning that engages people of faith in your city or neighborhood.

1. How effective is this campaigning?
2. How does it reflect the issue campaigning of Wilberforce and his friends?
3. How does it reflect the words of Paul to the Romans?

Move Forward

Talk about social issues that confront you in your community. What issues raise a desire in you to work for change? Pick one or two of the issues that surface and discuss what kind of campaign you would have to mount to accomplish change.

1. How would you bring the methods and strategies used by the Clapham Circle to bear on your issue?
2. What contemporary strategies could you use to work for change?
3. How would you communicate the need and mobilize the public to action?

Pray

Psalm 107 carries some of the sentiments that help in issue campaigning. Use the verses below as a source for prayer.

Give thanks to the LORD, for he is good;
his love endures forever.

Let the redeemed of the LORD tell their story—
those he redeemed from the hand of the foe,

those he gathered from the lands,
from east and west, from north and south.

Let them give thanks to the LORD for his unfailing love
and his wonderful deeds for humankind,

for he satisfies the thirsty
and fills the hungry with good things.

Some sat in darkness, in utter darkness,
prisoners suffering in iron chains.

Then they cried to the LORD in their trouble,
and he saved them from their distress.

He brought them out of darkness, the utter darkness,
and broke away their chains.

Let them give thanks to the LORD for his unfailing love
and his wonderful deeds for humankind.

Psalm 107:1–3, 8–10, 13–15

PART II

COMPLETING THE LEGACY
OF WILLIAM WILBERFORCE

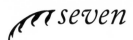

seven

The Unfinished Business of Abolition

By Beth Herzfeld

Beth Herzfeld has been the Press Officer at Anti-Slavery International since 1999. She has a BA and an MA in international relations and has written for numerous publications. Anti-Slavery International was founded in 1839 by the same abolitionists who successfully led the campaign in 1807 to abolish the Transatlantic Slave Trade in Britain and its colonies and fought for the abolition of slavery in 1833. The organization continues to work for an end to slavery throughout the world and is the leading organization in this field.

Millions of women, children, and men are living in slavery around the world. They are forced to work, they have no freedom, they are denied the right to make choices, and they are under the control of their masters. In a world where most nations guarantee human rights and slavery is purportedly illegal, people continue to be bought, sold, and exchanged. They are even given as gifts.

Today, most slaves do not wear chains or shackles, but still they are in bondage. In the twenty-first century slavery takes many forms. It is:

- **Bonded labor:** Millions of people are forced by poverty or are tricked into taking a small loan vital for their survival which can lead to a family being enslaved for generations.

- **Forced labor:** At least 12.3 million people throughout the world are forced to do work through the threat or use of violence or other punishment.

- *Forced marriages:* Girls and women are married against their will and are forced into a life of servitude often dominated by violence.

- *Work harmful to health:* An estimated 179 million children around the world are in work that is harmful to their health and welfare.

- *Human trafficking:* At least 2.4 million women, children, and men are trafficked throughout the world, taken from one area to another and forced into slavery.

- *Slavery by descent:* People are either born into a slave class or are from a "group" that society views as suited to be used as slave labor.

Slavery, servitude, and forced labor are violations of individual freedoms, which deny millions of people their basic dignity and fundamental human rights. (1)

The word "slavery" conjures up images of abuses that many believe were consigned to history by the victories of the nineteenth-century abolitionist movement. But in reality, slavery continues today.

At least 12.3 million women, children, and men throughout the world are being used as slaves. (2) They are forced to work through the threat or use of violence, are denied freedom or are physically constrained, dehumanized, and treated as property. No region is free from this abuse with slavery found in most countries, even though it is illegal under international law. It is defined and prohibited under the United Nations Supplementary Convention on the Abolition of Slavery, the Slave Trade and Institutions and Practices Similar to Slavery (1956) (33) and banned under the Universal Declaration of Human Rights (4) to which all members of the United Nations (UN) are subject. It is also prohibited under International Labor Organization core conventions, which most countries are obliged to implement, such as the Forced Labor Convention No. 29 (1930) and the convention on the Worst Forms of Child Labor No. 182 (1999).

Slavery takes many forms and affects people of all ages and races or ethnicities. Boys as young as four years old are abducted from their families in South Asia to be used as camel jockeys in the United Arab Emirates; young girls in West Africa are used as domestic slaves; young men in Brazil are used as forced labor to clear the Amazon making way for cattle farms; and women are trafficked to Western Europe and forced into prostitution.

Human Trafficking

One of the fastest growing forms of slavery is human trafficking, affecting at least 2.5 million people throughout the world. (5) Traffickers prey on people in impoverished areas who are excluded from opportunities or who are in societies destroyed by war and other turmoil. They promise well-paid work, education, and training that is unobtainable at home. Desperate to improve their lives, people are tricked or coerced into working away from their homes in conditions to which they have not agreed.

Mimin Mintarsih's experience is characteristic of this. When she was twelve years old, she began working as a domestic in Indonesia's capital, Jakarta. Five years later, her employer's sister, Dina Lam, took her to the United States to work for her. Lam paid Mimin's employer $8,000 for the visa, a false passport, and Mimin's return ticket. But when they arrived in the United States, she confiscated the travel documents and threw Mimin's ticket away.

Mimin was on call twenty-four hours a day. She had to do all of the housework in the Lams' mansion, including washing, ironing, cooking all meals, which sometimes required her to cook all night for parties the Lams held, and look after their children. In return, the Lams sent the equivalent of $1.96 per day to Mimin's family in Indonesia. Mimin was kept in isolation and subjected to constant fear and verbal abuse. When she pleaded to return home, the Lams refused. (6)

In 2004, the U.S. Government estimated that between 14,500 and 17,500 people were trafficked to the United States. (7) Although there has been some progress as governments pass legislation that criminalizes trafficking, many generally view the problem only as a law and order issue or one of organized crime. Trafficking is a human rights violation and the rights and welfare of the trafficked person must be at the heart of any counter-trafficking strategy. All too often, trafficked people are treated as criminals or illegal immigrants rather than as victims of a crime.

To address this, Anti-Slavery International not only presses for governments to adopt anti-trafficking laws but also sets measures, such as the Council of Europe's Convention on Action Against Trafficking in Human Beings, that will protect trafficked people's rights by guaranteeing at least a minimum standard of protection, such as thirty days to stay in the country to receive emergency medical assistance, safe shelter, and legal advice.

Born into a Slave Class

Trafficking is only one of the many forms of slavery in the world today. In Niger at least 43,000 people are enslaved as a result of being born into an established slave class. They are used as herders, agricultural laborers, and as domestic servants. Slaves carry out every task required by a highborn nomadic household. Many are subjected to torture and other forms of humiliating and degrading treatment, including rape, physical abuse, and threats.

Regardless of their age, they work every day without pay and are denied the freedom to make choices, whether it is deciding when to eat and sleep or whom they marry.

Assibit was a slave for fifty years:

> *I was born a slave just like my mother, my grandmother, my husband, and my children. We belonged to my Touareg master and lived with him, but my mother belonged to the master's wife. We did all of the work. I had to begin working at 5:30 A.M., pounding millet and milking the camels. Then I prepared breakfast for the master and his family. My family only got the leftovers. My husband and sons herded the cattle and camels while my daughter and I did all of the household chores including moving the heavy tent four times a day to ensure the mistress sat in the shade all day. I was my master's slave; that was my identity. We were never paid.* (8)

In addition to the violence and threats used to control these slaves, they are also tied to the master psychologically. The slave owner uses the belief that the master is god, and that slaves will only be able to enter paradise on his or her word.

But in spite of this, slaves manage to escape. Assibit finally fled after a violent storm throughout which she was made to stand serving as a support for her master's tent. She walked thirty kilometers to freedom; "I could take no more," she said.

The villagers who found Assibit took her to a non-governmental organization called Timidria. Timidria is Anti-Slavery International's local partner, which works to end slavery in Niger. It has offices throughout the country and helps slaves who have been freed or who have managed to escape.

To address this, in 2003, Anti-Slavery International and Timidria carried out the first nationwide survey of slavery in Niger, interviewing over eleven thousand people, the vast majority of whom were identified as slaves.

In response to the survey's results, the Niger Government introduced a law criminalizing slavery in 2003, making it punishable by up to thirty years in prison. It now has the chance to end centuries of slavery, but implementation is key if the law is to have any effect. Anti-Slavery International and Timidria continue to press for the law to be enforced.

Today, Assibit lives in freedom and survives with help from Timidria: "I have never known such kindness. They helped me buy seeds, and now I have a small plot near the water pool where I grow beans, pumpkin, and greens, and my sons are able to find paid work. Soon we hope to buy some goats and perhaps a donkey."

Bonded Labor

One of the most extensive forms of slavery is bonded labor, which affects millions of people. It is most prevalent in South Asia, and even though India outlawed this form of slavery almost thirty years ago, (9) followed by Pakistan (10) and Nepal, (11) the abuse remains widespread.

People become bonded when their labor is demanded as repayment for a loan. Usually they are forced by necessity into taking a loan in order to pay for such basic needs as food, medicine, and for social obligations such as the costs of a wedding or a funeral. To repay the loan, bonded laborers are typically forced to work long hours regardless of their age or health, for up to seven days a week, 365 days a year.

Entire families can be enslaved in this way, with the debt passed from generation to generation. Many bonded laborers work for no wages, and the food and clothing that are provided are added to their debt along with interest payments on the loan, thereby increasing the debt on a daily basis. And most are forced to carry out unpaid labor, on top of the tasks assigned against the debt.

Bonded laborers are traditionally used in agriculture, brick making, stone quarries, silk production, carpet weaving, and bidi (cigarette) making, but can be found in many other areas as well.

In India, Tyaiya Lal Shetha was twelve years old when he became a bonded laborer. His father had already worked as a bonded laborer for ten years after borrowing 3,000 rupees (US$65) from the same landlord. But when he became too old to work, he was told to send Tyaiya to work instead. Tyaiya is now twenty-five and has been working for thirteen years for a loan he never took out. He has to work from early in the morning to late in the day, plowing, planting, harvesting, and doing any other work the landlord demands, regardless of the hour. In return, he gets one-and-a-half kilograms of rice, which the landlord requires Tyaiya's mother to collect. However, before she is given the rice, she has to clean his house. (12)

Trapped in this cycle, bonded laborers find it almost impossible to pay off their debts. Poverty, long hours of hard labor, poor diet and lack of access to medical care mean they frequently become ill. Yet time off work due to illness is added to the debt, perpetuating the system of bondage.

Bonded laborers are routinely threatened with and subjected to physical and sexual violence. Their lives are controlled by those to whom they owe the debt, to the extent where those who use bonded labor sometimes sell the debts—and thereby the people— on to others. In Pakistan, brick kiln workers tell of being sold more than ten times.

To address this, Anti-Slavery International works with local organizations across India, Pakistan and Nepal to end bonded labor through pressing for the laws to be implemented, engaging the courts and police to help in the release of bonded laborers and helping former bonded laborers to release those who are enslaved. Also crucial to our work is the development of programs that can help former bonded laborers live free and independent lives once they are free.

Child Labor

Of the staggering number of slaves worldwide, it is estimated that some forty to fifty percent of them are children. (13) As with all slavery, child slavery takes many forms ranging from bonded labor, to descent-based slavery as found in Niger, to trafficking. Most are enslaved in the countries in which they were born.

Millions of children, as young as five years old, are enslaved as domestics throughout the world. Often this type of work is regarded as a safe form of employment, particularly for girls. But in reality girls are vulnerable to a wide range of abuses, including physical or verbal abuse and sexual violence. They are deprived of their right to education and rest, are isolated from their families and from opportunities to make friends, and are under the total control of their employers. (14) Child domestics are invisible and marginalized both economically and socially.

Mila is an example of the hundreds of thousands of girls in the Philippines who are working as domestic servants. (15) "During my time as a child domestic I worked for eleven employers. Only one of them gave me any salary, and that was just 500 pesos (US$9) a month," Mila said. "Each day I had to get up at 5:00 A.M., to carry out household chores such as taking care of my employers' children, cooking, cleaning, doing the laundry, and ironing. On top of this, I had to do additional work including making deliveries, and in one case, looking after pigs." (16)

She was kept in terrible conditions. "In one place I lived in a shed, with no light, no mattress, and only one bucket of water a week for washing." On two occasions she was sexually assaulted, once when she was twelve by her employer, a seventy-year-old man, and again when she was fifteen by the brother of her then-employer. Mila managed to escape and get help from Anti-Slavery International's partner, the local organization Visayan Forum. In 2005, she graduated from university and today is helping to empower other girls and women enslaved as domestics.

To address this, empowerment is a vital part in helping people become and stay free. Where child domestic workers are concerned, Anti-Slavery International works with local organizations throughout the world to help children know their rights and to protect them from abuse and exploitation.

End Slavery Now

Poverty, lack of political will, people's willingness to exploit those most vulnerable, and social acceptance all contribute to the survival of slavery. To end slavery, it is vital that the system as a whole is tackled. It is not enough to simply release someone; programs operated by non-governmental organizations, developed to help former slaves live free and independent lives, need to be supported by governments.

It is also vital that governments develop and implement laws that criminalize the specific forms of slavery in their countries, and ensure an end to the impunity that leaves those who use slaves unpunished. It is crucial that the root causes of slavery are addressed and societies understand that using human beings in this way will not be tolerated.

To achieve this, Anti-Slavery International works in a variety of ways, including helping local and regional organizations develop research to establish the forces behind slavery; to determine what form of slavery exists in a particular country; as well as to raise awareness of the current existence of slavery throughout the world, and how it can be stopped. Anti-Slavery International also supports the initiatives of local organizations to release people and presses for more effective implementation of international and domestic laws against slavery.

It has been two hundred years since Britain abolished the Transatlantic Slave Trade—an important step on the path to the total abolition of the slave trade and the liberation of those who were enslaved. It was an achievement that was only made possible by mass public action, challenging what was an accepted norm. As in the eighteenth and nineteenth centuries, the public has a vital role to play in demanding an end to this abuse once and for all.

Extended Observation

Reflection & Conversation

Discussions of slavery often are conducted in the past tense. Yet this chapter demonstrates that slavery remains an overwhelming problem in the present. Focus your thoughts and conversation on the need for Christians and all people of good will to rid the world of the evil of subjugation. The fact that millions of human beings are bought and sold for labor or for sexual pleasure means that the work of William Wilberforce is not yet complete.

Attend to the Word

Read Psalm 2 in its entirety. After the reading, spend a few moments in silence to let the meaning of the words sink in. Remember that this is one of the royal psalms, and it may have been composed for a coronation. It serves as a warning to rulers who would subjugate people, as Israel was so often subjugated.

Engage

The seeds of slavery are sown in human arrogance. That arrogance is willfully blind to the value of the lives of classes or groups of people in order to use them for pleasure or profit. Once a person sees each human being as one who is created in the image of God, enslaving another is no longer an option. The trafficking of human beings is but one step removed from murder, mass murder, or genocide. Examine your own attitudes toward others.

1. What is your reaction to stories about human trafficking? Do you feel outrage? Why or why not?
2. Where does accountability lie for the attitudes that tolerate human trafficking?
3. What warning for world leaders, for corporations, and for all humankind do you find in Psalm 2:7–12?

Move Forward

Most people cannot affect the behavior of others—especially those half a world away. And yet, if the legacy of William Wilberforce has any lesson at all, it is the lesson that people together, actively engaged with the issue, can effect major change. Reflect on and discuss your own resolve.

1. How can you change and improve your attitudes toward and the ways you treat others?
2. Realistically, how can you defend the rights of others?
3. As you work so that all may be free of subjugation and slavery, what will be your guiding principles?

Pray

Alone or in your group, use this responsive prayer to call to mind the plight of all those who are yet to experience freedom from slavery.

> *Lord, set free all those who are victims of human trafficking. Have mercy on those who are bought and sold for pleasure or for profit.*
>
> HAPPY ARE ALL WHO TAKE REFUGE IN YOU.

> *Lord, break the chains of all those who are born in bondage. Let them breathe the fresh and free air of your wonderful creation.*
>
> HAPPY ARE ALL WHO TAKE REFUGE IN YOU.

> *Lord, bless those who sweat and toil without pay in bonded labor. Let them know the value of their efforts and the dignity of a just workplace.*
>
> HAPPY ARE ALL WHO TAKE REFUGE IN YOU.

> *Lord, take special care of those children of yours who are pressed into servitude at a very young age. Let them experience again the wonders of childhood, of learning, and of playing together in joy.*
>
> HAPPY ARE ALL WHO TAKE REFUGE IN YOU.

> *Lord, give me the strength to speak up for those in bondage and slavery around the world. Let no voice be silent in the face of these grave injustices.*
>
> HAPPY ARE ALL WHO TAKE REFUGE IN YOU.

eight

Globalization: Incubator of a New Slavery

By Os Guinness

*Dr. Os Guinness is an author and speaker who has written or edited
more than twenty books, including* The America Hour, Time for
Truth, The Call, Invitation to the Classics, *and* Long Journey
Home. *His latest book,* Unspeakable: Facing Up to Evil in a World
of Genocide and Terror, *was published by Harper San Francisco in
2005. Previously, Os was a freelance reporter with the BBC.*

*Great-great grandson of Arthur Guinness, the Dublin brewer, Os
Guinness was born in China in World War II, where his parents were
medical missionaries. A witness to the climax of the Chinese Revolution
in 1949, he was expelled with many other foreigners in 1951 and
returned to Europe, where he was educated in England. He completed
his undergraduate degree at the University of London and his Ph.D. in
the social sciences at Oriel College, Oxford.*

*Since coming to the United States in 1984, he has been a Guest
Scholar at the Woodrow Wilson Center for International Studies and a
Guest Scholar and Visiting Fellow at the Brookings Institution. From
1986 to 1989, Os served as Executive Director of the Williamsburg
Charter Foundation, a bicentennial celebration of the First Amendment.
In this position, he helped to draft the Williamsburg Charter and
co-authored the public school curriculum* Living with Our Deepest
Differences.

*From 1991 until 2004, he was the founder and senior fellow of the
Trinity Forum, and a frequent speaker and seminar leader at political
and business conferences in both the United States and Europe. He has
also lectured at many universities, and has spoken at the White House,
Capitol Hill, and other public policy arenas around Washington, D.C.
As a European visitor to this country and an admirer but detached
observer of American culture today, he stands in the long tradition
of outside voices who have contributed so much to America's ongoing
discussion about the state of the union.*

Dr. Guinness has long been a great admirer of William Wilberforce, one of the most respected social reformers in history. The following essay is a transcription of an address given at "Socrates in the City" in New York in 2006.

In 1898, a friend of Otto von Bismarck, the German Chancellor, asked him what would be the decisive factor in the twentieth century. Bismarck answered, "The fact that Americans speak English." In his day, the British Empire was the largest, strongest force on earth. But within twenty years it declined and faded, and the vacuum was filled, not by the victor of a European conflict of powers, but by the United States. The last century was the American century.

In the same spirit, we might ask, "What is decisive today?" I am moved by the fact that three of the greatest questions have both a geo-political dimension and a spiritual dimension. But there is something that links them all. The first great question for the twenty-first century is, "Will Islam modernize peacefully?" The second is, "Which faith will replace Marxism in China?" The Communist Party is in power, but the ideology is hollow and China is on a search for an ethic and a philosophy to replace Marxism and guide China as she emerges as a great superpower again. The third great question for our time is, "Will the West sever or recover its roots?" No great civilization endures if it cuts its roots, yet we are on the verge of doing just that.

What accentuates and links these questions is Globalization. Now as soon as you mention Globalization, you are dealing with something that has been called a buzzword, a watchword, and a password. Globalization is a buzzword because people use it and never stop to think what it really means. It is a watchword in the sense that it is a word used to throw light on other things, but it very rarely has the light shone back on itself. And obviously, it is a password because it immediately splits people into camps—on one side, the cheerleaders who want to promote Globalization, and on the other, the curmudgeons who are protesting it.

I would like to set out a view of Globalization that is both more comprehensive than many people's and more critical. When you listen to people engaging with Globalization, many of them—say, readers of Tom Friedman's THE WORLD IS FLAT—have a blithely optimistic view of Globalization that sees only the winners and not the losers—those who are on the advanced end, not those on the losing end. But Globalization is much broader than this and much more challenging. So let me leave aside many of the obvious things about Globalization, which Friedman covers well, and look at some of the more challenging issues, and how it touches us all and raises issues for our world.

What Is Globalization?

We must start by asking, "What is Globalization?" But even before defining it, I would underscore the importance of humility in discussing it. The very term suggests its power. The word introduced originally was "universalization," which carried the idea that human beings could use reason, planning, and design to universalize what they wanted and stay in control of the process. Later, the word *Globalization* came in to underscore a different dimension. We have unleashed a force into the world that is affecting us all, and we are not fully in control of it. The simple fact is that when you think of a force that is truly global and globalizing, we are talking about something that no human can fully comprehend, and no leader, government, nation, or group of nations can fully control.

Obviously, none of us sees the world from nowhere. That is impossible. Equally, none of us sees the world from everywhere. That is incoherent. We all always only see the world from somewhere: from a place and at a moment that is finite and limited. This means that unless we have a word from God, which with Globalization we do not have, our views on something global are necessarily incomplete. So we all have to begin with a tremendous humility.

But what actually is Globalization? Contrary to many people's ideas, Globalization is not market capitalism. It is rooted in modern technologies of communication. So here is my definition: *Globalization is the process whereby, through the speed, the scope and the simultaneity of our communications we can conduct our human affairs anywhere in the world regardless of place, time, or government—so that for the first time in human history, in some rudimentary yet revolutionary degree, we are seeing the beginning of one world.*

Seen this way, Globalization can be called "Modernization, Mark Two." Modernization, Mark One was the Industrial Revolution, and at the heart of the Industrial Revolution was not communications, but production—the extraordinary new industrial capacity to produce on a scale never before seen in history. The factory epitomizes Mark One.

We have come a long way from that early stage, including a huge advance in communications. The first advance was marked by the combination of the steam engine and the telegraph, represented by the railroads. The second advance was marked by a combination of the telephone and the rocket, represented by the satellite. Our latest advance is marked by the combination of the microchip and the fiber optic cable, represented of course by the computer and the World Wide Web.

If this understanding is correct, the heart of Globalization is not market capitalism. That is just one of the forces that uses the technologies of communication; but communications themselves are at the very center of it all, and driving it forward in ways that are unprecedented. Thus, everything in our world depends on the twin currencies of conductivity (of information) and mobility (of people), both of which have reached unprecedented levels of advance.

Now when you look at the various forces that have taken advantage of these communications, you are obviously looking at capitalism, democracy, cultural products, and so on. I want to leave all of those at one side, because they are so well covered in much of the popular discussion. Instead, let me then pick out issues that are not so well covered, and in particular look at some of the broad consequences of Globalization. Now of course, Globalization is always a question of more or less. So what I am about to say applies more to people who are more modernized and globalized, and less so to those who are further behind. Living here in the United States, Globalization touches us all, as many people are just beginning to recognize.

The Consequences of Globalization

The first rather obvious consequence is that we are now in a world *on the move and melting down*. The surface sense of that is so obvious that it hardly needs saying. Connectivity and mobility have created a world in which distances do not matter, boundaries do not work as they used to, and traditional categories such as "close" and "faraway" are increasingly obsolete. To be sure, we have not reached "the end of history," but we have reached "the end of geography." Everyone is coming and going. We are all perpetual motion machines. Ours is a world of tourists and vagabonds.

But follow the idea down to a far deeper and more important level. A good description of the difference between the traditional world and the globalized world is that we have shifted from a "solid" world to a "liquid" world. You do not have to be a scientist to know that a solid is something that holds its shape at rest, whereas a liquid takes the shape of whatever it is in. A liquid flows, oozes, or trickles. And it is said that the effect of Globalization, because of the speed at which we move and the speed at which we communicate, is that the traditional bonds and ties that hold together social relationships have melted and become unglued.

An obvious example of such institutional meltdown is marriage. Fifty years ago, people said to each other "till death do us part." It was for the duration. It was for a lifetime bonded by the glue of covenant commitment. Then came serial monogamy— commitment "until further notice." And then came living together—"Let's see how this works out." The latest in European relationships are called SDCs, or "semi-detached couples." These are people who are together when they want to be together, but not together when they don't want to be together. In other words, ours is a world without firm ties and bonds, in which the institution of marriage is melting down.

Most people notice only the upside of this general institutional meltdown—a new freedom. "No ties, no tears" is the motto of those who are keen to solve all life's problems simply by "moving on." You have a problem? Move on. You want a fresh start? Move on. You would like a new relationship or a new job? Move on. But of course the downside of this "freedom" is restlessness, loneliness, heartache, and a harvest of dysfunctions.

The second grand consequence of Globalization is that we live ever more atomized lives. Communities, neighborhoods, and families are melting down, and what we are left with is an isolated individualism that is the atomic particle of society. The French author Michel Houellebecq captures this in his novel that has been called the Brave New World of our time: Elementary Particles. It is the story of two half brothers who are so isolated in their individualism that eventually they each have only themselves, and they end in atomic isolation.

Needless to say, this individual freedom is sold to us as new and unbounded freedom: "You can be anything you want to be," or "You have the right to be left alone." Put more technically, we are free because we have moved from a world of "ascription," in which our gender, class, and social roles are given to us as almost fixed to an "achievement" society in which all these same things are up to us. They are our task or our project, and we can choose and change at will.

In fact, the idea that "we can be anything we want to be" is one of the silliest ideas around, and also one of the most frustrating. And of course, the "frustration gap" between what we are told we can be and what we find we can actually be is filled in with shrinks and gurus, self-help formulae and self-improvement techniques—all designed to hide the fact that people in their lonely freedom are not doing as well as they are told that they really should be.

The third broad consequence of Globalization is that it is producing a world where *differences are dug deeper*. Put differently, we are seeing the rise of worldwide fundamentalism. At the elite level, Globalization means that people who were once apart are now brought together—for example, the "Davos man" who treks to the Swiss Alps every January to discuss the affairs of the world with others in the global elite. But at the bottom level, people who were once happy in their different ways of life are suddenly aware (through the media, and travel) of "all those others" and their very different ways of life, and how the modern world has a corrosive impact on them all.

Seen this way, fundamentalism is not traditional. It is a modern reaction to the modern world, and its cultural defiance and militancy can be seen in all the world's religions. For example, Japanese Buddhism has Soka Gakkai, Hinduism has the Hindu National Party, Islam has Islamism, and so on.

The Special Temptations of Globalization

Globalization raises three special temptations for the elites that are often overlooked. With the unimaginable fortunes they are able to make in the global era, it is often thought that the elites see only the blessings of Globalization, but this is not so. Even for them, the world is not all that flat. Let's take a look at the three temptations:

1. Lives without Any Reflection

As we all know, we are all going too fast, we know too much,
and we have far too much pressure on every second of our lives.
The speed and pressure of our lives are obvious. We may have
conquered geography and space, but while we have compressed
time, we have not conquered it. Time has conquered us. Labor
saving devices do not mean a world with more time, but less time.
Our 24 × 7 × 365 world is hurried and harried. As Kenyans say,
"All Westerners have watches; no Westerners have time."

Our information overload is obvious too. I read about a man
who did an online search for the word *waste*, and in less than
three seconds got more than 18 million references. As he said,
"What a waste." That amount of information is far more than
any human mind can digest or assess, let alone remember. It is
more than a library could contain. The only place that can handle
such an amount is the World Wide Web, which means that the
Internet is part goldmine and part garbage can.

How then can we be wise in such a world, when such
overloads have led to the age of the one-page executive summary,
the coach, the consultant, the one-minute manager, and so on?
Then there is the added pressure of impossible expectations. Take
the case of marriage again. If you say "until death do us part"
and you are married twenty, thirty, fifty, or even sixty years, the
husband doesn't have to be the ultimate Romeo every second of
life, nor does the wife have to be the ultimate Juliet. There is the
framework of the covenant that holds things together even when
you are not at your best. But without such a covenant framework,
you have to perform perfectly every second of the time, or there
is nothing to hold you together except the state of your love at
each moment, and either party can "move on" to relationships that
meet their needs better.

The same is true of business. Without any sense of loyalty
to, or from a corporation, everything is judged incessantly on
moment-by-moment performance. After the collapse of Enron, it
was said that there was an unremitting and unrealistic pressure on
those who worked there. A certain percentage of the workforce
was routinely fired every year, and another percentage was told
that they would be fired the next year unless they performed
better. Yesterday's success was never enough. All that matters
is today. Not surprisingly, many people said that it was a relief
to be fired by Enron, and the result of such a modern work

environment is a massive and dangerous loss of reflection and a corresponding lack of wisdom among leaders.

2. Loss of Responsibility

The second great temptation for the global elites is the loss of responsibility. If we are honest, moral responsibility has always been more than simply ethics, and closely linked to visibility. People were often good, or they weren't bad, because they were seen. Plato and many of the ancients discussed this, and there are examples in the Bible. In other words, responsibility was close to accountability because of visibility.

The trouble is that in the modern world, we are more anonymous in more situations than in any generation ever in human history. The question then is, what is the source of our integrity and responsibility when no one sees? The effects of anonymity play out in all sorts of ways. Let me mention one—the creation of absentee landlords. In the French and Russian Revolutions, the absentee landlords weren't always evil people. They were those who lived high on the hog in Paris or St. Petersburg off the backs of the peasants in rural France or rural Russia. They never saw the peasants and never gave a thought to them—and the outcome was injustice and oppression.

We have a new breed of absentee landlords today. There are major financial players in New York, London, Tokyo, or Shanghai, who every day manipulate trillions of dollars. And for many of them, their only consideration is the next quarter or the interests of their investors. In addition, you have business leaders, such Al "Chainsaw" Dunlap, who openly argue that CEOs should only think of the investor, never of the supplier, the workforce, the environment, or the outsource group. So you have the rise of new absentee landlords, people making decisions that touch the lives of thousands around the world, but they never think about these people, and they never see them; they narrow everything down to the financial decisions.

There is a fundamental irresponsibility in such relationships, and we need to remind ourselves that we are our brother's and sister's keeper, and we are the stewards of the earth. Any of us who have any influence in any area—a journalist writing articles in the press, or an investment banker making decisions that affect people on the other side of the world—we have a responsibility even where we do not see the effects of our decisions. The elite temptation to irresponsibility is a serious problem made worse by Globalization.

3. Loss of Roots & Realism

Globalization represents a massive erosion of roots and realism. We have shifted from the soul to the ego, from truth to spin, from the hero to the celebrity, from a world of neighborhoods to a world of networks, and from real relationships to virtual relationships. Put all that together, and you can see how profound is the erosion of roots and realism.

On the other hand, Globalization represents an equally massive inflation. Through the greatly expanded reach and resources of modern capital and technologies, an individual or a company can have an astonishing global influence—for example, Bill Gates in the business world or Rick Warren in the religious world. The result is what Carl Gustav Jung warned of years ago as "gigantism."

At the moment, thank God, most of the global giants are benevolent figures. But it is not hard to see how more malign figures could use the same globalized power for ill. And there is always the likelihood that otherwise reasonably good people will be corrupted by such global power. We would then be approaching a place close to the image in Nebuchadnezzar's dream in the Book of Daniel. The great king was warned against his own hubris through the vision of a figure with a head of gold but feet of clay. Without the face-to-face realism of having real face-to-face roots, Globalization will produce inflated people who are dangerous to the world. Lincoln's warning about the dangers of the "towering genius" makes sense in such a world. We need to be on the watch for malign global giants. A global Saddam Hussein or a global Hitler would be a frightening prospect.

The Blind Spots of Globalization

Globalization has three major blind spots that require attention because many secularists tend to make Globalization their gospel and their grounds for confidence. After the 1960s, many secular philosophies ran into the ground because they lacked any theoretical or empirical reason for optimism, but Globalization has breathed new life into secularism. The whole world is being linked, and becoming more free, more prosperous, and more democratic at the same time. Globalization is good news for humanity.

But people who speak like that usually overlook the blind spots of Globalization, and people who have a deeper concern for humanity must look out for the losers as well as the winners. There are three particular blind spots that we must be aware of.

1. Dislocation

The first blind spot is to the dislocations of Globalization. These are plain in the "first modernity" of the Industrial Revolution, as any reader of Charles Dickens knows well. Traditional ways of life were uprooted, dislocated, and disrupted. As Max Weber put it, the Industrial Revolution opened up a "separation" between the worlds of the household and work, and into that gap exploded vast growth in cities such as London, Paris, and New York with their sprawling slums, and countless forms of oppression. Even the greatest proponents of market capitalism admit that the first and second generations paid a high price in terms of dislocations. But as Globalization advances, we are seeing the same all over again; and any of you who have been to Manila, Cairo, or Mexico City, know the results: massive cities, horrendous slums, and a green light for all sorts of evils and injustices.

2. Contradictions

The second blind spot is the presence of contradictions within Globalization itself. In the West, we see market capitalism and democracy going hand-in-hand. But when they hit other parts of the world, they are often unequal partners and sometimes open enemies. Take the example of the Philippines. When democracy and capitalism were introduced into the Philippines after World War II, some of the communities there prospered unimaginably almost overnight. The Chinese, for instance, are brilliant entrepreneurs and natural business people. With cultural values that are congenial to capitalism, they took to it like ducks to water and made unimaginable fortunes overnight, whereas the majority of people, the native Filipinos, were left largely where they were. Not surprisingly, glaring inequities created resentments, suspicions and hostility, and then violence and terrorism. It was simply not true that the rising tide raised all boats.

3. Human Waste

The third blind spot is the worst: human waste, or what has been called "wasted humans." I am not talking about industrial waste, although that is a problem, but wasted human beings. Every social order creates its own disorder. There are people and things that do not fit in, and who either wish to leave or who are the "undesirables" whom the society wishes to get rid of. Thus, when the early modern world came in, the "unwanted" were shipped to empty "virgin lands" elsewhere in the world. For instance, the British shipped their unwanted convicts to Botany Bay and the French their les miserables to Algeria or Nova Scotia. There were certainly problems in this "waste management"—it is said that possibly 30 to 50 million human beings were slaughtered in the far from empty lands to which the emigrating or the expelled went. But on the whole there was room to send people.

This is no longer the case. In terms of empty land, the world is "full." There are no empty places to ship people to. As it is put bluntly, there is "a reduction of outlets and a reversal of flow." People from all parts of the world now want to come to the Western world, and we are seeing a massive "reverse colonization," as millions from Latin America try to enter the United States and people from Africa and Asia try to get into Europe. The net effect is a vast production of human waste—millions of unwanted human beings. There are nearly 30 million human beings in the vast archipelago of "nowherevilles," otherwise known as refugee camps. With no state to take them in, no jobs to fulfill, no roles to play, no income on which to live, and no community in which to gain security, the people there often have nothing but their bare-naked lives—and then they are vulnerable to exploitation and abuse, whether from their United Nations "safe keepers," as in Szrebenica and Darfur, or from outside predators, such as Joseph Koney and the Lord's Resistance Army in Uganda.

The Coming Perfect Storm

Finally, we need to recognize how Globalization is creating a "perfect storm" of contemporary evil. Each of the phases of modernity has its own characteristic form of evil. The English workhouse epitomized the early modern evils of the Industrial Revolution. The mid-modern evils, which arose in direct reaction to the early modern evils, were epitomized by the German death camps (the link between industrialization and Auschwitz is all too clear). And now the advanced modern evils are epitomized by the American shopping mall, or more accurately by the American-led Internet mall. In other words, we are witnessing the rise of one of the greatest human rights crises of all time, and a crisis that is the direct child of Globalization.

This perfect storm of evil is created by the convergence of three factors at the heart of Globalization: the vast expansion of freedom and mobility through technology—for example, travel and the Internet; the vast expansion of the profit motive through worldwide capitalism—for instance, the rise of illicit trade and illegal trafficking; and the vast expansion of human discontents and dysfunctions through the melting down of traditional human communities and institutions. Put differently, Globalization is stoking consumer demand for products and experiences once considered deviant, perverted, and wrong.

Many who hear of evils, such as human trafficking, tend to think only of the terrible sadness of the supply—for example, the millions of humans trafficked from Asia, Africa, and Eastern Europe. But the challenging fact is that while the supply comes from the less developed world, the demand comes from the modern Western world. It has been put very simply: It took 400 years for Europeans to transport 12 million Africans to the Americas, whereas in the 1990s alone, 30 million women and children were bought, sold, and trafficked from Asia alone. According to United Nations statistics, 27 million human beings are being held forcibly by criminal enterprises. Two to 4 million are added to their number every year. Ten million children under ten are prostitutes. Two hundred million children are in forced labor.

The moral scandal we must face is that while the supply comes from the third world, the demand is from the West. Almost every single country in the world has been touched by some form of this evil, but most of the demand is Western, the majority of the consumers are American, an extraordinary proportion of the victimizers are women, and the images are getting more graphic and the victims younger every year. The final tragedy is that other forms of illicit trade, such as drugs and arms, are nonrenewable, whereas trafficked humans can be used and re-used, abused repeatedly until worn out.

It is a great mistake and part of the self-congratulatory moral blindness of the West to think of evil as "way back then," whether in the eighteenth-century slave trade or the 1940s death camps, "way over there," such as Asian and African sex tourism. The "heart of darkness" today is not in the Congo or in imperialism; it is right at home in the West and in the Internet malls that are the cathedrals of consumption for our market-driven consumer-citizens. In short, in our new human rights crisis, we are the enemy.

Responding to Globalization

One last point to throw light on the debate opened up by the dark side of Globalization: There are three main ways forward in the debate, each of which is associated with a major worldview. When you look at the full scale of the challenges of Globalization, profound questions are being raised. As usual, there are only so many answers in the room and a limited number of suggestions as to the way forward.

1. Press On

The first possible outcome is to press on regardless. This is the usual position of those who are secularist. Their argument is that the crises have always been exaggerated, and always will be—for example, Thomas Malthus's fears about over-population. Besides, science and technology can always be counted on for an answer. And the final throw of the dice is that, in an extreme crisis for the earth, we can always create a post-human, artificial future, a world largely dependent on robots, which concentrates on the human mind, rather than the human body.

2. Look Elsewhere

The second possible outcome is to stop and look elsewhere, principally to the Eastern religions or to Native American ways of relating to the earth. In other words, the argument is that Judaism, the Christian faith, and the Enlightenment are responsible for the depredations and rapacity of our world bent on knowledge, power, and domination. Their solution is to turn towards views of wisdom, rather than knowledge; and equilibrium and balance, rather than domination, and so to Hinduism, Buddhism, and Shamanism, rather than Western beliefs. In 1978, for example, the Gaia Movement was launched when scientist James Lovelock chose as the title of his book GAIA: A NEW LOOK AT LIFE ON EARTH. His original title for the book had been boring and complicated, but his neighbor, the novelist William Golding, suggested that he use the name of the Greek goddess of the earth—Gaia. The book sold fabulously millions as a result, and launched the Gaia Movement.

3. Go Back a Bit

The third possible outcome is to go back where we went wrong. That is the broad position of Jews and the Christians. There is no question that the modern world came out of Judaism and the Christian faith, or what Prime Minster Benjamin Disraeli called "Judaism for the multitude." But somewhere in the seventeenth and eighteenth centuries, things went badly wrong and the Western world shifted from biblical "dominion" to "domination" and from stewardship to exploitation. Instead of seeing and treating the world as "God's handiwork," as Isaac Newton called it, we treated the earth as our property and our playground. Francis Bacon's "knowledge is power" became the watchword of the day, and there is no question that the West has raped and plundered the earth in a manner that is disastrous for humans, as well as for the earth.

This third position would require going back to where we have gone wrong. In Genesis, for example, we read of the covenant with Noah that was to include, not only humans, but also all the living species. By the terms of that covenant, it is clear that we have been and are today grossly delinquent as stewards.

The overall challenge of such outcomes is plain. Human beings must inevitably make grave decisions about our common future of the planet, and these decisions will inevitably be made out of the worldviews that we hold.

Conclusion

The deepest discussions of Globalization often come back to a very simple but fundamental crisis. The crisis of *trust* is far more than a philosophical problem, such as post-modernism. It is far more than an ethical problem, such we saw in the Enron Corporation. It is far more than a political problem, such as the post-Watergate cynicism. Globalization is creating a crisis of trust in the sense that the globalized world is an experience of such precariousness and anxiety that many people have lost a deep sense of trust in themselves, in their institutions, and in their future; and therefore in their agency and their ability to act constructively in the world.

The deeper I have explored the way in which Globalization is affecting our world, the more I am struck by a very simple conclusion. There is only one force or power on earth that is greater than Globalization—and that is God. This is what the prophet Isaiah of Jerusalem realized long ago. He lived in a day of vast empires and superpowers—Assyria, Babylon, Egypt, and Persia—and not surprisingly, people all around him were panicking, and trying to cobble together various defenses to give themselves some sense of security, however false.

Isaiah trusted none of them. He knew that if God is God, then God is greater than all, and God can be trusted in all situations. So there are two simple conclusions for people of faith in a day of vast forces, such as Globalization, and vast fears, such as terrorism, nuclear proliferation, and bird flu: We may be small, and we may be out-matched by the very forces and fears we have unleashed, but "Have faith in God," and "Have no fear."

Extended Observation

Reflection & Conversation

This chapter turns a critical light on Globalization. Focus your thoughts and your conversations on how you experience Globalization. As you review and debate the various observations presented in this chapter, keep your mind open to how you can work for a society that, though it may be global, needs to be enriched by the spiritual.

Attend to the Word

Read 1 Chronicles 29:14–18. These verses provide a warning for those who would give in to the temptations of Globalization, to keep their eyes closed to the dangers, or choose to go blindly forward. Take a few moments of silence to let the words find a place in your heart.

Engage

The chapter mentions three temptations, three blind spots, and three ways forward. Examine each of these in the light of the chapter and of the reading from 1 Chronicles. Articulate your own attitudes and test them against those of others.

Temptations	Blind Spots	Ways Forward
Life without Reflection	Dislocation	Press On
Loss of Responsibility	Contradictions	Look Elsewhere
Loss of Roots & Realism	Human Waste	Go Back a Bit

Move Forward

Obviously, an individual will not stem the tide of Globalization. Too much has happened already. Nonetheless, a willingness to reflect on the dark side of Globalization can keep individuals and groups from falling into the temptations, maintaining the blind spots, or abandoning traditional values and principles. Think back to the activities of Wilberforce and his circle of friends.

1. What can you do as an individual to maintain a consciousness of what is happening to human beings because of Globalization?
2. What can you do with a group of dedicated friends to affect the quality of human life and spirit in an increasingly global world and economy?
3. How can you best communicate with leaders and legislators to lobby for the good of humankind as the world gets smaller and smaller?

Pray

When Jesus opened the scroll of the Book of Isaiah in the synagogue at Nazareth, he gave a basic and fundamental antidote to what we see today as the dark side of Globalization. Use the words as a source of your prayer for this chapter.

> *The Spirit of the Lord is upon me,*
>   *because he has anointed me*
>   *to bring good news to the poor.*
>
> *He has sent me to proclaim release to the captives*
>   *and recovery of sight to the blind,*
>   *to let the oppressed go free*
>
> *to proclaim the year of the Lord's favor!*

Luke 4:18–19

nine

India: Peril & Promise

By Vishal Mangalwadi

Vishal Mangalwadi is an international lecturer and political columnist whom Christianity Today *has called "India's foremost Christian intellectual." Mangalwadi specializes in philosophical and political issues. Born and raised in India, Mangalwadi studied under Francis Schaeffer at L'Abri Fellowship in Switzerland.*

Mangalwadi is the winner of the Dr. Bhimrao Ambedkar Distinguished National Service Award and writes with a prophetic heart and a scholar's mind. He studied philosophy in secular universities, Hindu ashrams, and in L'Abri Fellowship before moving into a village in Madhya Pradesh. With his wife Ruth, he founded the Association for Comprehensive Rural Assistance to serve India's poor. From social work, he moved to political activism and served in the headquarters of two national political parties, organizing peasants and the "lower castes."

For some time now he has worked as a freelance writer and speaker, lecturing to illiterate peasants in India, as well as to university audiences. He loves simplifying complex ideas while filling despairing hearts with hope. Mangalwadi's books include The World of Gurus, Truth and Social Reform *and* Missionary Conspiracy: Letters to a Postmodern Hindu. *He has written a political column for the Dubai-based magazine* The International Indian.

India is hot today. Huge sums and private equity are now pouring into India because it is a land of great promise: the world's largest democracy with 1.1 billion potential consumers and a large, educated, English speaking, low-cost work force. Yet, this is not the first time India has appeared as a land of promise. The British East India Company established its first permanent base in India in 1612. It saw the possibilities as early as the seventeenth century, but by 1757 it found itself trapped in a quagmire. The merchants had turned into colonial masters.

It took 190 years for the British to extricate themselves from India. Ultimately, the price of India's independence (1947) was a million Hindus, Muslims, and Sikhs dead and ten million made homeless. That is an unpleasant saga: Its edifying feature is the story of the reformers: initially the British—Charles Grant, William Carey, and William Wilberforce—and eventually the Indians, from Rammohun Roy to Mahatma Gandhi.

Thanks to the British and Indian reformers, India is no longer as the British had found it. Yet, that saga teaches us that it is unwise to look only at the promise and ignore the perils. To the shareholders of the East India Company, the only thing that mattered was the profit. In contrast, the reformers also looked at the challenges. They struggled to bless India by changing both India as well as the British Empire.

Two men sounded the bugle for reforming India in 1792: Charles Grant (1746–1823) and William Carey (1761–1834). Grant had served in India and seen both the corruption of the East India Company as well as the quagmire that was India. His Observations on the State of Britain's Asiatic Subjects was written to help his friend, the Evangelical Member of Parliament, William Wilberforce, transform the very charter of the East India Company. For this reason, Grant's book circulated as a manuscript for a few years before it was printed.

Carey, in contrast, published An Enquiry into the Obligation of Christians to Use Means for the Conversion of the Heathens. The work discussed whether all Christians at all times were obliged to follow Christ's Great Commission to disciple all nations. If the Great Commission was still binding, then was it proper for the British Church to leave nations such as India at the mercy of unscrupulous merchants and soldiers? Shouldn't the Church be sending out missionaries as linguists, educators, and agents of socio-spiritual transformation?

Together, the two books, with help from men such as Wilberforce, won the argument that Britain must not see India merely as a territory to be exploited for economic gains. Britain must manage India as a steward of India's real sovereign—the almighty Creator. Today's India is a product of the battle these men initiated.

Human Waste Then

In 1793, three years after Charles Grant returned from India
to England, William Carey left England to serve as a Christian
missionary in India. He found, among other things, widespread
oppression and humans treated as waste and without dignity. He
was horrified by the treatment of untouchables, leprosy patients,
children, and women—specifically through infanticide, child
marriage, polygamy, widowhood, widow-burning (sati), and lack
of education.

1. Infanticide

The practice of exposing infants to death was a widespread
religious custom, which still exists today, though often
supplemented by abortions of female fetuses. Then, if an infant
was sick, it was supposed that the infant was under the influence
of an evil spirit. The infant was put into a basket and hung up for
three days. Only if the child survived were means then used to
save the infant's life. Every winter, children were pushed down
into mud banks into the sea to be either drowned or devoured by
crocodiles, all in the fulfillment of the vows that their mothers
had made. This was looked upon as a most holy sacrifice—giving
the Mother Ganges the fruit of their bodies for the sins of their
souls.

2. Child Marriage

To guard a young girl's safety and to uphold her family's honor,
getting her married at the earliest possible age was considered
the best safeguard. Childhood was thus denied to a girl. She
was to pass into motherhood before she had time to grow as a
person.

The last census of the nineteenth century in Bengal, India
revealed that, in and around Calcutta alone, there were ten
thousand widows under the age of four and more than fifty
thousand between the ages of five and nine. All these child
widows were victims of child marriages.

3. Polygamy

Polygamy was a common practice. Sometimes fifty women were given to one Brahmin man so that their families could boast that they were allied by marriage to a high caste.

4. Widowhood

When the much older husbands died, their widows were subjected to a terrible plight because they were perceived as bad omens that had brought about the death of their husbands. It was believed that a widow had "eaten her husband." One possibility was to live in widowhood without remarriage. But the widow was looked upon not as a precious individual in need of support to start a new life but as an economic liability. Her parents had already given the bride price (dowry); the in-laws were not willing to part with their "possessions" and return the dowry to get the young woman remarried. And, of course, the illiterate widow was in no position to earn and become an economic asset for a family.

To add insult to injury, the bereaved widow had to shave off her hair, remove all jewelry, and wear white, all to avoid attracting the other men in the family and causing them to go astray. She had to be kept indoors to keep her chaste. Often widows were required to cohabit with the brother-in-law or another male relative for the purpose of producing a son to offer religious obligations for the deceased husband if he had no sons of his own to undertake this important religious rite.

5. Widow-Burning

The other option for a widow was to be burned with her dead husband in a ritual known as sati. Many widows preferred a speedy death to the known and unknown life-long horrors of widowhood. They were deluded into thinking that the act of self-sacrifice would bestow celebrity status on the family and would take seven generations of their family, before and after them, to heaven. They were assured that the heroic act of self-immolation would deify them.

6. Female Education

Most men were illiterate and, as a rule, all lower caste men and all women were prohibited from studying. A Hindu father enlightened a missionary with his thoughts on education:

> *You may educate my sons, and open to them all the stores*
> *of knowledge: But my daughters you must not approach,*
> *however benevolent your designs, for they must marry at*
> *an age when your plans of education can hardly commence.*
> *Their ignorance and seclusion are necessary to the honor of*
> *my family, a consideration of greater moment with me than*
> *their mental culture.* (1)

South Asia's Linguistic Revolution

Carey recognized that the Indian sub-continent could not be reformed unless the people were educated in the knowledge of truth in their own languages. Pali, the sacred language of Buddhist scriptures, had been dead for almost a thousand years. The living literary languages were Sanskrit, Persian, and Arabic. But neither the Brahmin Pandits nor the Muslim Maulvies had a religious or secular motivation to turn the oral dialects of the people into literary languages and to translate their sacred literature into vernaculars. Therefore, Carey began the tedious task of translating the Bible into Indian vernaculars and developing their scripts, grammar, etc. Along with some protégés of Charles Grant, he raised a team of linguists and translators in Calcutta who created the national languages of modern India (Hindi), Pakistan (Urdu) and Bangladesh (Bengali).

A Better Hour for India

Carey's effort was heroic given the fact that he went to serve India in defiance of the British Parliament only months after it voted against Wilberforce's resolution that the East India Company must allow missionaries to serve India. Since Carey came to British India illegally, he was a fugitive and had to live in the Danish settlement of Serampore. He was welcomed in British

India only when the East India Company needed a teacher in Calcutta to teach Bengali at Fort William College. William Carey was hired as an Associate Professor and taught for thirty years, using his position to change India.

Before Charles Grant became a Member of Parliament, William Wilberforce was his spokesman, forcefully arguing in 1793 that England must assume the responsibilities of "uplifting" India. Wilberforce invited Grant to become a fellow resident of Clapham and supported his campaign to become a Director of the East India Company, and eventually a Member of Parliament. Grant believed that besides the corruption of the British Company, the chief problem of India's people was immorality and superstition in the guise of religion. Therefore, education— including moral education and religious re-education—had to be integral aspects of solutions. Good Chaplains were needed to meet the religious needs of the Company staff and missionary educators were needed to open the minds of India's masses. Everyone acknowledged that religious superstitions were terrible opium, yet the Company did not want missionaries to disturb the then existing religious tranquility.

However, by the early nineteenth century, the doctrine of religious liberty had already come to have two implications. One was that the power of the state should not be used to tamper with the religious conscience of the people. If social evils such as untouchability or destructive superstitions such as astrology had overt religious sanction, the state could not and should not erase them by mere force or legislation.

The other implication of the doctrine of religious liberty was that the removal of these religiously sanctioned evils had to be the work of counter-reforming religious or nonreligious ideas. Therefore, all ideas had to be given the freedom to compete in the marketplace of ideas to change people's beliefs and, thereby, their society.

Wilberforce argued that England should send missionary educators who could help "improve" Indian society. In 1793, he succeeded in pushing his proposals through the House of Commons, but unfortunately, the House of Lords, under the influence of the Directors of the East India Company, overthrew his proposals. In spite of this official rejection, Carey's sense of a divine call gave him the inner strength to set out for India in the same year.

It took twenty years of successful fieldwork by Carey and his fellow missionaries in India, lobbying within the East India Company by Charles Grant, and magnificent political work by Wilberforce, to persuade Parliament to assume its moral obligation to India. In 1813, when the Company's Charter came up for renewal, Wilberforce once again took up the challenge of transforming the Company's mission in India. This time his crusade was backed by the documentation supplied by Carey and others. These facts included lists of widows who had committed sati. Wilberforce had made a practice of reading their names at his dining table and praying for India. On July 1st and 12th, 1813, Wilberforce argued:

Let us endeavor to strike our roots into the soil by the gradual introduction and establishment of our own principles and opinions; of our laws, institutions, and manners; above all, as the source of every other improvement, of our religion, and consequently of our morals.

Wilberforce said that such a reforming effort, and not brute military force or political intrigue, would tie India to England with bonds of eternal gratitude.

The critics suggested that, through his advocacy of allowing missionaries to propagate Christianity in India, Wilberforce was counseling compulsory conversion. He rebutted the charge:

Compulsion and Christianity! Why the very terms are at variance with each other—the ideas are incompatible. In the language of inspiration itself, Christianity is the "law of liberty."

In those days many people in Britain believed that it was necessary to freely dialogue and debate truth. Freedom of conscience was incomplete without the freedom to change one's beliefs, to convert. A state that hinders conversion was considered uncivilized because it restricted the human quest for truth and religion.

In politics, however, arguments alone are rarely enough. Wilberforce's proposals regarding India had already been defeated in Parliament more than once. Therefore, in 1813, he took the precaution of mobilizing public pressure, particularly on the

House of Lords. The unsuspecting Lords were swept off their feet by the strength of public opinion. The public opinion, on which Wilberforce capitalized, was substantially a result of the publicity Carey's work had generated in England during the previous two decades. Today's commitment to pluralism and relativism would condemn Carey's effort to ban "religious" practices such as sati and untouchability; however, back then his work received positive publicity because the intellectual climate was shaped by books written by Grant, Carey, and Claudius Buchanan—THE CHRISTIAN RESEARCHES IN ASIA—which gave a vivid first hand account of the horrors of Indian society.

For India, Wilberforce's parliamentary victory had two immediate positive results: a) the East India Company had to allow missionaries freedom to work; and b) the Company was asked to earmark 100,000 rupees (around US$2,000) annually from its profits for public education in India. The consequence of the former was that great missionary educators such as Alexander Duff could freely come to India and open schools and colleges. It took twenty additional years of struggle to the next renewal of the Company's charter in 1833 before the reformers' viewpoint really began to determine British policy. The men who spearheaded the 1833 campaign for reforms were Charles Grant, Jr. and Lord Macaulay—both sons of the Clapham Sect.

William Carey's Efforts

William Carey, as the first missionary, addressed the issues of human waste that he found.

1. The British Governor asked Carey to inquire into the nature and reasons for infanticide. Carey's report resulted in the practice being outlawed.

2. Carey began to undermine the moral roots of child marriage through the teaching of the Bible and its social roots through female education. It took more than a century of sustained campaign for the practice to be made illegal in 1929 through the Child Marriages Restraint Act. Unfortunately, for many Indians, it is only "paper legislation." Even Cabinet Ministers in some states in India still marry off their underage daughters.

3. Carey began to help widows remarry—especially if they had become Christians. That small beginning ultimately resulted in the Widow Remarriage Act of 1856. The law overruled religious culture and, for the first time, it became a right for a Hindu widow to remarry. Until then the only options, especially for a high caste Hindu widow, was to suffer lifelong indignity and hardship or commit sati.

4. Carey began his famous campaign against sati after his horrible, first-hand experience in 1799. He saw a funeral pyre and a young woman who was about to commit sati. He sought to dissuade the widow and the family members from the sati but to no avail. He reasoned that the children, who had already lost their father, would now lose their mother, who could have taken care of them, to a practice based on silly myths. This awful practice would make those children orphans.

   In 1802, Lord Wellesley asked Carey to institute an inquiry into sati. Carey sent out people who investigated carefully the cases of sati within a thirty-mile radius of Calcutta and discovered 438 widow-burnings in a single year. Armed with these facts, Carey implored the government to ban sati, yet Lord Wellesley had to leave India before he could take action. Carey considered this battle against a social evil as a spiritual battle against religious darkness and the forces of death. He prayed and recruited others to pray. One of his prominent prayer partners in this matter was William Wilberforce.

   Carey's great day came when, on December 4, 1829, Lord Cavendish Bentinck, after one year of careful study, declared sati both illegal and criminal under the Bengal Code. The Edict was sent to Carey for translation two days later. Carey was overjoyed. At long last, widows were legally free to live as human beings and no longer would children be cruelly orphaned in the name of "religion."

5. William Carey was able to advance the education of women. One of Carey's colleagues, Hannah Marshman, took on the education problem. She started a boarding school for the children of missionaries and other Europeans. By the end of the first year in 1801, the

boarding school showed a profit. With this success, Mrs. Marshman was able to start schools for the Indian boys and girls.

The success resulted in the establishment of the Calcutta Baptist Female School Society in 1819 and an additional school for girls in Calcutta. From 1820–1830, Carey's mission took the lead in initiating the revolution of modern education for the women of rural Bengal. Their initiative, in turn, led to the founding of other girls' schools in Benares, Dacca, and Allahabad. These schools educated children who were picked up from the streets and of no caste. Free schools for the low castes and the outcastes were always a chief feature of Carey's work and these were started within a twenty-mile radius of his mission, where almost eight thousand children attended.

6. Carey encouraged a Scottish missionary, Alexander Duff, to start educational institutions that imparted European Education in the English language. Carey's own schools used vernacular languages as the medium or vehicle of imparting European education. Duff's efforts began to bring India into the family of English-speaking nations.

7. Carey focused on creating literary languages for the Indians. It was not English, but their native vernaculars, including Hindi. During India's great linguistic debate in the 1820s and 1830s, Carey's work was honored by both parties: the Classists, who argued that Sanskrit, Persian, or Arabic should be taught in order to enrich the vernaculars, and the Anglists, who argued in favor of English. Lord Macaulay, in many ways a protégé of William Wilberforce, finally ruled in favor of English, and did so in the spirit of William Carey. He wanted English literature to enrich Indian vernaculars.

Charles Grant's Observations on the State of Britain's Asiatic Subjects, which was well received in Britain's political circles, argued that the commercial interests of England would be better served by improving India, not by enslaving it. That this viewpoint finally won the day was illustrated when, forty years later, in a speech before Parliament in 1833, Lord Macaulay built upon Grant's thesis. In that historic speech, Macaulay argued that England must pursue this policy of improving India, even if improvement meant India's eventual independence. For, "To trade with civilized men is infinitely more profitable than to govern savages." The following is a sample of the power of Macaulay's language and logic that overwhelmed Parliament.

> It may be that the public mind of India may expand under
> our system till it has outgrown that system; that by good
> government we may educate our subjects into a capacity
> for better government; that, having become instructed in
> European knowledge, they may, in some future age, demand
> European institutions (of freedom). Whether such a day
> will ever come I know not. But never will I attempt to
> avert or retard it. Whenever it comes, it will be the proudest
> day in English history. To have found a great people sunk
> in the lowest depths of slavery and superstition, to have
> so ruled them as to have made them desirous and capable
> of all the privileges of citizens, would indeed be a title
> to glory all our own. The scepter may pass away from us.
> Unforeseen accidents may derange our most profound schemes
> of policy. Victory may be inconstant to our arms. But there
> are triumphs which are followed by no reverse. There is
> an empire exempt from all natural causes of decay. Those
> triumphs are the pacific triumphs of reason over barbarism;
> that empire is the imperishable empire of our arts and our
> morals, our literature, and our laws. (2)

Charles Trevelyan, Macaulay's brother-in-law, summed up the long-term aim of the Christian reform movement in 1838 in his pamphlet on Education in India. Macaulay and Trevelyan were articulating what Carey and Duff had already practiced and demonstrated. Trevelyan wrote:

> The existing connection between two such distant countries
> as England and India, cannot, in the nature of things, be
> permanent: No effort of policy can prevent the natives from
> ultimately regaining their independence. But there are two
> ways of arriving at this point. One of these is through the
> medium of revolution; the other through that of reform. . . .
> [Revolution] must end in the complete alienation of mind
> and separation of interests between ourselves and the natives;
> the other [reform] is a permanent alliance, founded on

mutual benefit and goodwill. The only means at our disposal
for preventing [revolution] and securing . . . the results
[of reform] is, to set the natives on a process of European
improvement. . . . The natives will have independence,
after first learning how to make good use of it; and we shall
exchange profitable subjects for still more profitable allies. . . .
Trained by us to happiness and independence, and endowed
with our learning and political institutions. India will
remain the proudest monument of British benevolence.

The long-anticipated day of India's independence and the triumph of the Christian reformers ultimately came in 1947. India asked for and became independent of the British Raj. Yet it retained and resolved to live by British laws and institutions, as a member of the British Commonwealth. For example, the Indian Penal Code of 1860, which is still the basis of law in Indian jurisprudence, was drafted by Macaulay himself as "Codes of Criminal and Civil Procedures" when he served as India's law minister.

Thus, India's independence in 1947 was not only a victory for Mahatma Gandhi and the "freedom fighters," but also even more fundamentally, a triumph for Carey's Christian England. It marked the victory of the early missionaries over the narrow commercial, political, and military vested interests of England, as well as a victory for the hearts and minds of India.

Need for Reform

Today, the long term results of the battles fought by Grant, Carey, Wilberforce, Macaulay, and Trevelyan are visible to everyone. Their educational, linguistic, moral, and socio-political mission was India's "Grand Experiment." Their success has become the bedrock for the limited success of the present and the unlimited promise for the future. Yet, it would be foolish to ignore Macaulay's wise words that none of us can predict or control the future, for "Unforeseen accidents may derange our most profound schemes of policy." (3) We need to follow these great men and look at the challenges of our times—the perils that can once again turn promises into quagmires. The following five challenges have the capacity to derange the calculations of our best economists:

1. The Caste Conflict

So far, the upper castes have been the primary beneficiaries of
education and democracy. However, enough has filtered down
to awaken India's lower castes. They are no longer prepared to
accept an inferior status. They have acquired enough strength to
challenge the Hindu social system and the philosophical ideas
of karma, reincarnation, and dharma that sustain Hinduism.
India has arrived at the point where France was before the
French Revolution. Interestingly, the main safety valve that
India has to escape a French Revolution is the one that William
Wilberforce fought for—individual liberty to reject a religion that
promotes inequality in favor of a religion that promotes equality.
Political democracy is fueling a hunger for social and spiritual
democracy—for human equality and "priesthood of all believers."
Brahmins have a vested interest in preserving their millennia-old
honor and privileges. They may even have the motivation to fight
to preserve the status quo. But an all-out clash of castes could
derail the India.com project.

2. The Communal Conflicts

India has become the biggest beneficiary of President Bush's war
on terror. That war turned the government of Pakistan against the
terrorists who used to intensify the Hindu/Muslim tensions in
India. However, there are good reasons to believe that the war on
terror has radicalized Pakistani Muslims. A democratic election
in Pakistan is likely to throw up a radical Muslim government,
which will have a vested interest in fueling communal tensions
in India. During the previous six decades, the frequent Hindu-
Muslim riots in India used to hurt the Muslim economy.
The future rioters and terrorists are likely to target the rising
economic power of the Hindus.

3. Urbanization or "Slumification"

The socialist economics made some difference to the traditional
Hindu economic order, but the socialist "land reforms" deceived
so many people that at least sixty percent of India's population
still experiences only a subsistence-level agricultural economy.

Technologically, India does not need more than ten percent of her population growing food for everyone. Should this come about, fifty percent of India's population (500 million people) will have to move from the village to the city. That could translate into one hundred cities receiving 4–5 million people each. That in turn means a slumification of our prestigious cities such as Bangalore. This projected slumification would lead to an all-around urban nightmare. It will have a bearing on caste and communal conflicts as well as on politics, corruption, and HIV/AIDS issues mentioned below. The challenge of this social chaos is that unless potential investors recover the mettle of earlier reformers, slumification would redirect the investors to more orderly cities in other countries.

4. Corruption

Corruption was a key factor that turned the promise of India into a great peril or quagmire for the East India Company. During the last decade, the corruption of India's political class played a significant role in ruining Enron. It will hurt many more multi-national companies in the days ahead. India's multi-party democracy is enabling new and small caste-based parties to acquire power. These parties may be small but they have a big appetite for power and bribes. Therefore, once a company sets up a significant base in a corrupt state, it has to appease potential troublemakers. It is a vulnerability to be bled to death by petty politicians. This factor implies that the mission of Grant, Carey, and Wilberforce—India's moral renewal—is as important today as it was in their day.

5. HIV/AIDS

Experts say that India is set to become the world capital of HIV/AIDS. This is no place to examine the implications of this fact, but it needs no imagination to understand that it would be hard for a nation to realize its potential if its workforce—the young adults—are laid off work in millions and if the state becomes responsible for millions of young orphans.

Conclusion

Although each of these problems requires distinct strategies and action programs, they are all intertwined and spring from deeper springs of culture and worldview. They reinforce and complicate each issue and have cumulative impact. Together they send out one message: India has always been a land of promise, but thanks to the new wave of "reforms," India has once again opened up to the world. However, the perils are as real today as they were in the eighteenth century. These perils call our generation to produce new heroes—men and women like Charles Grant, William Carey, and William Wilberforce.

Extended Observation

Reflection & Conversation

This chapter uses India as a specific example of societal needs. Although colonial rule in India had its own set of problems, many missionaries from Britain set out to improve conditions in India. Center your reflection and conversation around the problems articulated in the chapter. Note that Wilberforce was also concerned about India, and he urged Parliament to take responsibility for India and its problems.

Attend to the Word

Read 2 Chronicles 7:12–16 in the light of what you have learned in this chapter. Spend a few moments in silence to let these words sink in. Then read verse 14 again.

Engage

Review the missionary work of William Carey. Contrast the approach of the missionaries with the political and military realities of the Raj. Discuss how Hinduism is portrayed in this chapter.

1. How did the work of the missionaries heal the land of India?
2. What is your reaction to the impulse of the missionaries to convert India?
3. How has India been blessed by God today?

Move Forward

Review the five challenges faced by contemporary India. How is each challenge being met on a global stage? How is each challenge reflected in the lives of people here in America?

Challenge	Global Response	American Reflection
Caste Conflicts		
Communal Conflicts		
Urbanization		
Corruption		
HIV/AIDS		

1. Do an Internet search to discover more information on these challenges and how they are being met in India. How can you participate in the healing of the land—of India or of your own land?
2. Decide in what areas your land needs healing. How can you humble yourselves, pray, and seek the Lord's face? What difference will this make?

Pray

In considering the needs of the world and how to meet them, it is good to anchor one's prayer in the attitudes of Psalm 46. Use these verses as a source for your prayer for the healing of India and of your own land.

> *God is in the midst of the city: it shall not be moved;*
> *God will help it when the morning dawns.*
>
> *The nations are in an uproar, the kingdoms totter;*
> *he utters his voice, the earth melts.*
>
> *The Lord of hosts is with us;*
> *the God of Jacob is our refuge.*
>
> *Come, behold the works of the Lord:*
> *see what desolations he has brought on the earth.*
>
> *He makes wars cease to the ends of the earth:*
> *he breaks the bow, and shatters the spear:*
> *he burns the shields with fire.*
>
> *"Be still, and know that I am God!*
> *I am exalted among the nations,*
> *I am exalted in the earth."*
>
> *The Lord of hosts is with us:*
> *the God of Jacob is our refuge.*

Psalm 46:5–11 (NRSV)

ten

Slavery in the Sudan

By Elizabeth Ashamu

A Nigerian-American, Elizabeth Ashamu was born in Charlottesville, Virginia, but spent the first seven years of her life traveling between Nigeria and the United States. Her Nigerian ancestry has inspired her dedication to and interest in Africa. She received joint Bachelor's and Master's degrees in African studies from Yale University in 2006. As a student, she demonstrated a dedication to social justice and public service in her academic and extracurricular pursuits. She spent her junior year abroad in Egypt, and her experiences working with Sudanese refugees in Cairo inspired her interest in human rights advocacy, the Sudan, and forced migration. She was recently awarded the William E. Simon Fellowship for noble purpose to develop an oral history project devoted to documenting the experiences of the Southern Sudanese during the civil war in Sudan. Below is her prize-winning essay.

Rahib's description of the Janjaweed militia attacking and burning his village in Darfur, and Kirkek's account of the physical and psychological torture he was subjected to in a Khartoum prison remain etched in my memory. I heard and recorded the testimonies of these men last year in Cairo, where they had fled to escape the civil war in Sudan. The recurring themes of rape, violence, torture, and death in the stories of such refugees have had a powerful impact in shaping my future goals. Their accounts inspired in me a dedication to victims and survivors of similar events and circumstances and also left me with a belief in the importance of documenting the accounts of marginalized people, and the centrality of such testimonies in illuminating human rights violations.

Thus, with the support of the Simon Fellowship, I will initiate a project in Sudan dedicated to compiling collective social histories of Southern Sudanese communities. I will strive to use personal testimony not only as a way of promoting international human rights awareness and social action, but as a methodology in documenting the history of the civil war and as a way of providing detailed understandings of peoples' lives useful in shaping and directing humanitarian assistance and development programs. I also see the collection of testimonies as a tool to strengthen Sudanese communities and as a form of psychotherapy helpful for those individuals who give their testimonies.

My Motivation

Numerous previous experiences have played a role in motivating my desire to carry out this proposed project in Sudan. Although my fascination for knowing the details of others' experiences and course of events in their lives is long-held, it was my work transcribing Holocaust testimonies during my sophomore year at Yale that first revealed to me the social and historical value of personal testimonies and the possibility of directing this passion towards social action and scholarship. For nine months, I spent eight hours a week working for the Fortunoff Holocaust Archives. These archives contain a collection of over 4,300 videotaped testimonies of Holocaust survivors that are available to researchers, educators, and the general public. I listened to the videotaped oral testimonies of Holocaust survivors, typed detailed summaries of the content, and carefully identified and researched each geographical and camp location mentioned in the videos. Although this work was emotionally challenging, as all were survivors, each video was a testament to the strength of the human spirit and the power of the will to survive. My work was thus often equally as inspiring as it was distressing. And as each unique testimony stands for hundreds of others that will never be recorded, I felt that I had a role in an immensely valuable historical project that will continuously contribute to and enhance our understandings and memories of the Holocaust.

Watching the videos, I could sense the value of structured recording and documentation of testimonies for the survivors interviewed. As remembering is often painful, few of these survivors had shared such complete testimonies with the public or even with family and friends. Survivors rarely bring up their memories and experiences, and others avoid asking about them. Thus, many expressed relief in finally telling their stories, having them recorded, and the comfort and pride in contributing to a permanent historical record of the Holocaust.

My work with the Holocaust archives revealed to me the social and historical value of systematic collection of testimonies and thorough documentation of violence, war, and human rights violations. The repetition of incidents of genocide throughout history testifies to the ease in which atrocities slip out of our collective memory. It is therefore vital to the promotion of international peace to do all that is possible to document precisely the history of such events for scholars, researchers, and future generations. Such systematic gathering of testimonies has not yet occurred among survivors of the Sudanese civil war and my mission is thus to fill this gap in documentation.

Situation in the Sudan

Testimonies of Sudanese survivors of civil war have been recorded and documented in various contexts, and although these have contributed to educating the general public and moving people to care, as scattered accounts without context, most are lacking long-term historical significance and value for Southern Sudanese communities. In the United States, numerous authors, journalists, and filmmakers have recounted the lives of Sudanese "Lost Boys." These young refugees fled violence in Southern Sudan in the 1980s and trekked first to refugee camps in Ethiopia and then to the Kakuma refugee camp in Kenya. From here, approximately four thousand of them were resettled in the United States during the late 1990s, and they became the center of a large media campaign. Their stories inspired many to donate money, and volunteer time or support. Such reactions reveal the power of personal testimony to illuminate human rights violations and how, in bearing direct witness to events, testimonies instill a sense of personal connection that fuels and motivates audiences to learn, advocate, and serve. Yet more systematic and widespread collection is needed in order to develop a comprehensive historical record of the civil war.

Similarly, in Egypt, thousands of testimonies are recorded for private, legal, and administrative purposes. Yet these, at least in the near future, will be confined to file cabinets and hard drives. Accounts like Rahib's and Kirkek's made obvious the need to systematically compile such testimonies of human rights violations in the Sudan for public use and to assure that these occurrences remain a part of Sudanese collective memory, and are documented and available for use by historians, community members, human rights activists, and other interested organizations.

While in Cairo, I heard and recorded testimonies of Sudanese refugees in formal and informal contexts. I volunteered as an English instructor with the refugee education and assistance program at a local church and worked with the administrative staff in conducting brief biographical interviews for registering refugees at the church. I also conducted informal pre-orientations for refugees awaiting resettlement to the United States, and responded to their numerous questions and concerns. Through such activities, I developed close friendships with students and co-workers, and I became increasingly aware and knowledgeable of what refugees had experienced in the Sudan, and the challenges they faced in Cairo.

Getting Involved

Eager to provide other forms of assistance to refugees, I participated in a training course sponsored by the United Nations High Commissioner for Refugees (UNHCR) and Musa'ideen, a refugee assistance organization whose goal is to teach refugees to help each other by training community leaders to provide legal support. This course introduced me to the intricacies of international refugee law, UNHCR refugee status determination, and the resettlement process, as well as to other important subjects concerning refugee mental health. After successfully completing the course, I assisted refugees in writing and translating testimonies for the UNHCR from Arabic to English, and in preparing resettlement applications for Canadian and Australian embassies.

Through such activities, I gathered many personal accounts that I position in my mind temporally and geographically as I continuously attempt to detangle the complexities of the Sudanese civil war. Each narrative brought me to a closer and deeper knowledge of events and their effects, and catalyzed my personal, emotional and intellectual growth. Each story exposed me to cruelty, injustice or suffering; revealed courage and personal resilience; and inspired in me a growing dedication to working and advocating for refugees and the Southern Sudanese. I am convinced that these testimonies would have the significance for others that they have for me.

I have found in various courses an academic outlet for my interests in life history, the opportunity to explore the value and meanings of personal testimonies, and training in the methodology of collecting and recording people's stories. In a course on the psychosocial issues in forced migration, I explored issues of trauma in refugee populations and the benefits of giving testimony in the healing process. During a course on fieldwork methods, I studied interviewing techniques, the process of interviewing, and examined the use of personal accounts in anthropological works. For my final project, I collected testimonies of Sudanese Muslim refugees who converted to Christianity while in Egypt and wrote a paper in which I described their motivations for conversion to Christianity and discussed the role of churches in assisting refugees as well as the religious and racial climate of Cairo. I had yet other opportunities to develop interviewing and research techniques this past summer when I traveled to Guinea and to Senegal and conducted research on the history of Lebanese emigration to West Africa. I am currently compiling and analyzing the family histories and personal testimonies that I collected for use in my African studies master's thesis.

Goals in My Project

In preparation for my proposed project in Southern Sudan, I will spend a year in Kigali, Rwanda with African Rights, a London-based human rights organization whose work embodies my own vision of human rights advocacy. I am applying to several Yale fellowships that would fund this experience. African Rights documents the 1994 genocide and its aftermath by carrying out rigorous and extensive fieldwork that has included the gathering of thousands of personal testimonies of genocide survivors, witnesses and perpetrators. The organization employs local researchers and is devoted to documenting the experiences of ordinary people, whose voices are not often heard. African Rights uses these accounts to develop constructive and informed analyses of human rights violations. I am compelled by the participatory and community-based approach that characterizes African Rights' work and publications.

In my role with African Rights, I will research, analyze and collect testimonies, and prepare materials for publication. Specifically, I will write charge sheets, collective accounts, and a series called Tribute to Courage. Charge sheets are reports that summarize allegations against those accused of involvement in genocide, focusing on key perpetrators who have not yet been brought to justice. Collective accounts are based on compilations of individual testimonies, and provide detailed histories of events that occurred in specific sectors during the genocide. Both charge sheets and collective accounts are fundamental to African Rights' pursuit of justice. The aim of the African Rights series, Tribute to Courage, is to promote public recognition of acts of compassion and fortitude. This series speaks to the sacrifices and individual heroism of men and women who risked their lives to save others during the genocide.

In addition to such research and documentation, African Rights applies the knowledge gained through their collection of testimonies to shape practical assistance projects that aid survivors. I will help to maintain, monitor, and expand *The Gift for Life*, a program that assists women who were raped during the genocide and are now living with AIDS by extending to them financial, medical, and moral support. The project is structured around a community-based model of care and a detailed understanding of the histories and present circumstances of the individual women. I have been moved by progress reports that indicate the transformations that have occurred in the lives of these women and I look forward to contributing to such important work.

Besides allowing me to improve my interviewing and documentation skills, my year of work in Rwanda will expose me to using testimonies as a tool for advocacy and prepare me for graduate work in anthropology and human rights law. I will model my documentation and advocacy among communities in Southern Sudan after the work of African Rights. My experience with African Rights will help me to define and hone my methodology and lay down a course of action for work in the Sudan.

As in Rwanda, to an outsider, the events that occurred in Southern Sudan over twenty years of civil war might seem to be a chaotic continuity of violence, famine and destruction. Yet each prefect, city and village has its own story and timeline of events that directly affected it over the course of the war. Consultation with Sudanese living in the United States and Cairo has revealed to me the need to document with precision and detail what occurred in each area, and to map the dispersion of community members within and outside the Sudan.

My focus on personal testimonies and plan to work in the Sudan among communities of survivors makes my project unique among works of history and documentation of the civil war that have been carried out thus far. Through the writing of local histories, and incorporation of the testimonies of average people, whose experiences are often glossed over in historical records, this project will be invaluable for the memory and self understanding of future generations of Sudanese. Such histories and testimonies will serve as a means for Southern Sudanese to reconcile with past events, by certifying that their history, as told by themselves, is safeguarded. By preserving them in publicly available local and international archives, these documented histories will be useful in preserving events in Sudanese popular memory.

The process as well as the final product will be valuable for Southern Sudanese communities and individuals. As a collective effort that will call on Sudanese to involve themselves in interviewing, providing testimonies and documenting their own histories, it will assist in bringing communities together, and in the reintegration of returning internally displaced people and refugees from neighboring countries such as Uganda, Kenya, Egypt, and Ethiopia. Within communities of victims and survivors, the gathering of testimonies can develop collective understandings of history and communal identity that can better support peace and social trust. The documentation of these histories will also promote justice and accountability and will be useful in locating or accounting for separated family members. For individuals, the recording of testimonies can bring psychological benefits and serve as a means for recovery and healing from difficult or traumatic events. Through research and consultation with specialists, I hope to explore thoroughly the therapeutic benefits of testimony psychotherapy to take advantage of the potential ability of testimony to reduce individual suffering.

I am confident that my personal preparations, my upcoming experiences with African Rights in Rwanda, and the planning and organizing that I will begin in the United States and continue while in Rwanda, will assure the success of my project. I have begun discussing my proposed project with members of the Sudanese diaspora in the United States and Cairo, and will further expand my network of connections to gain support and advice from scholars and those involved with international non-governmental organizations operating in the Sudan. I will investigate the possibility of working within an existing organization, and research other funding sources that could make my project sustainable. While in Rwanda, I will travel in the region to meet and discuss my proposal with the large Sudanese refugee communities in Kenya and Uganda and connect with Sudanese civic and political organizations that could provide me with guidance and further expand my support network.

My Passion

Back in New Haven, I've been working with the Interfaith Refugee Ministry (IRM), a local refugee resettlement agency. I have been instrumental in the compilation of information guides and manuals for those resettling in Connecticut and have assisted the IRM in welcoming and working with their refugee clients. In the course of this work experience, I will gain a solid understanding of the post-resettlement situation of refugees, the work of U.S. resettlement agencies, and also be exposed to U.S. immigration policy. As a member of the Yale Association for Political Asylees, I have been providing general acculturation advice and support to a man from Guinea recently granted asylum through the Yale immigration clinic. I am also a volunteer at the African Community Center for Educational and Social Services where I have assisted with administrative and secretarial duties as well as in publicizing the work of the center among African immigrants in New Haven. With the director, Yasir Hamed, I organized an event during which Sudanese refugees from Darfur living in New Haven shared their testimonies with Yale students. Hearing their stories personalized the continuing genocide in Sudan for others, and inspired them to learn more about the situation and take action.

Personal testimonies of marginalized and oppressed people cultivate my dedication to public service, advocacy, and devotion to helping others. My passion for life history and conviction in the social and historical importance in knowing, understanding, and recording personal stories is indicative of my general approach to life and interactions with others. I value individuals' unique life experiences, and approach each relationship I enter as an opportunity to learn about another history, culture, and about how best to lead my own life. Stories of others' lives have encouraged, impassioned, guided, and directed me as I make my way through my own, inspiring me to social action and grounding me in the reality of human experience. Testimonies from survivors of war and violence like Rahib and Kirkek compel me to act. With the help of the Simon Fellowship, I will begin a career devoted to human rights advocacy, historical documentation, and the promotion of international peace.

Extended Observation

Reflection & Conversation

This chapter is a very personal essay by a young Nigerian-American woman. Reading her account can be a bit breathtaking and maybe even a little awe-inspiring. Focus your reflections and conversations on some of the actions this woman took, especially her attempt to document the evil of slavery taking place in the Sudan. Share your own experiences of working for the good of others.

Attend to the Word

Read John 8:31–37 slowly and thoughtfully. Notice the short memory of Jesus' audience. The children of Abraham spent generations enslaved in Egypt. Spend a few moments in silence considering how the truth is the ally of freedom.

Engage

Action for the good of others begins with knowledge. So far in this book, you have learned that the legacy of William Wilberforce—freedom from bondage—is an unfinished legacy. In light of your biblical reflection, discuss the following:

1. Why do you think that there is such a great lack of understanding about modern forms of slavery?
2. What is the media saying about modern slavery? (You may have to do a bit of digging on this one.)
3. What do the words "everyone who sins is a slave to sin" mean to you? In what respect do people who are not interested in the truth about modern forms of slavery in turn enslave themselves?

Move Forward

The author of this chapter learned a lesson from her studies of the Holocaust. She learned that it is important never to forget. She is concerned that unless she and others document the slavery that exists in Africa, people in later generations (not unlike the children of Abraham who were questioning Jesus) may forget that this slavery happened.

1. How can you and your group aid awareness of modern slavery in Africa?
2. What are some related issues that need to be presented truthfully and openly?
3. Decide on one or two actions you and your group can take that will help people know the truth about slavery and be set free by what they learn.

Pray

In Luke's Gospel, Zechariah—the father of John the Baptist—focused the longings of generations in a glorious canticle. Use his words as a source for your prayer.

> *Let us praise the Lord, the God of Israel.*
> *He has come to the help of his people and has set*
> *them free.*
>
> *He promised through his holy prophets long ago*
> *that he would save us from our enemies,*
> *from the power of all those who hate us.*
>
> *He said he would show mercy to our ancestors*
> *and remember his sacred covenant.*
>
> *With a solemn oath to our ancestor Abraham*
> *he promised to rescue us from our enemies*
> *and allow us to serve him without fear,*
>
> *so that we might be holy and righteous before him*
> *all the days of our life.*

Luke 1:68, 70–75 (GNT)

eleven

Slavery of the Mind

By Nina Shea & R. James Woolsey

Nina Shea is the Director of the Hudson Institute's Center for Religious Freedom. She is also a Vice Chair of the U.S. Commission on International Religious Freedom, on which she has served since its creation in 1999. A human rights lawyer, she has been an international religious freedom advocate for over twenty years and is nationally known for her book on anti-Christian persecution, In the Lion's Den. *In 2005, she edited a path-breaking study,* Saudi Publications on Hate Ideology Invade American Mosques, *and in 2006, authored the report* Saudi Arabia's Curriculum of Intolerance.

R. James Woolsey is Co-Chair of the Committee on The Present Danger. He was Chairman of the Board of Freedom House when it published Saudi Publications on Hate Ideology Invade American Mosques, *and he authored its foreword. He practiced law for twenty-two years and has held a variety of senior government positions, including Director of Central Intelligence from 1993 to 1995; he is now a consultant. He writes as a private citizen.*

───────────────────────────────── What would William Wilberforce do about the rising new political movement to highjack the world's second largest religion—Islam? What would Wilberforce say about a movement to enslave the mind by extremists within the Islamic world who are motivated by a radical political doctrine that some are calling Islamofascism, but can be best thought of as Islamist totalitarianism?

The twentieth century saw the rise and fall of dangerous political ideologies: fascism, Nazism, Japanese imperialism, and communism. These movements produced tens of millions of deaths and were responsible for World War II, various regional guerrilla wars, and the Cold War. By the beginning of the 1990s, these totalitarian "isms" had generally been defeated militarily, intellectually, or both. Some were calling it the "end of history," meaning that liberal democratic capitalism, which is based on the "self-evident" principles of equality, individual freedom, and human rights, had prevailed in winning the minds and hearts— if not the governments—of all humanity. Then, it would have been almost inconceivable to believe that another "ism" with the power to enslave millions would re-surface. But that is now the case.

Since the attacks of September 11, 2001, it has become quite clear that Islamist ideologies grounded in extreme versions of Islamic law, known as sharia, have been gaining adherents throughout the world. These laws create a brutally-enforced hierarchy of group rights, favoring Muslims over non-Muslims, men over women, and a dominant Muslim sect over other Muslims, with individual rights and freedoms subordinated for all. Such extreme laws lie at the heart of the Islamist terrorists' radical agenda. Where implemented, they have produced outlaw states, such as Afghanistan under the Taliban, repressive societies, and areas that are breeding grounds for terrorism. (Such enslavement of the mind is distinct from the actual physical enslavement of thousands of Christians and other non-Muslims in present-day Sudan, discussed elsewhere in this book by Baroness Caroline Cox.) This retrograde Islamist political ideology, rejected by most Muslims throughout the world today, destroys freedom and human rights, democracy, equality, the rule of law, and economic growth based on human effort and ingenuity. It is a principal barrier to a free and peaceful world.

Suppression of Democracy in the Middle East

Worldwide, the number of countries whose citizens have basic political rights and civil liberties has been growing. Freedom House indicates that there were ninety such "Free" countries and fifty-eight others qualifying as "Partly Free," together accounting for seventy-seven percent of the world's nations in 2006. (1) The trend is clear—the world has increased the number of liberal democracies by an order of magnitude during the twentieth century.

Islam is not inconsistent with democratic freedom. The majority of the world's Muslims enjoy individual liberties in democracies, such as in Indonesia, Bangladesh (assuming the recent takeover by the military is only temporary and leads to prompt elections), India, Turkey, the Balkans, Senegal, and Mali, as well as in Western countries. What we often describe as a freedom deficit in the Muslim world is in fact largely a problem of the Arab world, a world that contains only one-quarter of the world's Muslims. In the seventeen Arab states, there are no "free" countries and no real democracies. Only a handful (in the Gulf, Lebanon, Jordan, and Morocco) can effectively guarantee a few basic liberties, such as relative press freedom. The "Arab Human Development Report 2002," authored by a brave group of Arab intellectuals for the United Nations Development Program, indicated some of the reasons for this situation: approximately half of Arab women are kept illiterate, there are only one-fifth as many books translated into Arabic every year as are translated into Greek, and Arab per capita income growth has shrunk to a level just above sub-Saharan Africa.

There is no single reason for the Middle East's recalcitrant resistance to the movement toward human rights, democracy, and the rule of law that has swept the planet. However, the influence of Iran's mullahs and of Saudi Arabia's Wahhabi sect, with their followers' wealth and hatred of modernity and openness of every kind, has been one of the largest factors in the growth of repressive laws and the suppression of democracy and human rights. This is not only true in the Middle East, but in much of Asia and Africa.

The watershed year was 1979, when Ayatollah Khomeini came to power in Iran and extremists took over the holiest of Islam's shrines, the Great Mosque in Mecca, which was under the protection of the Saudi King. In subsequent years, in return for protecting their own privileges, the Saudi royal family chose to turn over many aspects of life in the kingdom to the Wahhabi. The Saudi funded, with over $75 billion, the expansion throughout the world of the Wahhabi's extreme, hostile, anti-modern, and anti-democratic form of Islam. Since over eighty percent of the world's Muslims identify with the Sunni branch of Islam rather than the other large branch of Shi'a Islam, the Sunni Wahhabi have a built-in advantage over the Shiite Iranians in this competition for dominance of the Muslim world.

Background

Since the Saudi conquest of the Hejaz from the Hashemites in 1924 and the formal establishment of the state of Saudi Arabia in 1932—more or less occurring simultaneously with the discovery of huge oil deposits in the kingdom—Saudi Arabia has been of substantial importance in the world. Although the Saudis have existed as a tribe and a family in control of a small portion of Arabia for centuries, their influence, even their existence as a nation, has come about within the lifespan of many now living. Until less than thirty years ago, U.S. relations with the Saudis were generally smooth. The United States and Saudis were on the same side of the Cold War, and the Saudis valued U.S. support (and the United States valued theirs) against Soviet influence in the Middle East. Of course, the oil embargo of 1973 created major stress, but the watershed year, as noted above, was 1979.

Prior to 1979, a number of Saudis prominent in government, the military, and the oil business had been educated in the West and were on easy terms, at least privately, with Western values and ways. When R. James Woolsey was Under Secretary of the Navy in the late 1970s, he was invited to a Saudi home for dinner. There were several Saudi men there, all of whom had been educated in the West. Their wives, who had spent substantial time in the West and wore modest Western dresses, accompanied them. Everyone had an aperitif before dinner. Their conversation about world events was informed, sophisticated, and urbane. That sort of evening would not occur in today's Saudi Arabia. The dinner would be all male (and certainly no aperitifs or alcohol of any kind would be served). We would judge that the Saudi participants would be far less likely to have either studied in the West or be familiar with many issues from a Western perspective.

A major part of the reason for this and other important changes in the Kingdom was the Saudi royal family's reaction to the tumultuous year of 1979. After the twin shocks of the rise of Ayatollah Khomeini and the attack on the Great Mosque at Mecca, the Saudis chose a Faustian bargain with the Wahhabi sect. The Saudis accommodated their views about proper behavior and Islamic law and effectively turned over education in the Kingdom to them. The Saudis would later fund the expansion into Pakistan and elsewhere their extreme, hostile, anti-modern, and anti-democratic form of Islam. The other side of the bargain was that if the Wahhabi would concentrate their attacks on others, particularly the United States and Israel, the Saudi elite would more or less get a free ride from the Wahhabi. The corruption within the Kingdom would be overlooked. Former secretary of state George Shultz, not known for either a propensity for overstatement or for hostility to the Saudis, calls this deflection of Wahhabi anger toward the United States "a grotesque protection racket." (2)

What began 250 years ago within a fringe sect in a remote part of the Arabian peninsula has been given global reach through Saudi government sponsorship and money, particularly as the Wahhabi have competed with Iran in spreading their versions of the faith. With its vast oil wealth and its position as guardian of Islam's two holiest sites, as well as its being part of the most populous Sunni branch of Islam, Saudi Arabia now lays claim to being the leading power within Islam. It also claims to be the protector of the faith, a belief stated in the Saudi Basic Law. Saudi Ambassador to the United States Adel al-Jubeir publicly states, "the role of Saudi Arabia in the Muslim world is similar to the role of the Vatican." (3)

Wahhabi Extremism

The 1979 Faustian bargain by the Saudi royal family has had a huge effect on opinion in the Kingdom. Bernard Lewis points out that throughout much of Islamic history in many parts of the Muslim world before the eighteenth century, Muslims have often been more tolerant than many other religions. Jews and Christians, "People of the Book," were indeed limited and taxed as dhimmi, but still their worship services were tolerated. However, young people in the Kingdom today are systematically infused with hostility for all infidels and for other Muslims, such as Shi'a and Sufis. Christian churches and Jewish synagogues, along with all other non-Muslim places of worship, are banned.

Furthermore, most young Saudis are not equipped when they graduate from school to perform the jobs necessary to operate a modern economy. Instead, many are employed, if that is the right word, as "religious police"—walking the streets to harass women whose veils may not fully cover their faces, for example. The anger of young Saudis due to the lack of useful work, and their indoctrination, is palpable. It is not coincidental that fifteen of the nineteen terrorists who attacked the United States on September 11th were Saudis. The NEW YORK TIMES cited a poll conducted by Saudi Intelligence and shared with the U.S. government that over ninety-five percent of Saudis between the ages of twenty-five and forty-one have sympathy for Osama bin Laden. (4) Whether this report from the Saudi government of their young adults' views is accurate or distorted, it makes an important point about hostility to the United States either by the government, the people, or both. The Saudi-funded, Wahhabi-operated export of hatred reaches around the globe.

It is well known that the religious schools of Pakistan that educated a large share of the Taliban and al-Qaeda are Wahhabi. But Pakistan is not the sole target. Wahhabi extremism has spread throughout parts of Africa and Asia. The Wahhabi-funded textbooks flooding the world teach that the obligation of all Muslims is to consider all infidels the enemy.

One analogue for Wahhabism's political influence today might be the extremely angry German nationalism in the period after World War I. Not all angry and extreme German nationalists or their sympathizers in that period were or became Nazis. But just as angry and extreme German nationalism of that period was the soil in which Nazism grew, Wahhabi and Islamist extremism today is the soil in which al-Qaeda and its sister terrorist organizations are growing.

Worldwide Education Based on Hate

Something like the following has occurred on many occasions: In late 2004, a recently arrived Arab exchange student walks down a palm-lined boulevard in a working class neighborhood of Los Angeles. Since it is Friday, he bypasses the Hispanic restaurants, the convenience and sporting goods stores, and enters the King Fahd mosque—an elegant building of white marble etched with gold and adorned by a blue minaret. The mosque is named after its benefactor, the Saudi monarch, who died in mid-2005. Later he will join some five hundred other California Muslims in prayer. Because it is early, he visits the mosque library where he picks up several books on religious guidance, written in Arabic, that are offered free to Muslims like him — newly arrived and uncertain on how to fit into this modern, diverse land.

The tracts he opens are in the voice of a senior religious authority. They tell him that America, his adoptive home, is the "Abode of the Infidel," the Christian and the Jew. He reads:

Be disassociated from the infidels, hate them for their religion, leave them, never rely on them for support, do not admire them and always oppose them in every way according to Islamic law. There is consensus in this matter, that whoever helps unbelievers against Muslims, regardless of what type of support he lends to them, he is an unbeliever himself.

The new student looks carefully at one book's cover: GREETINGS FROM THE CULTURAL DEPARTMENT. The book is from the Embassy of Saudi Arabia in Washington, D.C., and published by the government of Saudi Arabia. The other books are textbooks from the Saudi Education Ministry and collections of fatwas (religious edicts) issued by the government's religious office, or published by other organizations based in Riyadh, Saudi Arabia. The student's experience is repeated today, in Saudi Arabia, the notorious madrassas of Pakistan, and even here at some sites in America. To be sure, not all the books in such mosques espouse extremism, and not all extremist works are Saudi. However, Saudi Arabia is overwhelmingly the state most responsible for these publications that support the ideology of hate. National security analyst Alex Alexiev estimates that Saudi Arabia expends several times more than what the Soviet Union spent at the height of the Cold War on external ideological propaganda. (5)

The Center for Religious Freedom gathered samples of over two hundred such texts from 2003 to 2004—all from American sites and all spread, sponsored, or otherwise generated by the government of Saudi Arabia. They instruct that it is the Muslim's duty to adopt the hostility and belligerence of the hard-line Wahhabi sect of Islam. In 2006, the Center reported that the Saudi state religious curriculum, which is also used in the official Islamic Saudi Academy near Washington, D.C., teaches the Wahhabi doctrine of religious hatred. A twelfth grade textbook published by the Saudi Ministry of Education, for example, asserts that "jihad to spread the faith of God is an obligation," and that jihad, which is defined in this text as "battling" infidels, is the "summit of Islam." An eleventh grade textbook in the Saudi curriculum instructs that "raising women's issues" is part of a modern Crusade. A tenth grade textbook asserts that there is a Jewish conspiracy to dominate the world. According to a ninth grade textbook, "the hour [of judgment] will not come until the Muslims fight the Jews and kill them." (6)

The Wahhabism that the Saudi monarchy enforces and on which it bases its legitimacy is shown in these documents as a fanatically bigoted, xenophobic, and sometimes-violent ideology. These publications articulate its wrathful dogma. The publications gathered for the Freedom House 2005 study state that it is a religious obligation for Muslims to hate Christians and Jews. They warn against imitating, befriending, or helping such "infidels" in any way, or taking part in their festivities and celebrations. They instill contempt for America because the United Sates is ruled by legislated civil law rather than by totalitarian Wahhabi-style Islamic law. These textbooks and documents preach a Nazi-like hatred for Jews and avow that the Muslim's duty is to eliminate the state of Israel. Regarding women, they instruct that women should be veiled, segregated from men, and barred from certain employment and roles.

Since 2004, the U.S. Department of State has annually designated Saudi Arabia as a "Country of Particular Concern" under the International Religious Freedom Act, after finding for many years that "religious freedom did not exist" in the Kingdom. (7) The Saudi policy of denying religious freedom is explained in one of the tracts in a study published by the Center for Religious Freedom as follows:

> *Freedom of thinking requires permitting the denial of faith and attacking what is sacred, glorifying falsehood and defending the heretics, finding fault in religion and letting loose the ideas and pens to write of disbelief as one likes, and to put ornaments on sin as one likes.* (8)

This means that Muslims who openly disagree with Wahhabi rulings are also denounced, discredited, and intimidated. In these documents, other Muslims, especially those who advocate tolerance and reform, are condemned as infidels and blasphemers. The opening fatwa in one booklet distributed by the Saudi embassy responds to a question about a Muslim preacher in a European mosque who taught that it is not right to condemn Jews and Christians as infidels. The fatwa rebukes the Muslim cleric: "He who casts doubts about their infidelity leaves no doubt about his." Since, under Saudi law, "apostates" from Islam can be sentenced to death, this is an implied death threat against the tolerant Muslim Imam, as well as an incitement to vigilante violence. Other Saudi fatwas in the same collection declare that Muslims who engage in genuine interfaith dialogue are also "unbelievers." Sufi and Shiite Muslims are also viciously condemned. As for a Muslim who fails to uphold Wahhabi sexual mores through homosexual activity or heterosexual activity outside of marriage, the edicts advise that it would be lawful for Muslims to spill his blood and to take his money.

Reaction by Moderate Muslims

Sheikh Muhammad Hisham Kabbani, the Lebanese-American Chairman of the Michigan-based Islamic Supreme Council of America, has stated that he was shocked to learn that Wahhabism is active in America. After he arrived in America in 1990, he says he heard Wahhabism being preached in a number of American mosques.

Saudi dissidents Ali al-Ahmed of the Washington-based Gulf Institute and Ali Alyami of the Center for Democracy and Human Rights in Saudi Arabia, the Carnegie Endowment scholar Husain Haqqani, Dr. Zuhdi Jasser of the American Islamic Forum for Democracy, and author and Muslim convert Stephen Schwartz are among other Muslim leaders and intellectuals who have courageously spoken out and written about the threats posed by Wahhabi hate ideology and its global expansion. Within worldwide Sunni Islam, followers of Wahhabism and other hard-line movements are a distinct minority. This is evident from the many Muslims who have chosen to make America their home and are upstanding, law-abiding citizens and neighbors. In fact, it was just such concerned Muslims who first brought these publications to our attention. They decry the Wahhabi interpretation of Islam as being foreign to the toleration expressed in Islam and its injunction against coercion in religion.

These moderate Muslims believe they would be forbidden to practice the faith of their ancestors in today's Saudi Arabia. They are grateful to the United Sates and other Western nations for granting them religious freedom. They also affirm the importance of respecting non-Muslims, pointing to verses in the

Koran that speak with kindness about non-Muslims. They raise examples of Islam's Prophet Mohammed visiting his sick Jewish neighbor, standing in deference at a Jew's funeral procession, settling a dispute in favor of a truthful Jew over a dishonest person who was a Muslim, and forming alliances with Jews and polytheists, among others. These moderate Muslims criticize the Wahhabi for distorting and even altering the text of the Koran in support of their bigotry. They say that in their tradition jihad is applicable only in defense of Islam and Muslims. They say that it is commendable, not an act of "infidelity," for Muslims, Jews, and Christians to engage in genuine dialogue. Some moderate Muslims are beginning, in spite of intimidation, to make these points publicly.

Conclusion

Encouraging individual rights, the rule of law, and democracy in the Muslim world will take decades as it did with Europe throughout most of the twentieth century. There will also be great challenges. Yet, there is hope. Since 1945, by Freedom House's calculation, more than one hundred democracies have been established. Many, indeed most, of these countries are places where self-appointed experts have said time and again that freedom would not take root. As Germany, Japan, Taiwan, South Korea, Thailand, India, the Philippines, Spain, Portugal, much of Latin America, important parts of the sub-Saharan Africa, almost all of Eastern Europe, and many other states have moved toward respect for human rights, the rule of law, and democracy, the experts have grown silent about their past misjudgments. They now focus on the Muslim world, particularly the Arab portion, and tell us that it is hopeless to believe that it can ever be moved effectively toward freedom and democracy. We believe they are wrong.

But to defeat the Wahhabi ideology, we must know what it is. In the words of Abdurrahman Wahid, a former President of Indonesia and a Muslim scholar who heads the world's largest Muslim organization, Nahdlatal Ulama, Wahhabism is:

> . . . *claiming to restore the perfection of the early Islam*
> *practiced by Muhammad and his companions, who are*

*known in Arabic as al-Salaf al-Salih, "the Righteous
Ancestors"; establishing a utopian society based on these Salafi
principles, by imposing their interpretation of Islamic law on
all members of society; annihilating local variants of Islam
in the name of authenticity and purity; transforming Islam
from a personal faith into an authoritarian political system;
establishing a pan-Islamic caliphate governed according
to the strict tenets of Salafi Islam, and often conceived as
stretching from Morocco to Indonesia and the Philippines;
and, ultimately, bringing the entire world under the sway of
their extremist ideology.* (9)

In combating this reactionary force, we must make common
cause with the hundreds of millions of decent and reasonable
Muslims in the world. They too want peace and prosperity for
themselves and their families and are not interested in either
supporting terror or living under repressive laws. They have no
more wish to be stoned or beheaded or to be put to death for
criticizing the government and its laws than we do. In supporting
their struggle for freedom and against Islamist totalitarianism
and extreme sharia, we are helping secure a more peaceful and
prosperous world.

Extended Observation

Reflection & Conversation

In this chapter, you learned that ideologies that enslave the
mind can be as dehumanizing as physical slavery. The means
for portraying that repression was one of the most perplexing
phenomena of the contemporary international landscape—
Islamofascism. Center your reflection on what you learned about
this phenomenon. Reflect on other manifestations of this kind of
slavery that you have observed.

Attend to the Word

Read John 15:12–27. It would be good to read the entire passage aloud—slowly and with meaning. The passage first lays down the law of love and proceeds to a warning against persecution. Imagine that someone who has been the victim of slavery of the mind is hearing these words. What possible reaction would such a person have to these words of Jesus? Spend a few moments in silence. Let the message and its meaning soak in.

Engage

In stark contrast to Jesus' message, slavery of the mind begins with the suppression of democracy and spreads an ideology based on hate, separation, and fear.

1. Spend some time talking about the freedoms you treasure most. Why do you treasure them? What would cause you to relinquish those freedoms?
2. Individual rights, democracy, and the rule of law are alien to those regimes and movements that enslave the minds of their members. How can those three constituent elements of freedom be eroded even in free societies?
3. In your view, what are the limits of personal freedom? Where do these limitations come from? Why are these limitations necessary?

Move Forward

Understanding the dynamics of enslavement of the mind is one of the first steps to preventing it. It is also important for combating it. Dismissing this kind of enslavement as "craziness" is not helpful—even dangerous.

1. What steps can you take to be informed and aware of enslavement of the mind experienced by many people around the world?
2. What actions can you take in your life to combat this slavery, including the minor signs of it—even in your local community?

3. In what ways can you test whether or not a political group or some organization is engaging in ideologies that attempt to enslave the mind in order to control its members?

Pray

One of the great enemies of the enslavement of the mind is the gift of wisdom. When that gift is shared, it can serve to inoculate groups against those who would enslave the mind. Use these words from Wisdom of Solomon as a source for your prayer.

> *Wisdom rescued from troubles those who served her.*
>
> *When a righteous man fled from his brother's wrath,*
> *she guided him on straight paths;*
> *she showed him the kingdom of God,*
> *and gave him knowledge of holy things;*
> *she prospered him in his labors and increased the fruit*
> *of his toil.*
>
> *When his oppressors were covetous,*
> *she stood by him and made him rich.*
>
> *She protected him from his enemies,*
> *and kept him safe from those who lay in wait for him:*
> *in his arduous contest she gave him the victory,*
> *so that he might learn that godliness is more powerful*
> *than anything else.*
>
> *Wisdom of Solomon 10:9–12 (NRSV)*

PART III

WILBERFORCE AS A MODEL
FOR EFFECTING CHANGE

twelve

The Reformation of Manners

By Don Eberly

Don Eberly is a nationally recognized voice on issues of citizenship and community, and a leading contributor to the growing debate over how to strengthen the social institute in America. His writings on issues of society and culture include dozens of essays and articles and four books, most recently America's Promise: Civil Society and the Renewal of American Culture. *Don has founded or co-founded several nationally recognized initiatives promoting civic, democratic, and economic renewal, including the Commonwealth Foundation and the National Fatherhood Initiative, a non-partisan civic initiative seeking to renew responsible fatherhood in American society.*

Don is an affiliate scholar at the Institute for American Values, and a fellow at the George Gallup International Institute. He has held key staff positions in Congress and the White House, and regularly advises senior officials in national and state government. His work has been covered by many of the major media outlets in the country, including the Wall Street Journal, Newsweek, *the* Washington Post, *the* L.A. Times, *National Public Radio, and CNN. He speaks regularly to business, civic, and policy groups. Don holds graduate degrees from George Washington University and Harvard University.*

William Wilberforce's two great objectives—ending slavery and reforming the moral climate in Britain—seem to be separate and even disparate goals. However, the two objectives are inextricably linked. Wilberforce knew that government action against slavery was impossible without a massive shift in the moral attitudes, actions, and habits of the British people. That shift could and did lead to a more positive engagement in the task of improving the world, including the abolition of slavery.

How does abolishing the British slave trade relate to manners, or to what English poet William Cowper called "the better hour"? The answer is that the two are inextricably linked. Wilberforce knew that government action against slavery was impossible short of a massive shift in the moral attitudes and habits of the people themselves. It was necessary for people to make a positive engagement in improving the world around them.

As impossible as the job of abolishing the slave trade appeared, the remaking of a decadent English society seemed even more daunting. The times were characterized by high rates of crime, drunkenness, and general disregard for moral standards. Public confidence in the laws was at an all time low, and there was widespread economic and political corruption. The sophisticated classes mocked religion and embraced skepticism toward moral truth as the fashionable outlook, while malicious and lewd behavior was commonplace.

Remaking English Society Then

Over the course of his decades-long campaign, Wilberforce was able to renew English society. He did this by several means. Wilberforce created, led, or participated in at least sixty-nine benevolent societies (what we would call non-profits) that promoted social reformation in dozens of areas, including public health, aid to the poor, education reform, and the humane treatment of animals. He also wrote a book about the Christian faith that had been so influential in his life. Its title was twenty-four words long: A PRACTICAL VIEW OF THE PREVAILING RELIGIOUS SYSTEM OF PROFESSED CHRISTIANS, IN THE HIGHER AND MIDDLE CLASSES IN THIS COUNTRY, CONTRASTED WITH REAL CHRISTIANITY. It was a best seller in the UK and in the United States for fifty years.

Some of the societies that Wilberforce was involved were religious, but some were secular, including the Society for the Reformation of Manners. When he set out to reform the manners and morals of the people, he did not draft legislation or form a political action committee. There was already plenty of that. Instead, he collaborated with social reformers in developing society-wide campaigns to affect attitudes and behavior.

Proclamations promoting public virtue had been issued by the kings of England since the mid-seventeenth century, but were widely ignored. Wilberforce persuaded King George III to reissue one such proclamation, bearing the ungainly name "A Proclamation for the Encouragement of Piety and Virtue and for the Preventing and Punishing of Vice, Profaneness, and Immorality." This time, Wilberforce decided to accompany the proclamation with the creation of local "societies" for the purpose of reforming manners in localities all across England.

Wilberforce added real community-based campaigns to an otherwise abstract and largely ignored official declaration, and the result was an elevation of the people's conduct and refinement of their tastes. The reform campaigns provided direct help to "persons of dissolute and debauched lives." The theory behind these reform societies was that seemingly small things, including manners, matter. Minor offenses against the common good were seen as the fertile ground for more serious crimes.

Slavery Linked to Moral Indifference

Slavery, according to Wilberforce, could not be understood in isolation from these debauched conditions. Moral indifference toward the evil of slavery, he discerned, was nourished in a cultural environment of coarseness and crudeness. The systematic misery of slaves was considered but one or two links in the chain removed from the habitual immorality and degradation that characterized the masses in society at the time.

By recognizing this linkage, Wilberforce was merely reflecting what others from different places and times in history had observed: that laws are, to a very large extent, a reflection of the culture. Perhaps Edmund Burke offered the most famous encapsulation of this: "Manners are of more importance than laws. Upon them, in a great measure, the laws depend." Burke continued, manners are "what vex or soothe, corrupt or purify, exalt or debase, barbarize or refine us, by a constant, steady, uniform, insensible operation, like that of the air we breathe in."

This being the case, Wilberforce concluded that to change the law he had to go "upstream" to the tributaries of moral beliefs and conduct. He had to confront the moral ethos in which the slave trade was nourished. Uprooting a corrupt law required reforming the debased culture that legitimated it.

Wilberforce also recognized that, unlike passing anti-slavery legislation, the work of reforming manners and morals was not the work of the state; such a task would have to be carried out by various voluntary associations within civil society. Over the course of three decades, Wilberforce's founding of and participation in voluntary associations resulted in one of the most dynamic chapters in the history of voluntary reform societies. His success at achieving the twin goals—reforming manners and, in turn, eradicating slavery—stands as a monument to the power of voluntary associations and reform societies in bringing social and moral uplift to a debauched culture.

Voluntary Rules of Behavior

What Wilberforce understood in his day, and what growing numbers of Americans are coming to appreciate today, is that there is an unbroken link between uncivil and ill-mannered behavior of the milder variety and tolerance for the more barbaric treatment of human beings, illustrated in Wilberforce's time by the slave trade. The corruption of superficial and seemingly harmless behavior can have a far deeper corrupting effect. The attempts by some organizations and movements today to restore civility and recover manners should be seen as an attempt to renew the linkage between freedom and its responsible use with the aid of social rules and restraints. Manners, in other words, serve important purposes in maintaining an ordered freedom in a democratic society.

Manners have a unique history as an informal and voluntary tool for shaping individual behavior and social standards. In 1530 the philosopher Erasmus wrote in his etiquette book, DE CIVILITATE, that a young person's training should be in four important areas: religion, study, duty, and manners. Another book on manners from the same era, written by French Jesuits in 1595, was translated into English and was adopted by George Washington two centuries later.

John Moulton, a noted English judge, speaking in 1912 on the subject of "law and manners," divided human action into three domains. The domain of law essentially compels people to obey, without much choice in the matter, while the domain of free choice grants the individual unconstrained freedom. Between these two domains lies a third domain that is neither regulated by the law nor free from constraint.

This "domain of obedience to the unenforceable" was what Moulton termed manners. Manners were about proper behavior, of course, but they also entailed a larger concept of moral duty and social responsibility. They involved "doing right where there is no one to make you do it but yourself," where the individual is "the enforcer of the law upon himself." (1)

What Moulton understood was that cultural conditions could not be reversed by government action or changes in the law alone, but by a recovery of manners. Moulton saw the domain of manners as "the whole realm which recognizes the sway of duty, fairness, sympathy, taste, and all other things that make life beautiful and society possible," things which can be easily corrupted but not so easily corrected, at least not by laws. (2)

While the state is in no position to restore manners, the quality of public life and government is inextricably linked to them. Government is forced to deal with the consequences of the breakdown of manners and moral norms. The erosion of cultural norms practically ensures that the state becomes the arbiter of conflict, and will thus continually expand.

Less Need for Government

Every society, to function as a society, must settle on some basic notion of right behavior that is regarded as important and legitimate enough to enforce. Societies have basically two means to enforce right behavior. One method is the law, which is a clumsy, heavy-handed, and often inappropriate tool. The second method, as Lord Moulton pointed out, is manners. As many observers have noted, there is an inverse relationship between the widespread practice of manners and the intrusiveness of law.

When the rules for determining what conduct is proper are no longer set by custom, morality, and religion, the rules of society become decided through politics alone.

Judith Martin, leading etiquette expert, sees manners fulfilling a "regulative" function, similar to that of the law. Where manners function properly, the conscience is informed and behavior is constrained without having to resort to policy or the courts. Martin says that manners work to "soften personal antagonisms, and thus to avert conflicts," so that the law may be restricted to "serious violations of morality." (3) Social rules bring respect and harmony to daily situations.

The wide practice of manners can make the job of governance easier. Political philosopher Thomas Hobbes understood manners as "small morals," and no small protection for a society against what he famously described as "state of nature." (4) Manners were part of the routine of an ordered society, where civility and respect were practiced voluntarily apart from the compulsion of law. They are the bridges between private freedom and public duty.

A system of manners is a way for a free society to induce people to act respectfully by voluntary means. As Hobbes pointed out, manners contribute to the maintenance of order and balance in society: safeguarding society from the nasty, brutish conditions that characterized man in his uncivilized state while minimizing the need for a highly intrusive state.

As individuals make their decisions less in accordance with either private conscience or widely accepted moral standards and more on the basis of the law, society becomes legalistic in its approach to behavior; the law, not morality, guides behavior. Under this law-based system of regulating conduct, many are prone to resort to the law in sorting out differences and to assume that whatever the law does not formally forbid must therefore be permissible. In other words, when the law is the principle arbiter, other gentler forms of regulation—such as ethics and manners— tend to recede.

Judith Martin explains it this way: on the one hand, she says many Americans have come to believe and to put into practice "the idea that any behavior not prohibited by law ought to be tolerated." On the other hand, she says people resort to the law to correct minor offenses that should be socially regulated by manners: "people who found rude but legally permitted behavior intolerable have attempted to expand the law to outlaw rudeness." (5)

Ultimately, says Martin, attempts to eradicate rudeness or obnoxiousness through the law poses a threat "to the freedoms guaranteed by the constitution."

Flexibility

Social regulations, such as manners, not only govern more softly than the law, but they are more flexible. Social regulation leaves room for nonconformity, which the law does not, and requires no costly governmental apparatus. The state's rules are absolute and binding, enforceable through arrest and imprisonment.

Thus, when conflicts arise in a society governed by a pervasive law rather than social constraints, these conflicts—whether on highways, school playgrounds, or in malls—quickly escalate and must be resolved by external authorities. The increased number of security personnel serving in locations where they were never needed before, such as in schools and at sporting events, illustrates this phenomenon.

Balance

In many respects this need to balance order and liberty by voluntary means was seen by the framers of the U.S. Constitution as the central challenge for the Republic, and one that they hoped and expected succeeding generations would take up. The framers frequently used terms such as *habits, dispositions, sentiments,* and *manners* to describe the kind of self-regulating behavior that would maintain public order while minimizing the need for costly, intrusive government. A free society requires a capacity not only to regulate one's own passions, but also to have regard for the rights and opinions of others.

At least two founders, George Washington and Benjamin Franklin, contributed their own original thoughts and writings on manners. As noted earlier, Washington translated onto a small plain notebook 110 "Rules of Civility and Decent Behavior in Company and Conversation." In Washington's day, civility was furthered through a set of voluntary rules whereby a person seeking social advancement and distinction learned to display deference to the interests and feelings of others.

Rules of civility were consciously adopted by Washington to win the respect of his fellows and to advance in leadership. (6) By means of a strict code of courteous behavior, Washington established a towering command as a leader on the battlefield. The first principle of manners, according to Washington's rules, had to do with public leadership and conduct: "Every action done in company ought to be done with some sign of respect for those who are present."

Manners and simple courtesy added grace to what was a natural gift for iron-willed leadership. Manners also helped him master what was widely known to be a severe temper.

Moral Habits Need to Be Internalized

As mentioned above, when rules are established by law they can produce superficial compliance where the person is motivated by avoidance of punishment. By contrast, there is evidence in the case of manners of some internalization of the values. Aristotle held that people are essentially conditioned to be good by developing positive habits, what some modern sociologists refer to as "habituation." He said: "only a blockhead can fail to realize that our characters are the result of our conduct." In other words, people become good by doing good. (7)

Edmund Burke, writing in the eighteenth century, said much the same thing in pointing out that morals, to some extent, depend upon the maintenance of manners. Manners, he said, "give their whole form and color to our lives." He continued, "According to their quality," he said, "they aid morals, they supply them, or they totally destroy them." (8)

Mark Caldwell, in his book A SHORT HISTORY OF RUDENESS: MANNERS, MORALS AND MISBEHAVIOR IN MODERN AMERICA, supplies evidence of this connection between manners and morals, although he says the connection is "deceptive, sinuous, and complicated." He cites a variety of examples in history of how attitudes and beliefs adjusted themselves according to newly expected behavior. For example, the movement to consider racial discrimination unacceptable has led to improved moral attitudes about race. Caldwell concludes that attempts to turn "optional niceties into duties in the hope that this will stiffen our moral spines" is supported by history. (9)

Critics of manners are quick to cast doubt upon this phenomenon by suggesting that rather than supporting moral attitudes, manners are merely a cover for hypocrisy and repression. In other words, manners are discounted as phony because they are thought to bear no relationship to inner character. The defenders of manners will readily admit that hypocrisy is one human behavior that does exist, but will then quickly add that it is not entirely lacking in social usefulness.

University of Texas Associate Professor of Government J. Budziszewski is among those who believes that practicing courtesy will not only take the edge off some of society's coarseness, but it will begin to fundamentally change people. Though courtesy can "mask" some of the unpleasant things one might feel, Budziszewski says this type of mask is not hypocritical, as many would define it, because it has a high purpose. "Masks, of course, can be used to deceive, but in courtesy that is not the aim." (10) It is to guard against wanton disrespect of human beings.

As C.S. Lewis, Gilbert Meilaender, and a host of other scholars and social critics have explained, masks are worn partly in hopes that our true faces will gradually grow to fit them, and partly to set a good example in the meantime. "If you please," "thank you," and "the pleasure is mine" may be mere formulae, says Budziszewski, but "they rehearse the humility, gratitude and charity that I know I ought to feel and cannot yet." Courtesy, he says, finds its place in a world where people "would like to be better than they are." (11)

Cultural Forces Behind the Corruption of Manners

The wide acceptance of manners has always waxed and waned throughout society. Their waning in recent decades has been brought about by cultural and philosophical influences, some of which may have been inherent in the American system from the beginning, and some of more recent origins.

Alexis de Tocqueville praised many aspects of the American system of democracy, especially its driving impulse toward equality, but wondered how a society that would do away so completely with social distinctions could preserve a sense of mutual respect and obligation when it came to social conduct. Tocqueville speculated that America's incessant drive toward equality would produce a dynamic, opportunity-rich society, but that it would do so at the expense, in effect, of manners. He warned that Americans would use their freedom not merely for purposes of individual industry, but in pursuit of "petty and paltry pleasures." (12)

Weakening Institutions

Another factor of more recent origin is the weakening of those institutions that typically transmit manners and morals. Michael

Sandel states that worries about incivility exposes a deeper fact that the moral fabric of community is unraveling around us. "From families and neighborhoods to cities and towns to schools, congregations, and trade unions, the institutions that traditionally provided people with moral anchors and a sense of belonging are under siege." (13)

As Sandel and others argue, it is not enough to have a clear concept of what manners and morals are. They depend upon effectively functioning value-shaping institutions, with real legitimacy and authority, to be transmitted. "You can't have strong virtues without strong institutions," says University of Chicago ethics professor Jean Bethke Elshtaine, "and you can't have strong institutions without moral authority." (14)

The erosion of authority and community norms picked up momentum in recent decades as an ideology of individual autonomy became widely embraced in the culture. The objective has been to liberate the individual from all inner and outer restraints, including commonly held social standards.

Much of the authority that was once enjoyed by family, religion, and the civic community has been transferred to the individual. According to Allen Ehrenhalt, "there may be a welter of confused values operating in the 1990s, but there is one point on which all Americans speak with unity and unmistakable clarity." We have become, he says, "emancipated from social authority as we once used to know it." (15) This is true, says Ehrenhalt, throughout every segment of America, in the lower, middle, and upper classes, and it is grounded in an excessive orientation toward individual autonomy. The worship of individual autonomy and the suspicion of authority "has meant the erosion of standards of conduct and civility, visible mostly in the schools where teachers who dare to discipline pupils risk a profane response." (16)

A culture that is in search of greater emancipation from all restraints is likely to see such things as manners as a barrier, not an aid, to individual development. According to Bill Bennett, former Secretary of Education, "the messages being so powerfully promulgated is basically this: the summum bonum of life is self-indulgence, self-aggrandizement, and instant gratification; the good life is synonymous with license and freedom from all inhibitions; rules are undesirable and made to be broken; and self-fulfillment is achieved by breaking them." (17)

Repudiating an Older Culture of Conformity

Some would say that the erosion of social standards over the past several decades is an understandable, if somewhat excessive, reaction to a culture that previously erred on the side of a conformity that stifled individual expression. The excessively constrictive standards of the 1950s were thrown off by the "baby boom" generation, which is now demographically dominant. For many in this generation, the call to manners cannot be confused with a return to a previous era with all of its limits and social rigidity. Many in this generation have second thoughts about the social revolution they spawned, but few are willing to go back to where things were.

And how different those social standards were. Writing in the fall of 1996 in the WILSON QUARTERLY, James Morris describes films from the postwar era that show Americans in public places, such as baseball games, almost as though "they're under the sway of an alien force. The women wear blouses and skirts or dresses or, more formal still, suits—and hats, hats, hats. The men are suited too, and hatted row after row to the horizon with brimmed felt jobs, deftly creased." Rules were set by people in communities, not the halls of Congress: "The kids you were told not to play with, the people who could not be invited to dinner, the topics that could never be discussed, the Sears-sized catalogue of actions that were 'shameful' and 'unforgivable' and 'unmentionable.'"

Morris doubts Americans will exchange the present for a past considered "speciously safe, ignorant and restricted." Manners depend on acknowledging authority, but authority is hard to come by in "a vigorous strutting democracy." No one, Morris adds, "wants to make a judgment, to impose a standard, to act from authority and call conduct unacceptable." Until standards of intelligence and behavior are defined and defended once again, "we had better be prepared to live with deterioration." (18) Modern skepticism toward moral values has reduced what was once widely considered objective standards of morality to matters of personal taste, preference, and individual choice.

If the 1950s were stifling, as most would agree, Morris says the present age is its radical opposite. "In this age of 'whatever,' Americans are becoming slaves to the new tyranny of nonchalance." For thirty years, every facet of the culture has steadily coarsened. Movies, music, television, newspapers, and magazines dwell routinely on topics that, according to Morris, were "once too hot for whispers."

An older culture of almost stoic self-denial, which erred on the side of restraint, has been traded in for a culture of self-realization and sensuality in which there are no universal values to which all consent—only individual preferences and desires. Popular culture broadcasts this new tendency by encouraging everyone to ignore the rules. Calvin Klein targets secularized images of youth as "people who do only what they want to do." Saab sells cars by telling us to "peel off inhibitions; find your own road." Nintendo urges children to "be heard; play it loud" as a boy spits at the camera. Healthy Choice Cereals suggests that to be happy "you gotta make your own rules."

If manners are about anything, they are about concealment of what is private, especially one's body and its functions. Manners, much like clothing for the body, provide an outer covering for unpleasant or debased tendencies. Most will acknowledge that up until perhaps the mid-twentieth century, American culture encouraged people to repress aberrant thoughts and behaviors. Now, says James Wolcott, "the problem is the opposite; getting people to put a cork in it. What was once quite possible to accomplish has become impossible to stop." Even our deepest, darkest secrets, "our once hidden shames," become easy pickings for publicity hounds. Because popular culture is now filled with "so many memoirs covering so many addictions and afflictions, the confessions have gotten kinkier and more gossipy, as writers add extra salsa to stand out from the growing herd." (19)

Closely linked to manners is the capacity for shame and the desire to achieve respectability. "Like any other tool, it can be abused, but that doesn't make it wrong in principle. Compared to jail, shame is a very benign tool." (20)

The loss of interest in manners can be tied directly to declining concern about respectability in any number of areas, including such basic things as fashions. For example, Mark Caldwell describes designer jeans as "a skeleton key to the mystery of manners." For the lower classes, the jeans are merely tacky. For others, however, the imitation of their economic inferiors becomes a social statement. In other words, a lowering of dress standards and a lowering of manners and language can, and do, go hand in hand. (21)

The Anonymous Society

Another factor in the loss of manners is the speed and rootlessness of modern life. People are less inclined to worry about manners when they aren't personally known, or when they are under pressure. People may simply have less time to be well mannered, says Ted Anthony. "Technology, mass media, and a desire to do more, do it better and do it yesterday have turned us into hurriers." He describes the twentieth century as "a hundred-year madness." He explains how "it started with horses and hours. It ends with Maseratis and microseconds, with cars speeding across highways, airplanes streaking across skies, microprocessors burning across desktops. This century's mad dash of innovation has produced all of these things—and the most frantic human era ever." Anthony continues, "This overwhelming desire to get from A to B, it's madness," causes us to be oblivious to one another. (22)

Technology itself, which is driving this accelerating process, may be a factor in our declining regard for others. Says David Masci, "something as frivolous as a Walkman brings millions of people pleasure every day. But by shutting out the people we encounter on the street, we inhibit an essential piece of what we think of as our humanity. Compassion, generosity, and empathy are all in part tied to our ability to find common ground with those around us. And it is much harder to find common ground without common courtesy." (23)

Added to speed is the anonymity that exists in a transient, uprooted society. Americans simply don't know each other the way they did when they had less busy lives and when most lived in one community for a lifetime. "Hello" and "excuse me" are less likely to be said among perfect strangers. When you know fewer people, the world is bound to appear riskier. According to Mark Caldwell, "Learning manners and living with their consequences would be easy if people and their social systems would only stay put. Most group relations are never stable anywhere; America is and always has been more volatile than the world average." Mobility and the technology that made it possible, says Caldwell, "heightened civilization in one way, but put the skids to it in others." (24)

America's Moribund Manners

Whether America has, in its current ill-mannered state, reached the same low-water mark as Britain at the turn of the nineteenth century is open to debate. Judging from the assessment that Americans themselves make of their current condition, it would appear that this is so.

A survey by U.S. NEWS AND WORLD REPORT and Bozell Worldwide indicates that many people believe that the behavior of Americans has worsened. Large majorities of Americans feel their country has reached an ill-mannered watershed. Nine out of ten Americans think incivility is a serious problem, and nearly half think it is extremely serious. Seventy-eight percent say the problem has worsened in the past ten years. (25)

Americans do not see rudeness merely as a private irritant. They see that disrespectful behavior portends a more worrisome social disintegration. More than 90 percent of those polled believe incivility and rudeness contribute to the increase in violence in the country; 85 percent believe it divides the national community, and the same number see it eroding healthy values such as respect for others. (26)

In other words, the abandonment of responsible behavior is no longer seen as isolated to an occasional episode, nor is it viewed as a matter of merely private concern with no social consequences; it is thought to be both pervasive and to be affecting the nation's social health.

A recent Gallup poll showed that a large majority of Americans believe that society has "a harsh and mean edge." Pollster George Gallup notes that the United States has become "a society in which the very notion of a good person is often ridiculed," where "retribution is the operative word." (27)

Columnist Michael Kelly describes a "Gresham's law in aesthetics" that operates manners just as in economics, which he says works with "breathtaking, ruthless rapidity." Nothing, he says, "is not fit to print," not even the act of the nation's highest leader and chief living symbol of democracy soiling the dress of his adulteress. Kelley proclaims: "The Marxist ideal is at last reached. We live, finally, in a classless society: No one has any class at all."

Kelly cites as evidence of his "classless society" thesis a number of cultural trends which have been adopted by the demographic mainstream, including fashion and the use of vulgarity. What is remarkable about this, he says, is not that deviance is being used to offend the sensibilities of the refined, which has occurred for centuries, but that deviancy may no longer exist as a category. The offenders are not cultural rebels; they are the mainstream culture. "The horror," he says, "is that we are fast approaching a culture where it is impossible to offend." (28)

A New Beginning for Manners

Stories of America's slipping manners are regularly captured in our headlines and decried by columnists. Language and behavior standards on film, television, and popular music have eroded to an unprecedented degree. Nearly every community in America has witnessed increased anger and rudeness in public places, and of road rage occasionally turning violent. (29)

Soccer moms and dads have become so loudmouthed and ill-mannered on the sidelines that one youth soccer league in West Palm Beach has adopted a policy of requiring the parents of all kids who sign up for the league to complete an ethics class. The Juniper-Tequesta Athletic Association, which serves six thousand kids ages five through eighteen, is now requiring parents to take an hour-long class in ethical conduct, including training in how to show positive support and good sportsmanship. "We just want to try to de-escalate the intensity that's being shown by the parents at these games," says the volunteer athletic league president. (30)

Few public spaces are seen as unsuitable for broadcasting ideas and images once widely thought of as reflecting bad manners. For example, bumper stickers have always been around, advertising one's favorite politician or rock band, or promoting a charity or social cause. It has been commonplace to broadcast offbeat ideas and causes via this medium. Today, however, bumper sticker messages carry sexual references and insults, the "F" word, and cartoon characters urinating on anything they find unacceptable. (31)

In an article entitled "A Small Plea to Delete a Ubiquitous Expletive," in U.S. NEWS AND WORLD REPORT, Elizabeth Austin plaintively suggests that if American society can agree on nothing else, perhaps establishing the goal of removing the now common use of the "F" word from polite circles might be a modest start. Everyone, including people who never use bad language, is now forced to hear it frequently used "on the street, on the job, at the health club, at the movies—anywhere two or three disgruntled citizens might gather."

Austin adds that the need to work for the elimination of the English language's most vulgar word would have been seen as preposterous a couple of generations ago since neither it nor any comparable word would ever have been used in polite company. (32)

Renewal Movements

In Wilberforce's time, and periodically throughout American history, society has realized the importance of "the unenforceable" social rules and embraced renewal movements to revive them. In nineteenth century America, for example, books and manuals for the application of manners to every aspect of life flourished. One bibliography assembled during this period counted 236 separate titles on manners. (33) When Emily Post's famous book, ETIQUETTE, was published in 1922, it became such a publishing success that it rivaled Sinclair Lewis' BABBIT, also published that year.

Today's manners movement has arisen in very much the same fashion. Manners are offered as at least a partial corrective to the excesses of a generation that spent its youth determined to throw off social conventions and constraints. A growing interest in manners is reflected in the popularity of books on the subject and a widening network of civility advocates. These contemporary authors carefully avoid appearing stiff or Victorian, and instead link manners to a widely expressed desire for greater social harmony and mutual respect.

Modern day manners philosopher Judith Martin, who has written extensively on the subject, says manners are defined as that "part of our fundamental beliefs or wants that include such notions as communal harmony, dignity of the person, a need for cultural coherence, and an aesthetic sense." (34) Etiquette is the set of rules that emerges from these fundamental beliefs.

Evidence that a search is on for more civilized social customs can be found in the popularity of films, such as the Jane Austen series, based in highly mannered societies. The characters suppress their emotions and urges, and express fastidious regard for others. Further evidence can be found in the astonishing success of THE RULES, a runaway best seller which establishes for women new (actually old) rules of conduct in courtship in order to secure the respect and fidelity of one's suitor.

The return to manners reflects a growing awareness that the loss of standards in courtship have been costly, especially to women. In her book A RETURN TO MODESTY, Wendy Shalit describes the dreadful consequences of declining respect for women in areas of courtship and sex, and predicts a counterrevolution in women's attitudes: "In the face of all the cultural messages that bark at them that promiscuity and exhibitionism are liberation, they are slowly but surely coming to think the opposite."

Promoting the rules of respect may also be good for commerce. Sensing that courtesy might strengthen the city's tourism industry, New York City civic leaders launched a campaign to encourage its citizens to be nicer to the twenty-five million visitors who visit the city each year. "Instead of Making a Wise Crack, Smile" the campaign encourages, and "Turn your Back on Tourists and They'll Turn Their Backs on New York." Thanks to the program, cabbies get a new supply of air fresheners, while cops, airport personnel, and subway workers get sensitivity training.

Conclusion

The history of manners suggests that they inevitably rebound. Mark Caldwell describes an "innate and unconscious human law" that seems to conserve manners, even against the odds. (35)

Wilberforce's many councils were usually organized around odd bedfellows and peculiar coalitions. Wilberforce insisted that his "measures, not men" motto would be the means by which persons of all persuasions and stations in life could be recruited to social reform. He believed that it could change everything, as it indeed did in England. It can also do that today.

Extended Observation

Reflection & Conversation

It is not difficult today to create a list of personal observations regarding rudeness or offensive behavior. Shoving ahead in line, abusive language, littering, speeding, and road rage are all symptoms of a fundamental disrespect for the rights of others. Center your reflection and conversation on an honest appraisal of your own "manners"—your own behavior toward others and their rights as individuals.

Attend to the Word

Read Romans 12:9–21. The sentence of this passage is a universal antidote for incivility. Listen carefully to the words of the passage. Spend some moments in silence extending the admonitions in this reading into the contemporary world. For example, hear in the words of the passage phrases such as—"be patient and wait your turn," "follow the rules of the road," "do not cheat on your taxes," "watch your language," "don't play your stereo too loud," and so forth.

Engage

A basic premise of this chapter is that the corruption of superficial and seemingly harmless behavior can have a much more sinister and corrupting effect.

1. What specific examples in your own experience speak to the truth of the author's premise?
2. Why are those who campaign for a more civil society seen as weak or intrusive?

3. What role does language play in a civil society? How does language betray attitude?

Move Forward

Accountability seems to be the missing factor in disrespectful and uncivil behavior. No one is more important than I am. No one needs my deference. In the interests of my own peace, I am not going to demand much of anything of others. If no one feels accountable, almost any behavior becomes allowable.

1. What practical means can you employ to become accountable for the behavior of others? How can you be a messenger for a new civility?
2. How important is it to work together to attain this accountability? What are ways that a group of people will be heard more loudly than an individual will?
3. If you had the opportunity to eradicate one form of rudeness or incivility, what would it be? How would you attack this corrupting behavior?

Pray

Use the following words as a source for your prayer.

Fools say in their hearts, "There is no God."
They are corrupt, they commit abominable acts:
There is no one who does good.

God looks down from heaven on humankind
to see if there are any who are wise,
who seek after God.

They have all fallen away, they are alike perverse;
there is no one who does good, no, not one.

Have they no knowledge, those evildoers,
who eat up my people as they eat bread,
and do not call upon God?

Psalm 53:1–4 (NRSV)

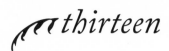

thirteen

Making Goodness Fashionable

By Mark Rodgers & Bill Wichterman

Mark Rodgers and Bill Wichterman have each worked as congressional staff and as policy advisors to the U.S. Congress for nearly twenty years. Bill Wichterman has recently joined a law firm. Both men have a great admiration for William Wilberforce and his leadership as a statesman, particularly in leading the changes in society that were necessary for changes in legislation.

Much has been made of William Wilberforce's effort to abolish the slave trade, what he referred to as one of his Great Objects. His work to abolish the slave trade and ultimately slavery transformed Western Civilization, and rightly has been recorded as one of the great crusades of modern times. But his lesser-known second Great Object, the reformation of manners (or, in modern language, the reformation of morals) was inextricably linked to his first, and in many ways made possible the demise of slavery. For a nation to countenance the destruction of an entire industry that served to enrich the Empire meant that money and selfish ends must be subjugated to the common good—a common good that transcends place and time.

The Culture: Upstream from Politics

As men who have each spent almost twenty years working as policy advisors in the U.S. Congress, we are committed to making just laws. We are passionate about the process and the aims of politics. We are deeply involved in the day-to-day business of lawmaking, and we each feel a strong calling to the political realm as a means of improving our nation. Yet we recognize that politics is not sufficient to bring about justice and promote liberty. We write this not because we are discouraged with the political process. To the contrary, we believe that national politics is portrayed in the media far too negatively. In our experience, most people in policy-making, on the Left and the Right, are chiefly motivated by a desire for just and compassionate policies.

Still, many important "Great Objects" cannot be pursued through political and policy activity alone. Indeed, many of our policy objectives will only be achieved by a prior or concurrent change in the cultural norms that shape the political realm. Legislation is never created in a vacuum, but in a "cultural context" in which people's beliefs and worldviews have largely already been shaped at a foundational level. Surveys consistently show that opinions are molded by one's family, religion, education, and by the news media. But more dominant now than ever, especially for those growing up in the "infotainment age," is the role of entertainment. The culture-creating sector that manufactures fine art, fashion, movies, television shows, console games, graphic novels, extreme sports, streaming video shorts, and pop music is not just consequential to our post-Baby Boomer generations, but as our most influential export to the world at large.

In short, the culture, both broadly and narrowly defined, is upstream from politics. Politics is more about reflecting the beliefs forged in other, more powerful "gate keeping" institutions. Though we may trace our history by political events—Jacksonian Democracy, Jim Crow laws, the New Deal, the Great Society, the Civil Rights Movement, *Roe v. Wade*, etc.—it was the culture of the time that made each development possible, for good or for ill.

Wilberforce's two Great Objects reflected this understanding. As a Member of Parliament, he sought to change the laws of the nation. But he leveraged his work in the political sphere by seeking to renew the culture of his times, to shape hearts and minds through other institutions, both as a means to an end and an end in itself. The success of his efforts is a model for us as we seek to fashion just laws and renew American culture. Examining how Wilberforce changed England will help guide today's reformers in their efforts to create a better society.

Wilberforce's Focus on Society

At twenty-eight years old, Wilberforce wrote in his diary on October 28, 1787, "God Almighty has set before me two great objects, the suppression of the Slave Trade and the Reformation of Manners." True to his intent, Wilberforce would spend the next forty-six years working to accomplish these lofty goals. To the surprise of many, he would achieve both.

Looking back from our age plagued by child pornography, gambling addictions, and Enron scandals, we might wonder what morals Wilberforce thought needed to be reformed. After all, wasn't eighteenth-century England a tame and cultured time?

Actually, no! Wilberforce had witnessed first-hand the degradations of the age, which included drunkenness among Members of Parliament in the House of Commons, frequent duels, debauched lifestyles among the rich and famous, a corrupt clergy, and bribery among elected officials. Fatherless families, alcoholism, and the grinding effects of the nascent industrialization that was swelling urban centers afflicted the lower classes. The social injustices were grave, with workers, especially children, exploited and abused.

Wilberforce's driving concern in his campaign to reform England's manners was to improve the welfare of the entire society, especially the poor and the powerless. He was distressed at the cavalier imposition of the death penalty and the effects of crime on the lower classes. "The barbarous mode of hanging has been tried too long and with the success which might have been expected from it: the most effectual way of preventing the greater crimes is punishing the smaller, and endeavoring to repress that general spirit of licentiousness which is the parent of every species of vice." (1) Mayor Rudy Giuliani transformed New York City by enforcing laws against petty crimes, such as public urination, graffiti artists, and subway gate-hoppers, which in turn caused the serious crime rate to plummet. This is a modern-day attempt at what Wilberforce accomplished two hundred years earlier.

In a letter dated September 27, 1787, Wilberforce found that "there is always a great deal of religious hypocrisy: we have now an hypocrisy of an opposite sort, and I believe many affect to be worse than in principle they really are, out of deference to the licentious moral [sic] of the fashionable world." He was disturbed by the moral slide from which he had only recently emerged himself, and he set out to change the moral climate of the time. And yet, "the profligacy and moral decay . . . when Wilberforce first entered public life gave way to the moral integrity and concern for the welfare of others that was the hallmark of the Victorian era" shortly after his death. Wilberforce truly made goodness fashionable in the course of his life.

The question was how? How did an obscure politician get traction to turn around an entire culture? Wilberforce had a plan that he executed for decades to come.

How the Clapham Circle Helped

Although William Wilberforce was an extraordinary man, he did not achieve his objectives alone, but in community. Wilberforce understood that humans are made to live in fellowship with one another, not as isolated individuals. He personally relied on his own tight-knit circle of family, friends, and neighbors to help him achieve his dreams and strive to accomplish the two Great Objects. He also depended on communities to implement the reformation of manners throughout England.

Wilberforce lived in the rural village of Clapham, just outside London, with his cousin Henry Thornton and several other close friends who also served in Parliament. Thornton and Wilberforce started this intentional community of like-minded men and women to help strengthen their respective callings. They became known as the Clapham Circle. Wilberforce relied on these friendships as a brain trust, an operational nerve center, an in-house think tank, and a personal support to help him through the rough and tumble of public life, including the sometimes-fierce criticism he received from his political opponents. When several of his colleagues in the House of Commons committed suicide, he challenged others to rely on a circle of friends to help them avoid a similar fate.

One key member of this community was poet and author Hannah More, one of the most successful writers, and perhaps the most influential woman, of her day. She entered the social and cultural scene in the 1770s by writing for and engaging with the theater. Through a gradual conversion, she became aligned with Evangelicalism, and wrote poetry and essays targeting the upper class on matters of manners and religion. However, she also weighed in on the great debates of the day, including slavery and the French Revolution. She published VILLAGE POLITICS in 1793 to counter the arguments of RIGHTS OF MAN by Thomas Paine. She wrote a series in THE CHEAP REPOSITORY TRACTS to promote the plight of the working lower class, who were virtually enslaved by their economic conditions. Her work was so consequential that when the Cheap Repository was closed, the Religious Tract Society was founded to continue her work.

One of her early social commentaries was published anonymously in 1788 as THOUGHTS ON THE IMPORTANCE OF THE MANNERS OF THE GREAT TO THE GENERAL SOCIETY. Many believed the author to be William Wilberforce himself. The book was phenomenally popular: the second edition sold out in six days, the third in four hours, and an eighth edition appeared in 1790. In admonishing the upper classes, More made clear her belief in a hierarchical and deferential society. She argued that a reformation of manners could be achieved only if the leaders of society reformed themselves. This belief was shared by Wilberforce and the Clapham community, and would influence their tactical engagements and priority of projects.

This community of like-minded conviction and faith was central to the pursuit and accomplishment of Wilberforce's two Great Objects. But it is important to note that dozens of initiatives were born out of the fellowship, from efforts to reform the Church and promote the Christian faith to efforts to protect animal welfare. It has been said that more than sixty different initiatives, projects, and societies were operating simultaneously out of the Clapham circle.

First Steps: The Proclamation of Manners

In 1769, King George III issued the "Proclamation for the Encouragement of Piety and Virtue and for the Preventing of Vice, Profaneness and Immorality." It was routine for new monarchs to issue such proclamations, but they were usually ignored. The Proclamation is strict by today's standards. It forbade playing cards or dice on Sundays, drunkenness, blasphemy, profane swearing and cursing, lewdness, pornography, and required church attendance.

Wilberforce, More, and their colleagues saw potential
in the Proclamation, and successfully petitioned the King to
reissue it on June 1, 1787, eighteen years after his ascension to
the throne. They used the re-issuance of the Proclamation as a
springboard to launch a campaign to make a kinder and gentler
society. King William and Queen Mary's moral proclamation
almost a century earlier had been successful, thanks to the
formation of local societies to encourage recognition of the
Proclamation. Wilberforce and his community sought to
repeat history by creating nationwide voluntary associations
of "Great" men and women to ensure that the Proclamation
was not ignored. These so-called Proclamation Societies
were comprised of community leaders, most of whom were
morally upright, though some were notoriously dissolute—
much like enlisting today's celebrities, such as Madonna or
Kid Rock.

The Proclamation Society movement also reflected
Wilberforce's understanding that people learn what to love and
what to hate in communities of like-minded people. The myriad
meetings that took place surrounding implementation of the
Proclamation were designed to develop positive peer pressures
to adhere to moral standards. Inherent in the notion of "making
goodness fashionable" is the belief that people pay attention to
what others think. If some people followed the new and more
upright norms of behavior solely out of concern for what their
friends thought of them, that was for Wilberforce one step on
the road to real virtue. Although he didn't want just superficial
compliance with the Proclamation, he did recognize that norms
and mores could lead to the embrace of the underlying virtue
motivating the norm. Where the adherence was superficial,
a sort of "positive hypocrisy" might develop so that at least
others might be less tempted into wrong behavior by degraded
mores.

Today's counterparts to the Proclamation Society are small
groups. Some studies estimate that as many as 40 percent of
Americans are involved in small groups, from scout troops to
Bible studies. While these groups are formed around many
diverse aims, they are an essential part of the glue of a healthy
society. They knit us together as a nation.

The Role of "The Great"

Wilberforce and More understood the role and the power of the elite in shaping society, and consciously integrated this appreciation into their efforts. Their aim was to make goodness fashionable or "cool." By enlisting the elites, they ensured that their movement would have the support of the Establishment.

> *[M]en of authority and influence may promote the cause of good morals. Let them in their several stations encourage virtue and [discourage] vice in others. Let them enforce the laws by which the wisdom of our forefathers has guarded against the grosser infractions of morals. Let them favor and take part in any plans which may be formed for the advancement of morality.* (2)

Wilberforce was not interested in simply putting a veneer of goodness over corruption and licentiousness. He was no fan of hypocrisy. Instead he aimed to reduce the allure of debased morals by lifting up the good, the true, and the beautiful as a model to be venerated. His aim was to restore genuine virtue and refinement at the core, not just on the surface.

The core for Wilberforce was the soul. His conversion to Christianity was central to his life and what he believed necessary for the renewal of the culture. In 1797, he wrote a book entitled A PRACTICAL VIEW OF THE PREVAILING RELIGIOUS SYSTEM OF PROFESSED CHRISTIANS, IN THE HIGHER AND MIDDLE CLASSES IN THE COUNTRY, CONTRASTED WITH REAL CHRISTIANITY. He was passionate about reinvigorating what he believed was a calcified Anglican Church that was more cultural than it was authentically spiritual. It would be difficult to underplay the pervasive influence of his faith on everything that Wilberforce did. Though he was a man comfortable among the non-religious—friends like Jeremy Bentham—his devotion to God permeated every aspect of his life, from his daily Bible study and prayers to his scrupulous attention to his personal habits. His faith was well known and an object of admiration and sometimes derision. Towards the end of his life, it became fashionable in the upper classes to have lengthy family prayers as was patterned by the Wilberforce family.

Wilberforce and company believed that voluntary associations were more effective at encouraging adherence to the Proclamation than law enforcement, but they were not grassroots populists, per se. The societies held numerous meetings all over the country on the implementation of the Proclamation. These included parish officers, constables, and churchwardens. And this was not without practical impact. For example, licenses were no longer renewed for businesses that promoted immorality. But it was more by positive example than by threats of retribution that the Proclamation began to be more widely observed in daily life. Just as smoking has declined in recent years—less by the passage of anti-smoking laws for public places and more by the powerful ad campaigns and the example of famous athletes and Hollywood stars—so Wilberforce managed to strategically use the levers of power to persuade people to project goodness and morality. He recognized the power of law to change behavior was not as great as the power of fashion and culture, and the elite who define it.

There were some critics of Wilberforce's campaign, including those who said that the poor were targets of the campaign. This was never Wilberforce's intent. He believed that effective moral renewal required renewal within the upper strata of society. In fact, he made great in-roads with the elite, including Princess Victoria through her tutor, an Evangelical clergyman. He also captured the imagination of the young social elite, so much so that he had to encourage them not to be self-righteous or "preachy" with their parents. In later years, it would actually be considered old-fashioned in the upper classes to curse.

In her book THOUGHTS ON THE IMPORTANCE OF THE MANNERS OF THE GREAT TO GENERAL SOCIETY, Hannah More made the direct connection between the positive and negative "pattern" set by society's elite:

> *Reformation must begin with the Great, or it will never be effectual. Their example is the fountain whence the vulgar draw their habits, actions, and characters. To expect to reform the poor while the opulent are corrupt is to throw odors into the stream while the springs are poisoned. . . . If, therefore, the rich and great will not, from a liberal spirit of doing right, and from a Christian spirit of fearing God, abstain from those offenses, for which the poor are to suffer fines and imprisonments, effectual good cannot be done.* (3)

The effects of the moral reforms would be far-reaching and enduring. By strategically recruiting powerful cultural, political, and religious leaders in his campaign and by extending its reach to the grassroots, England would eventually become known as a society of gentility, refinement, and moral uprightness—all of the things it was not during Wilberforce's youth.

The Importance of a Moral Society

Wilberforce's second Great Object, the reformation of manners, reflected the truth that law alone is not sufficient to bring about a more just society. There must also be just people to enact, implement, and obey just laws. Laws are not self-enforcing, and robust law enforcement is not sufficient to ensure compliance. Creating a just society is only partially a function of law, and much more a product of other institutions—family, religion, education, entertainment, journalism, civic associations, etc.— institutions that help us to shape what we love and what we hate.

It is unlikely that Wilberforce would have been successful in abolishing slavery without a corresponding, or perhaps even antecedent, renewal of the moral foundation for British society. The interdependence of the two Great Objects seems more than coincidental. Instead, it reflects the reality that the passage of just laws requires a virtuous citizenry. In Wilberforce's words,

> *It is a truth attested by the history of all ages and countries . . . that the religion and morality of a country, especially of every free community, are inseparably connected with its preservation and welfare; that their flourishing or declining state is the sure indication of its tending to prosperity or decay. It has even been expressly laid down, that a people grossly corrupt are incapable of liberty.*

The abolition of slavery with all of the economic sacrifice that it required would only be possible if people were motivated by something better than crass self-interest. Ensuring that the British people would be prepared to accept the abolition of the slave trade meant that the morals of the nation must be the soil in which the laws would take root. Remaking those mores was Wilberforce's second Great Object, but not necessarily second in importance.

We are not suggesting that politics is just a reflection of culture. Law is a teacher, and the passage of just laws has an effect on people's behavior. Legal sanctions help to inform and guide the conscience of a nation. Everything from abortion laws to tax policy play a role in shaping culture. Our personal political involvement for decades underscores this conviction. Voter guides, congressional hearings, petition drives, debates, and political campaigns are integral to a healthy republic.

But, as Wilberforce teaches us, law and politics only go so far. No matter how large a political party's majority in Congress, there are certain legislative goals that remain elusive absent cultural change. King George's initial Proclamation issued in 1769 was widely ignored. But when it was issued a second time in 1787, it was taken more seriously thanks to the Proclamation Society making its adherence compelling. The Society breathed life into the Proclamation by giving it what sociologists call "plausibility structures"—systems that make rational the passage, implementation, and compliance with law. Just look at all of the old and widely ignored laws throughout the United States, such as gum chewing, that no longer make sense to a new generation. Compliance with a particular law presupposes a certain kind of civilization. Once that civilization morphs into something new, old laws fall into disuse. In short, cultural mores dictate which laws pass and are obeyed, and which laws are defeated or ignored.

The tendency for many people is to overstate the importance of politics in shaping culture. As two men who have spent our careers in the halls of power, we are convinced that law and politics play a relatively minor role in forming culture when compared to religion, Hollywood, academia, media, or the family. Law, while it may appear to be at the vanguard of a society, is more like the infantry. Law stands at the front lines, but is directed from the rear by the culture. Its prominence in ongoing battles over abortion, same-sex marriage, stem cell research, and Supreme Court nominations may deceptively suggest that the battle rages there. Because our history is often a record of government, one may think that law and politics lead our society. Instead, law and politics protect a particular social order, but do not primarily lead or guide it.

Wilberforce's contemporary and fellow Member of Parliament Edmund Burke wrote, "Manners are of more importance than laws." (4) Individuals rarely change their lives based on a political speech or a government act. An individual may be inspired to work for a political candidate who reflects what he finds most important in preserving or creating a certain kind of culture. But, more often than not, a cultural consensus precedes the enactment of laws.

Across the sea in the former British colonies, the Framers of the U.S. Constitution had concluded the same thing. John Adams, a friend of Wilberforce, had said that "our Constitution was made only for a moral and religious people. It is wholly inadequate to the government of any other." It is entirely possible that Adams and Wilberforce had discussed this very thing. President George Washington in his Farewell Address of 1796 said, "Of all the dispositions and habits which lead to political prosperity, Religion and morality are indispensable supports." (5) John Witherspoon, a signer of the Declaration of Independence, said, "Corruption of [morals] make a people ripe for destruction. A good form of government may hold the rotten materials together for some time, but beyond a certain pitch, even the best constitution will be ineffectual." (6)

It is not enough to craft a government that relies on checks and balances, the separation of powers, an independent judiciary, and a strong legislative branch. The American Experiment required the right kind of people to create and sustain it. The old adage that "you get the government you deserve" was as fundamental to the American Framers as it was for Wilberforce.

The Two Great Objects as One

Wilberforce's reformation of England's decaying morals made possible the abolition of slavery. Wilberforce biographer Kevin Belmonte maintains that Wilberforce understood the connection between the first and second Great Objects, and that "the linkage was deliberate and Wilberforce believed abolition [of the slave trade] could not have taken place without a concurrent moral reformation to strengthen the consensus that the [British] slave trade was a tragic national sin." (7)

It is not clear, however, that Wilberforce understood at the outset how necessary cultural reformation was to the success of the abolition of the slave trade, and eventually slavery. As a legislator, his instinct was to win the old-fashioned way, through power and petition. But as Ernest Howse observed in his book SAINTS IN POLITICS:

> *All the workers were being gradually convinced that their*
> *only hope lay in an appeal from Parliament to the people,*
> *an appeal that would be viewed with little favor in*
> *eighteenth-century England. Wilberforce at first had been*
> *suspicious of such tactics. He approved of promoting petitions*
> *to Parliament. . . . In his first labors, however, Wilberforce*
> *"distrusted and disowned the questionable strength which*
> *might be gained by systematic agitation." He did not then*
> *favor the use either of corresponding societies or of public*
> *meetings. Be he was to be taught by his cause. He found that*
> *his hope lay only in the people; and in a short time he and his*
> *friends became the most persistent agitators in all Britain.*
> *"It is on the general impression and feelings of the nation we*
> *must rely," Wilberforce confessed early in 1792. "So let the*
> *flame be fanned. . . ." (8)*

Consider the civil rights laws of the 1960s. These laws
would not have passed without the prior decade of an active civil
rights movement. The countless personal sacrifices of African
Americans who bravely endured the retributions of water hoses,
police clubs, dog bites, and church bombings—broadcasted on
the nightly news to the outrage of a nation—changed the minds
of enough Americans to demand the abolition of Jim Crow laws.
It's true that the Civil Rights Act of 1964 and the Voting Rights
Act of 1965 continued to change hearts and minds, but their
effect was predicated on a prior reformation of manners. In the
end, filibustering Southern politicians were unable to stand in the
way of the cultural demand for change. The law simply reflected
the growing culture of racial equality.

Culture is upstream from politics. Certain legislative goals
from either political party are impossible absent a change in the
culture. And when a political party gets out-of-step with the
prevailing cultural ethos of the nation for a sustained period of
time, voters are apt to vote them out of office. It's no wonder that
politicians are constantly polling their constituents on every issue
under the sun: they are trying to stay in step with their electorate.

This intuitively rings true for us, after almost two decades
on Capitol Hill. Legislating is not conducted in a vacuum, but
in a cultural context in which people's foundational beliefs have
already been shaped. The sectors that are intrinsically world-view
shaping include the family, religion, academia, peer groups and
associations, the news media, and entertainment. Wilberforce

and his colleagues engaged virtually every one of these sectors to "reform the manners" of their cultural context, making their legislative goal to end the slave trade eventually achievable.

Arts, Entertainment, & the Elites

Several years ago, as we surveyed our political relationships and networks, we realized that there was one sector with which we had virtually no strategic engagement: the only inherently "culture-creating" sector, arts and entertainment. This was not the case for the Clapham Circle. William Wilberforce the politician knew he needed more than bills in Parliament and a general improvement in the moral climate to change people's hearts and minds about slavery. He and his fellow abolitionists turned to the arts to set forth the case for change. They understood that it takes more than abstract propositions or personal piety to change culture. It requires images and creative words to stir people's souls.

Ernest Howse continued his observation regarding the effort to shape broad public opinion regarding slavery:

> *The flame was fanned accordingly. New experiments were attempted. Even before his time the abolitionists had adopted unusual methods of propaganda. . . . Cowper's poem, "The Negro's Complaint," has been printed on expensive paper and circulated by the thousand in fashionable circles, and afterwards set to music and sung everywhere as a popular ballad. Wedgwood, the celebrated potter, had made another effective contribution to the cause. He designed a cameo showing, on a white background, a Negro kneeling in supplication, while he utters the plea to become so famous, "Am I not a man and a brother?" This cameo, copied on such articles as snuffboxes and ornamental hairpins, became the rage all over England. . . . (9)*

On the eve of the first debate on slavery in 1788, Hannah More published the poem entitled "Slavery." The abolitionists commissioned a print of a slave ship visualizing how Africans were abused. A few decades later in America, a novel called UNCLE TOM's CABIN would help to ignite the abolitionist movement that would lead ultimately to the Civil War.

It is a timeless truth that art shapes belief at a deep and often subconscious level. Damon of Athens wrote, "Give me the songs of a nation, and it matters not who writes its laws." And what was true for the Greeks and for Wilberforce's time is no less true today, and perhaps more so. Arts and entertainment, especially in commercial "pop culture," have an enormous impact on what we think today. The notion that entertainment is "just fluff" or a "wasteland" betrays a profound misunderstanding of how the creative side of our brains shapes what our logical side believes.

If you are like most people, you may be hard-pressed to recall more than a few political events or speeches. In contrast, think about how many songs you know by heart, how many movies you watched, and what commercials and TV shows you remember. Far from diverting our attention, it was, and still is, stories that shape us. They teach us what to love and what to hate. They inspire us, enrage us, and help us to understand complex issues. It is no wonder that Jesus taught in parables: narratives speak to our souls in ways that abstract propositional truths cannot.

So what are the cultural artifacts today that shape hearts and minds? Podcasting, streaming music videos (even on your cell phone), comic books, novels, video games, magazines, and sitcoms—the list is endless. Perhaps more today than ever before, our society is captivated by arts and entertainment. It is not enough for academic lectures to be informative: the professor has to be "culturally relevant." Commercial ditties stick in our minds. The television is stuck in the "on" position. And our iPods are stuck in our ears.

Our media elites are our "Greats" today. And like eighteenth century European elites, in many cases they are "patterning" lives and behavior that promote vice rather than virtue. Even more disconcerting, the cultural artifacts they create do the same. A disturbing fact is that much of today's ubiquitous entertainment industry is leading to the coarsening of American society. Musicians who sing songs glorifying violent rape win Grammies. Movie directors who marry their stepchildren are lifted up as avant-garde. Films that make light of bestiality and glamorize prostitution are "edgy." Hotels make their profits by in-room pornographic videos. Many people of all political and ideological stripes worry about the corrosive effect of the entertainment industry on our society. They worry that far from being innocuous fun that exposes the hypocrisy of Victorian ethics, the entertainment is leading us to become numb to things we should hate. Some people fear that we are reaping domestic violence, child abuse, pedophilia, as well as disregard for the weak and vulnerable.

Any effort to address the social pathologies that plague our nation must involve the "Greats" of arts and entertainment. Thankfully, many do take on ills such as global AIDS and drug abuse. Rather than just cursing the darkness, many of today's Wedgwoods are seeking to reform the manners of our civilization by working with and through the arts. Tom Wolfe, Bono, Bill Cosby, Oprah, billionaire Phil Anschutz, and even Angelina Jolie are using their craft and position to promote the common good. They aren't perfect, but they are cognizant that with their public profile comes public responsibility.

The Great Objects Applied

As political animals, we believe the battles over who controls the Congress, who sits on the Supreme Court, and who sits in the White House are vitally important. We think it is a shame that too many Americans do not vote. But we are clear-eyed about the limits of politics—not just what the limits should be, but what they are. Law will continue to be more of a reflection of the soul of a people than its shaper. Plato was right when he said that the government is simply the soul of a people written in large letters.

Once one understands the primacy of culture and joins in the effort to renew it according to transcendent standards, the question of one's political label becomes less important. A healthy culture is about lifting up the good, the true, and the beautiful. These are not ideological categories. There is plenty of common ground for cultural renewal among individuals who differ on the particular role law should play. Some citizens may join in the cultural fight against social pathologies, even though they oppose legal restrictions on those pathologies. This applies to violent prime time television, pornography, divorce, and many other social maladies. This is not to say that the policy differences are inconsequential. But renewal can be furthered even without political agreement, again, because culture trumps politics.

America in 2007 is very much like England in 1807. We have elites, a culture that often promotes vice rather than virtue, and social pathologies such as high out-of-wedlock birthrates and sexually transmitted diseases that threaten the public health. We need a reformation of manners. Let us suggest several lessons that we could apply from Wilberforce and his colleagues' successful enterprise:

1. Elites Must Be Recruited

Our entertainment elite set trends, shape behavior, and fashion beliefs. The PBS FRONTLINE show "Merchants of Cool" documented the way in which corporate America taps pop culture icons to sell their products. Just as the landed gentry and upper society were recruited to use their power and prestige as a public good, our elites must be recruited to do the same. In addition, we must encourage our best and brightest to go into the culture-shaping sectors to become the next elites, and we need to build the institutions to support them in their vocational pursuits. Non-profit groups like Act One, which mentor young aspiring filmmakers on how to write high-quality scripts that tell the truth about the world and are accessible to a wide audience, need to be encouraged and supported.

2. Earnest Dialogue Must Be Initiated

A community needs to be created that allows conversations to take place between poets and politicians regarding the great objects we face as a culture today. For example, when one catalogues the cost of the sexual revolution (out of wedlock births, sexually transmitted diseases including AIDS, abortion, and marital infidelity), there is an obvious public policy consequence. But how can the consequences of the sexual revolution be addressed without engaging arts and entertainment—the very vehicles through which the revolution was first propagated? We have been privileged to be part of a dialogue with artists in New York, Hollywood, and Nashville. Many writers, singers, and filmmakers realize that they are no less in the field of justice than those of us in policy. Policy-makers may have a larger impact on next year's election, but artists will have a huge impact on elections ten and twenty years from now. We need to be in conversation with each other.

3. Promote Virtue Rather Than Vice

When the cover of Forbes magazine announces that "Bad Ass Sells," we know that the wrong thing is being exalted. Essayist and author Walker Percy said that bad books lie, and good books tell the truth. More and more artists are producing works to tell the truth, to restore cultural health and wholeness. Alternative rock bands like Switchfoot and P.O.D. are making Top 40 songs that speak to the consequences of the sexual revolution and no-fault divorce. Their impact may not be felt for a generation, but they cannot help but make a difference. U2 has been doing this important work for almost 30 years and is still going strong.

4. Capital Must Be Invested

Over the course of our conversations with "culture creators," the refrain we keep hearing is "investment and distribution." The issue is not simply creating ennobling art, but finding the means to disseminate it to the public. The Internet, technology, and grassroots marketing may address the distribution question over time, but investment will undoubtedly continue to be a challenge. It is critical that wealthy individuals do more than just donate money to worthy causes, but also choose to invest wisely in entertainment that will positively shape society. eBay founder Jeff Skoll started Participant Productions, a film development company that has as its mission not to make blockbusters but messages—movies that promote social and economic justice. "I think of this as philanthropy," he said in WIRED magazine. "Participant is the only production company in town that has a double bottom line: social good plus financial returns. It's too early to tell how our returns are going to look—though all signs are promising—but social good is what we're really after." (10)

Conclusion

The reformation of manners was not just a project for Wilberforce's time, but for every time and every culture. His courageous and visionary life spent working to free the slaves and renew the culture is instructive in our fresh attempts to restrain evil and exalt the good.

Politics is not enough. William Wilberforce is our patron saint in this regard. He led with both political conviction and recognition that political activity is not conducted in a cultural vacuum. An exclusive or even primary focus on law to transform society is shortsighted. It is the cultural fields, long overgrown with tares from decades of neglect, which need to be plowed and re-sown. We who care about cultural renewal must learn it is the unwritten constitution of culture that shapes the written constitution of a nation. The sooner we get this straight, the sooner our efforts will produce lasting fruit.

We cheer the rediscovery of William Wilberforce. His tireless years devoted to the reformation of manners bore rich fruit, from the abolition of slavery and a deepened concern for justice in the public square to a greater attention to personal virtue. His strategic use of law, and much more his engagement of the arts, civic associations, and the natural aristocracy of his day instruct us how to pursue today's objective of a more just and compassionate society as we, too, seek to make goodness fashionable.

Extended Observation

Reflection & Conversation

This chapter provides a more detailed look at today's culture in relationship with William Wilberforce's two Great Objects. The authors suggest that these two objects really are one because without a change in moral behavior, people would have remained deaf to the plight of the slaves. In a culture where the outlaw is more fashionable and more appealing than is the good person, it is difficult to hear and to heed the cries of anyone in need. Focus your reflection on the observations in the chapter. Consider or share more examples of how "bad manners" are fashionable in today's society.

Attend to the Word

Read Philippians 4:4–9. The first four verses of this passage radiate an attitude of joy. The next four verses are an exhortation to do what is true, honorable, and just. After the reading, spend a few moments in silence to let the words of the passage nourish what you have learned from reading the chapter.

Engage

Wilberforce used the royal proclamation encouraging virtue as a springboard for his campaign to create a kinder and more "moral" society. He and his colleagues in his Clapham Circle formed voluntary associations to insure that this royal proclamation was not ignored.

1. What were the effects attained by the efforts of Wilberforce and his circle of friends? What difference did their efforts make?

2. If you and your friends were to make similar efforts in today's society, what would be your objectives? Limit yourself to three. Tell why you chose these objectives.
3. What do you consider the greatest obstacles are to building a community where virtue is "in" and vice is "out?" Who decides what is virtue and what is vice?

Move Forward

The authors of this chapter chose four lessons from the tactics of Wilberforce and his colleagues. Review the tactics, and use them to propel you and your group into action on some clear steps toward making goodness fashionable in the parts of society where you have influence.

1. *Recruit Elites:* Which people in your community can you get involved in making it a more civil and friendly place to live? What do these leaders bring to the table that will help you?
2. *Earnest Dialogue:* How, when, where, and with whom will you begin a very serious conversation about what in the atmosphere of your community needs to be improved?
3. *Promote Virtue:* In what creative and noticeable ways will you tell virtue's story for your community and improve its cultural health and wholeness? What is your goal?
4. *Invest Capital:* What kind of money does your effort need? How will you raise it? How will you spend it? What other types of capital are needed to address the need for goodness in your community?

Pray

Use the following words from the Book of Sirach (found in the Apocrypha) as a source for your prayer. Let them lead to a spontaneous declaration of your desire for goodness to regain a prominent place in the culture of your community.

Watch for the opportune time, and beware of evil,
and do not be ashamed to be yourself.

For wisdom becomes known through speech,
and education through the words of the tongue.

Never speak against the truth,
but be ashamed of your ignorance.

Do not be ashamed to confess your sins,
and do not try to stop the current of a river.

Do not subject yourself to a fool,
or show partiality to a ruler.

Fight to the death for truth,
and the Lord God will fight for you.

Do not be reckless in your speech,
or sluggish and remiss in your deeds.

Do not be like a lion in your home,
or be suspicious of your servants.

Do not let your hand be stretched out to receive,
and closed when it is time to give.

Sirach 4:20a, 24–31(NRSV)

fourteen

Eleanor Roosevelt & Human Rights

By Mary Ann Glendon

Mary Ann Glendon is Learned Hand Professor of Law at Harvard University and the author of A World Made New: Eleanor Roosevelt and the Universal Declaration of Human Rights. *In that book, Professor Glendon tells the story of Eleanor Roosevelt, former first lady of the United States for nearly sixteen years, who was asked by President Harry Truman to lead a controversial commission under the auspices of the newly formed United Nations to forge the world's first international bill of human rights. Eleanor Roosevelt followed in the footsteps of William Wilberforce. She talked publicly about her deep faith in Jesus Christ and her concern about the rights of poor and oppressed peoples. The issues were complex and difficult. It took statesmanship to negotiate the path towards an agreement. It took a team of skilled and persuasive people to bring along the many countries into an agreement that would set international standards—standards which today provide a basis for international engagement on the huge issues of slavery worldwide, both narrowly and more broadly defined.*

Professor Glendon has been deeply involved in the issues of human rights as a law professor. She was the first woman to lead a Vatican delegation as the Vatican's representative to the Beijing Women's Conference in 1995. Professor Glendon has been featured on Bill Moyer's World of Ideas. *She has written a number of books and received the Scribes Book Award, in addition to the Order of the Coif Prize, the legal academy's highest award for scholarship. She is a member of the American Academy of Arts and Sciences and a former president of the UNESCO-sponsored International Association of Legal Science.*

The moral terrain of international relations was forever altered late one night in Paris, on December 10, 1948, when the General Assembly of the United Nations adopted the Universal Declaration of Human Rights without a single dissenting vote.

In early 1947, with the horrors of two world wars fresh in their memories, a remarkable group of men and women gathered at the behest of the newly formed United Nations, under Eleanor Roosevelt as chair, to draft the first "international bill of rights." So far as the great powers of the day were concerned, the main purpose of the United Nations was to establish and maintain collective security in the years after the war. The human rights project was peripheral. It was launched as a concession to small countries in response to the demands of numerous religious and humanitarian associations. It tasked the Allies to live up to their war rhetoric by providing assurances that the community of nations would never again countenance such massive violations of human dignity. Britain, China, France, the United States, and the Soviet Union did not expect these assurances to interfere with their national sovereignty.

In the years that followed, to the astonishment of many, human rights would become a political factor that not even the most hard-shelled realists could ignore. The Universal Declaration would become an instrument, as well as the most prominent symbol of change that would amplify the voices of the weak in the corridors of power. It challenged the longstanding view that a sovereign state's treatment of its own citizens was that nation's business and no one else's. It gave expression to the diffuse, deep-seated longings of movements that would soon bring down colonial empires. Its thirty concise articles inspired or influenced scores of postwar and postcolonial constitutions and treaties, including the new constitutions of Germany, Japan, and Italy. It became the polestar of an army of international human rights activists who pressure governments to live up to their pledges and train the searchlight of publicity on abuses that would have remained hidden in former times. Confirming the worst fears held in 1948 by the Soviet Union and South Africa, the Declaration provided a rallying point for freedom movements that spurred the collapse of totalitarian regimes in Eastern Europe and the demise of apartheid. It is the parent document and the primary inspiration for most rights instruments in the world today.

Together with the Nuremberg Principles of international criminal law, developed by the Allies in 1946 for the trials of German and Japanese war criminals, and the 1948 Genocide Convention, the Universal Declaration of Human Rights became a pillar of a new international system under which a nation's treatment of its own citizens was no longer immune from outside scrutiny. The Nuremberg Principles, by sanctioning prosecutions for domestic atrocities committed in wartime, represented a determination to punish the most violent sorts of assaults on human dignity. The Genocide Convention obligated its signers to prevent and punish acts of genocide, whether committed in times of war or in peace. The Universal Declaration was more ambitious. Proclaiming that "disregard and contempt for human rights have resulted in barbarous acts which have outraged the conscience of mankind," it aimed at *prevention* rather than punishment. (1)

It Almost Didn't Happen

On New Year's Eve, 1945, after the photographers that had surrounded such notables as senators Thomas Connally and Arthur Vandenberg finally dispersed, a tall woman in a black coat boarded the Queen Elizabeth bound for Southampton, England. Eleanor Roosevelt, along with Connally, the Texas Democratic Chairman of the Senate Foreign Relations Committee, and Vandenberg, the Michigan Republican who was the Committee's ranking minority member, were headed for the first meeting of the UN General Assembly in London. Neither she nor anyone else suspected that, at age sixty-two, she was on a course that would lead to the most important achievement of her already distinguished public life.

When President Harry Truman had asked her to be a member of the U.S. Delegation to the United Nations, the widow of the wartime president was doubtful: "How could I be a delegate to help organize the United Nations when I have no background or experience in international meetings?" Many members of the foreign policy establishment shared these reservations. The opposition to her nomination included not only prominent Republicans, but also distinguished Democrats. The former regarded her as too liberal, the latter as too inexperienced. Senator William Fulbright was concerned that her presence on the delegation would signal a lack of seriousness about the United Nations.

There was also the risk, from the perspective of these foreign-policy professionals, that the outspoken former first lady would be a loose cannon in her new environment. As a political activist and popular journalist, she had developed a formidable reputation for her independence of mind and determination to champion progressive causes. During her White House years, she had even used her newspaper column to criticize decisions of her husband's administration, such as the provision of his economic recovery program that resulted in the layoff of married women. Franklin Roosevelt accepted these public disagreements with equanimity.

The decision, however, was Truman's. And he was less concerned with possible risks than with keeping the prestige of the Roosevelt name associated with his administration. Besides, Truman was the last person in the world to be dissuaded by Mrs. Roosevelt's inexperience in foreign affairs. When he was thrust into the highest office in the land the preceding April, he had to work hard to bring himself up to speed on foreign policy. Truman, therefore, pressed Mrs. Roosevelt to accept the UN assignment.

What overcame Mrs. Roosevelt's hesitation was the belief, shared by family and friends, that the UN appointment might be the best solution to the problem with which she had been wrestling since the death of her husband in April: how to make a new life for herself. From the time she had been a young woman, she had thrown herself into helping the most neglected members of society. Her empathy was aroused, perhaps, by her own experiences as a lonely, unloved child whose mother had regarded her as an ugly duckling. After years of involvement in Democratic Party politics at all levels, in which she had spoken out on behalf of her favorite causes—women's rights, the end of racial discrimination, and the improvement of working and housing conditions—she was resolved to remain active in public life. But since the death of her husband, she could not see her way forward clearly. The new international organization might, she thought, be a place where her talents and energies would be useful and where she could pursue her lifelong interest in humanitarian causes.

Despite misgivings about her abilities, she wrote to her daughter Anna from the ship en route to the first United Nations meeting in England: "just a line from the ship to tell you I am comfortable & tho' the responsibility seems great I'll just do my best and trust in God."

The Challenges

The challenges were enormous. There had been several great charters to declare humanity's first rights movements in the seventeenth and eighteenth centuries. The British Bill of Rights of 1689, the U.S. Declaration of Independence of 1776, and the French Declaration of the Rights of Man and Citizen of 1789 were born out of struggles to overthrow autocratic rule and to establish governments based on the consent of the governed. They proclaimed that all men were born free and equal and that the purpose of government was to protect man's natural liberties. They gave rise to the modern language of rights.

From the outset, that language branched into two dialects. One, influenced by continental European thinkers, especially Rousseau, had more room for equality and "fraternity" and tempered rights with duties and limits. It cast the state in a positive light as guarantor of rights and protector of the needy. Charters in this tradition—the French constitutions of the 1790s, the Prussian General Code of 1794, and the Norwegian Constitution of 1815—combined political and civil rights with public obligations to provide for the relief of the poor. In the late nineteenth and early twentieth centuries, as continental European Socialist and Christian Democratic parties reacted to the harsh effects of industrialization, these paternalistic principles evolved into social and economic rights.

The Anglo-American dialect of rights language emphasized individual liberty and initiative more than equality or social solidarity and was infused with a greater mistrust of government. The United States invoked God-given rights to humans:

> *We hold these truths to be self-evident, that all men are created equal, that they are endowed by their creator, with certain unalienable Rights, that among these are Life, Liberty and the Pursuit of Happiness.—That to secure these rights, Governments are instituted among Men, deriving their just powers from the consent of the governed,—that whenever any Form of Government becomes destructive of these ends, it is the Right of the People to alter or to abolish*

*it, and to institute new Government, laying its foundation
on such principles, and organizing its powers in such form,
as to them shall seem most likely to effect their Safety and
Happiness.* (2)

When Latin American countries achieved independence in
the nineteenth century, these two strains began to converge. Most
of the new nations retained their continental European-style
legal systems but adopted constitutions modeled on that of the
United States, supplementing them with protections for workers
and the poor. The Soviet Union's constitution took a different
path, subordinating the individual to the state, exalting equality
over freedom, and emphasizing social and economic rights over
political and civil liberty.

The brief interlude between the end of World War II and the
definitive collapse of the Soviet-American alliance lasted barely
long enough to permit major international institutions such as
the United Nations and the World Bank to be established and
for the framers of the Universal Declaration to complete their
task. The members of the first Human Rights Commission were
well aware that they were engaged in a race against time: around
them, relations between Russia and the West were deteriorating;
the Berlin blockade raised the specter of another world war; the
Palestine question divided world opinion; and conflict broke
out in Greece, Korea, and China. Shortly after the Declaration's
adoption, the window of opportunity closed and remained shut
for forty years.

The growing hostility between the United States and the
Soviet Union was one of the many daunting obstacles confronted
by the Declaration's drafters. They had to surmount linguistic,
cultural, and political differences and overcome personal
animosities as they strove to articulate a clear set of principles
with worldwide applicability. Their final product, they all
acknowledged, was imperfect, yet they succeeded well enough
to give the lie to claims that peoples with drastically opposed
worldviews cannot agree upon a few common standards of
decency.

For everyone who is tempted to despair of the possibility of
crossing today's ideological divides, there is still much to learn
from Eleanor Roosevelt's firm but irenic manner of dealing
with her Soviet antagonists and from the serious but respectful
philosophical rivalry between Lebanon's Charles Malik and

China's Peng-chun Chang. There is much to ponder in the working relationship between Malik, a chief spokesman for the Arab league, and Rene Cassin, an ardent supporter of a Jewish homeland who lost twenty-nine relatives in concentration camps during the war. When one considers that two world wars and mass slaughters of innocents had given the framers every reason to despair about the human condition, it is hard to remain unmoved by their determination to make the postwar world a better and safer place.

Teamwork

In the end it was teamwork that brought together the Universal Declaration, not unlike the teamwork that Wilberforce brought to the issues of his day. Most of the members of the committee that shaped the Declaration are now little remembered. Yet they include some of the most able and colorful public figures of their time: Carlos Romulo, the Filipino journalist who won a Pulitzer Prize for his articles predicting the end of colonialism; John P. Humphrey, the dedicated Canadian director of the UN's Human Rights Division who prepared the preliminary draft of the Declaration; Hansa Mehta of India, who made sure the Declaration spoke with power and clarity about equal rights for women well before they were recognized in the legal system; Alexei Pavlov, brilliant nephew of the conditioned-reflex scientist who had to dispel suspicions that he was still bourgeois; and Chile's Hernan Santa Cruz, an impassioned man of the left who helped assure that social and economic rights would have pride of place in the Declaration along with traditional political and civil liberties.

Among the Declaration's framers, four in particular played crucial roles: Peng-chun Chang, the Chinese philosopher, diplomat, and playwright who was adept at translating across cultural divides; Nobel Peace Prize laureate Rene Cassin, the legal genius of the Free French who transformed what might have been a mere list or "bill" of rights into a geodesic dome of interlocking principles; Charles Malik, existentialist philosopher turned master diplomat, a student of Alfred North Whitehead and Martin Heidegger, who steered the Declaration to adoption by the UN General Assembly in the tense Cold War atmosphere of 1948; and Eleanor Roosevelt, whose prestige and personal qualities enabled her to influence key decisions of a United States that had emerged from the war as the most powerful nation in the world. Chang, Cassin, Malik, and Roosevelt were the right people at the right time. Without the unique gifts of each of these four, the Declaration might never have seen the light of day.

The Achievement

In 1948 the framers of the Universal Declaration achieved a distinctive synthesis of previous thinking about rights and duties. After canvassing sources from North and South, East and West, they believed they had found a core of principles so basic that no nation would wish openly to disavow them. They wove these principles into a unified document that quickly displaced all antecedents as the principal model for the rights instruments in force in the world today.

When read as it was meant to be, namely as a whole, the Declaration's vision of liberty is inseparable from its call to social responsibility, inspired in part by Franklin Roosevelt's famous "four freedoms"—freedom of speech and belief and freedom from fear and want. Its organic unity was, however, one of the first casualties of the Cold War.

The Universal Declaration charted a bold new course for human rights by presenting a vision of freedom as linked to social security, balanced by responsibilities, grounded in respect for equal human dignity, and guarded by the rule of law. That vision was meant to protect liberty from degenerating into license and to repel the excesses of individualism and collectivism alike. By affirming that all of its rights belong to everyone, everywhere, it aimed to put an end to the idea that a nation's treatment of its own citizens or subjects was immune from outside scrutiny.

When the Declaration was adopted, friends of human rights were of different minds about its prospects. Many regarded it as a milestone in the history of freedom, but to others it seemed to be just a collection of pious phrases—meaningless and without courts, policemen, and armies to back them up. The latter view was common among men impatient for action and progress.

Eleanor Roosevelt saw the matter differently. Her confidence was due in part to her lively sense of the Declaration of Independence as a bright thread running through American history. That document, too, had proclaimed certain truths as self-evident and declared certain rights to be unalienable. It too was nonbinding.

In the April 1948 FOREIGN AFFAIRS, Eleanor Roosevelt wrote of her hopes for the Declaration then nearing completion:

> *In the first place, we have put into words some inherent rights. Beyond that, we have found that the conditions of our contemporary world require the enumeration of certain protections which the individual must have if he is to acquire a sense of security and dignity in his own person. The effect of this is frankly educational. Indeed, I like to think that the Declaration will help forward very largely the education of the peoples of the world.* (3)

In 1986, Charles Malik, who had been one of the staunchest supporters of human rights covenants, had come around to Roosevelt's view, admitting: "Whenever the question of human rights has arisen throughout the world, the appeal has been far more to the Declaration than to the covenants." He now appreciated, he said, that "[i]n the long run, the morally disturbing or judging is far more important than the legally binding." (4)

The Declaration over the Years

From the early years after the Declaration, the United States and the Soviet Union could not resist treating the Declaration as an arsenal of political weapons. Each nation yanked its favorite provisions out of context and ignored the rest. What began as expediency hardened into habit until the sense of an integrated body of principles was lost. Today, the Declaration is almost universally regarded as a kind of menu of rights from which one can pick and choose according to taste.

The fact that nations and interest groups increasingly seek to cast their agendas or justify their actions in terms of human rights is one measure of the success of the human rights idea. Nearly every international dispute today sooner or later implicates human rights; nearly every exercise of military force claims some humanitarian justification. Yet the more the Declaration is pulled apart and politicized, the higher the risk that the protection of human rights will become a pretext for imposing the will of the strong by armed intervention or economic pressure.

One of the most common and unfortunate misunderstandings today involves the notion that the Declaration was meant to impose a single model of right conduct, rather than to provide a common standard that can be brought to life in different cultures in a variety of ways. This confusion has fostered suspicion of the Universal Declaration in many quarters and lends credibility to the charge of Western cultural imperialism so often leveled against the entire human rights movement.

Eleanor Roosevelt understood these dangers. She was fond of saying that documents that express ideals "carry no weight unless the people know them, unless the people understand them, unless the people demand that they be lived." (5) In a world marked by homogenizing global forces on the one hand and rising ethnic assertiveness on the other, the need is greater than ever for clear standards that can serve as a basis for discussions across ideological and cultural divides. Until something better comes along, it is, as Mrs. Roosevelt once remarked of the United Nations itself, "a bridge upon which we can meet and talk."

Thus, today, the Declaration is the single most important reference point for cross-national discussions of how to order our future together on our increasingly conflict-ridden and interdependent planet. But time and forgetfulness are taking their toll. Even within the international human rights movement, the Declaration has come to be treated more like a monument to be venerated from a distance than a living document to be re-appropriated by each generation. Rarely, in fact, has a text been so widely praised yet so little read or understood.

Yet, one of the most basic assumptions of the founders of the United Nations and the framers of the Declaration is hugely important today: the root causes of atrocities and armed conflicts are frequently found to be in poverty and discrimination. That is why Franklin Roosevelt included the "freedom from want" among the four freedoms. That is why Harry Truman took the occasion of the signing of the UN Charter to connect this root cause directly to war: "Experience has shown how deeply the seeds of war are planted by economic rivalry and social injustice." (6) Those ideas found expression in the Declaration's insistence on the link between freedom and social security and on the relation of both to peace. That aspect of the Declaration, unfortunately, is commonly ignored today—just at a time when the poorest people and countries, a quarter of the world's population, are being increasingly marginalized in the global economic order. A pressing challenge for the future is to reunite the sundered halves of the Declaration—its commitment to individual liberty and its acknowledgement of a link between freedom and economic opportunity.

Like the U.S. Declaration of Independence, the Universal Declaration was radically ahead of its time. After nearly sixty years, its transformative potential has still barely begun to be realized. However, the further progress of its principles will be complicated by globalization and the upsurge of regional and ethnic conflict. The world seems to have entered upon a new phase of upheaval.

The principal framers, though they differed on many points, were unified in their belief in the priority of culture. Rene Cassin, though a strong backer of international criminal law, wrote, "In the eyes of the Declaration's authors, effective respect for human rights depends primarily and above all on the mentalities of the individuals and social groups." Malik, who labored long and hard on the Covenants, agreed. "Men, cultures and nations must first mature inwardly," he wrote, "before there can be effective international machinery to adjudicate complaints about the violation of human rights." (7) Chang, citing a Chinese proverb, wrote, "Laws alone are not sufficient to bring about results by themselves." He went on to say that the Declaration's main goal was "to build up better human beings, and not merely to punish those who violate human rights." (8)

Eleanor Roosevelt was of the same mindset. In one of her last speeches at the United Nations, she emphasized the importance of the small settings where people first learn of their rights and responsibilities.

> *Where, after all, do universal rights begin? In small places, close to home—so close and so small that they cannot be seen on any maps of the world. Yet they are the world of the individual person: the neighborhood he lives in; the school or college he attends; the factory, farm or office where he works.* (9)

The hopes and fears of the men and women who framed the Declaration were grounded in their understanding of human nature. The events of their times had shown them human beings at their best and worst—with their potential for good and evil, reason and impulse, trust and betrayal, creativity and destruction, selfishness and cooperation. They had seen governments at their best and worst—capable of atrocities at home and abroad, but also of restoring their former enemies to a dignified place in the community of nations. The framers took encouragement from the fact that human beings are capable not only of violating human rights, but also of imagining that there are rights to violate, of articulating those rights in declarations and constitutions, of orienting their conduct towards the norms that they have recognized, and of feeling the need to make excuses when their conduct falls short.

Future generations will judge whether our generation has enhanced or squandered the inheritance handed down to us by Eleanor Roosevelt, Charles Malik, John Humphrey, Peng-chun Chang, Rene Cassin, and other large-souled men and women who strove to bring a standard of right from the ashes of terrible wrongs. How we measure up will depend in part on today's leaders, especially those who chart the course of the world's one remaining superpower. But what will be decisive is whether or not sufficient numbers of men and women in "small places, close to home" can imagine, and then begin to live, the reality of freedom, solidarity, and peace.

Extended Observation

Reflection & Conversation

This chapter gives a specific example of cultural change—the Universal Declaration of Human Rights. It pays tribute to the courageous work of Eleanor Roosevelt, but it also gives a paradigm for great change on an international scale. Focus your reflection on just what the Declaration means for the world. How has the realization that every human person has the right to liberty shaped the contemporary world? How is this great ideal being tarnished?

Attend to the Word

Read Isaiah 42:1–7. Listen to this passage in light of what you
have learned about the work on the Universal Declaration of
Human Rights and on the efforts it takes to work constantly so
that justice prevails. Spend a few moments in silence to let the
power of these words sink in.

Engage

Liberty is at the heart of human rights. Without freedom, the
other rights are impossible, and the pursuit of happiness elusive
at best.

1. What was the challenge that Eleanor Roosevelt had in
   bringing together the various viewpoints on human rights
   in the post-war world?
2. What value does the declaration have in today's world—
   filled as it is with the fear of terrorism, with corporate
   greed, and with contemporary slavery in all its forms?
3. How can the declaration be helpful to those who would
   want to "faithfully bring forth justice?"

Move Forward

It has been said in many ways that the most certain guarantee
of the triumph of evil is for people of good will to do nothing.
Engraved on the Liberty Bell, the icon of freedom for the people
of the United States, are words from the Book of Leviticus
(25:10): "Proclaim liberty throughout the land unto all the
inhabitants thereof."

1. How can you, by the way you live and act, proclaim
   liberty?
2. What groups working for human rights and liberty
   can you, and will you, support? (This question may take
   some research. Seek help from people who can help you
   separate the wheat from the chaff of action groups.)

3. Eleanor Roosevelt understood that the ideals in the Universal Declaration would "carry no weight unless the people know them . . . unless people demand that they be lived." How can you help in this great task?

Pray

The following words from Isaiah can be the source of your prayer for this chapter.

> *In the wilderness prepare the way of the Lord;*
> *make straight in the desert a highway for our God.*
>
> *Every valley shall be lifted up,*
> *and every mountain and hill be made low;*
> *the uneven ground shall become level,*
> *and the rough places plain.*
>
> *Then the glory of the Lord shall be revealed,*
> *and all people shall see it together,*
> *for the mouth of the Lord has spoken.*

Isaiah 40:3–5 (NRSV)

Fighting Slavery
in Africa

By Baroness Caroline Cox

Baroness Caroline Cox became a created life peer in 1982 and has been
Deputy Speaker of the House of Lords in the United Kingdom since
1985. She was Founder Chancellor of Bournemouth University from
1991–2001 and is Vice President of the Royal College of Nursing. Her
international humanitarian work includes serving as non-executive
director of the Andrei Sakharov Foundation, trustee of both MERLIN
(Medical Emergency Relief International) and the Siberian Medical
University, and Chief Executive of HART (Humanitarian Aid Relief
Trust).

Baroness Cox has been honored for her humanitarian work
with the Commander Cross of the Order of Merit of the Republic
of Poland, in addition to the Wilberforce Award. She has also been
awarded an Honorary Fellowship of the Royal College of Surgeons
of England and Honorary Doctorates by universities in the United
Kingdom, the United States, the Russian Federation, and Armenia.
Baroness Cox's humanitarian work has taken her on several missions
to conflict zones, including Armenia, the Sudan, Nigeria, the Burmese
jungles, and Indonesia. She recently visited North Korea to help
promote parliamentary initiatives and medical programs. She has been
instrumental in helping change policies for orphaned and abandoned
children in the former Soviet Union.

William Wilberforce's
parliamentary successes and the political achievements of the
Clapham Circle were accomplished by a powerful combination
of passionate commitment to basic values, political integrity, and
realistic pragmatism.

However, their mission to abolish slavery is still unfinished—nowhere more so than in Africa. Attempts to expose and eradicate the continuation of this barbaric phenomenon require comparable political initiatives. The reality and the inhumanity of modern slavery need to be demonstrated; measures to free those enslaved need to be implemented—urgently; and the underlying causes need to be understood and addressed.

In attempting to address the horrors of modern slavery, I have endeavored to use the privileges of speaking on these issues in Parliament, having been appointed to the House of Lords as a life peer. I believe that, in order to speak with maximum effectiveness, it is important to speak with the authenticity of first-hand evidence, to be able to say, "I have been, I have seen—and this is how it really is."

I have also given evidence in U.S. Congressional briefings on the Sudan and Slavery on March 13, 1996 and at the UN Human Rights Commission in Geneva in April 1996. I am a frequent speaker on this subject at universities, schools, and churches in the United Kingdom and the United States.

In my testimony before the U.S. Congress subcommittees on International Relations and on Africa, I said, "the government of Sudan continues to try to transform by force the ethnically and religiously diverse country into an Arab, Islamic state against the wishes of the vast majority of its population, both North and South. The devastating effects of this policy in the South and the Nuba Mountains are tantamount to genocide."

In order to fight slavery in Africa, I have many times visited areas where slavery is entrenched, systematic, and widespread. I have also been active in helping to free those who have been enslaved, obtaining testimonies of their experiences as slaves and witnessing the joys and tribulations of their homecomings. Our policies of redemption—buying slaves to set them free—have been criticized, but my colleagues and I have no compunction about freeing those it is possible to free.

While many people talk of metaphorically being shot at, I have been shot at for my work, which is my passion. The Government of Sudan has told us that they would shoot us out of the sky if we persisted in going to airstrips they had designated "No Go" locations for UN Operation Lifeline Sudan. These were precisely the locations where the government was undertaking its military offensives against innocent civilians. The government denies access to these areas because it does not want anyone to witness its activities or to take aid to its victims. We naturally persisted in visiting these locations despite the threat of bombardment or our aircraft being shot.

Therefore, in my contribution to this tribute to William Wilberforce, I hope to show how, as a contemporary British parliamentarian, I try to follow, albeit very humbly, in the footsteps of William Wilberforce. I do this with a passionate commitment to the fundamental values of human freedom and dignity, political integrity based on authenticity of evidence, and political pragmatism grounded in realism. In so doing, I will give a very brief overview of some manifestations of slavery in Africa today and an account of my own political and practical activities in response to this phenomenon. Most important of all, I will provide an opportunity for the slaves to speak for themselves so that their voices can be heard and some of their testimonies made known. They provide the greatest challenge to us all to increase our endeavors to accomplish William Wilberforce's mission in our day.

Contemporary slavery in Africa takes a number of different forms in Sudan, Mauritania, Senegal, Mali, and northern Uganda. (1) As my commitment to speaking with the authenticity derived from first-hand evidence has taken me to Sudan many times and, more recently, to Uganda, I will focus on the reality of slavery as I have witnessed it in those two countries. (But I do not wish to underestimate the seriousness of the continuation of slavery elsewhere. Slavery is among the very top priorities that I have, and I have been very outspoken on other related issues such as sex slaves in Burma.)

Sudan

I first became interested in the issue of modern slavery during my visits to Southern Sudan beginning in 1996. I visited Nyamlell in Northern Bahr-El-Ghazal very shortly after the first systematic slave raid was undertaken in that region in April and May. Subsequent visits to that area and other parts of Southern Sudan provided evidence of the systematic nature of the use of slavery as a weapon of war by the regime in Khartoum, the capital.

Sudan has a long history of inter-racial and inter-tribal slavery as part of a historical tradition of Arab enslavement of Africans in many parts of Africa. It is estimated that the numbers of Africans enslaved by Arabs over the centuries exceeds that of the numbers enslaved in the transatlantic slave trade. (2)

Attempts to eradicate such slavery were made during the era of British colonialism. (3) But in Sudan, bitter civil war has raged for all but 10 years since independence was gained in 1956. In the 1980s, systematic slavery of Africans by Arabs began to re-emerge. In 1989, the Islamist regime National Islamic Front (NIF) seized power by military coup and declared Islamic military jihad (holy war) against all who oppose it, including many Muslims, Christians, and traditional believers. The weapons of the jihad were threefold: military offensives against civilians, the manipulation of aid (the declaration of areas as "No Go" to Operation lifeline Sudan and all the aid organizations working under its umbrella), and slavery.

Typically, the regime would carry out systematic, large-scale offensives against innocent civilians, simultaneously declaring the areas affected as "No Go" to aid organizations. Nobody could take aid to the victims or witness the atrocities the regime perpetrated.

In some areas, such as the borderlands between northern and southern Sudan in Bahr-El-Ghazal and in the Nuba Mountains, the raids would typically involve the slaughter of men and the abduction of women and children into slavery. Apart from the economic "benefits" of free hard labor, slavery served the purposes of the jihad. These included the forced Islamisation of those not already Muslim and the forced Arabisation of the Africans. Children who are abducted from their families can be brought up as Muslims and women can be sexually exploited, changing the genetic identity of their children.

However, there are peaceable Arab Muslim traders who, from time immemorial, come south in the dry season to trade and to graze their cattle. Many are friends of the local Dinka people, and, at considerable risk, tried to find, buy, and bring back women and children who had been captured and enslaved. They had to charge a price for redemption because they had to pay the ransom to free the slaves and feed them during the escort home.

I have witnessed again and again the complete devastation of the scorched earth policy inflicted on the African communities during these military offensives. Combined NIF Government forces, the special Popular Defense Forces (PDF) who were trained as mujahadin or "jihad warriors," and the murahaleen— the local tribesmen who were recruited, armed, and supported by the professional troops—perpetrate this violence. On many occasions, I have landed at small "No Go" airstrips. Flying in, I have seen the smoke of burning villages spreading from horizon to horizon. On landing, I have seen emaciated, harrowed people come running to the airstrip, thankful that we have come, grateful for the medical supplies we have brought, and desperate to show us what has happened. Again and again, we have gone "footing" (as they call it) through miles of carnage and devastation. Human corpses intermingled with slaughtered cattle. We have seen burnt villages and crops. We have met the remnants of families whose loved ones have been taken away as slaves.

Sometimes, we have given advance notice of our coming, so arrangements have been made for us to meet Arab traders and to pay for the freedom of slaves—usually several hundred at a time. We systematically have interviewed random samples of those who have returned. On some visits, we have checked translations with independent interpreters afterwards to ensure validity. And we have often seen the physical scars that are evidence of reported maltreatment.

Testimonies of Those Put into Slavery

Here are a few testimonies that we collected. Akuac Mathiane is female, aged about thirty-four. This is her story:

In May 1998 Sudanese Popular Defense Forces, together with murahaleen, came on horseback and attacked my village, Aweng (Bahr-El-Ghazal). They killed many people, mainly men, including my brother and my nephew. Some of those killed were fighting the forces but many were unarmed civilians. I was taken captive with two of my three children and a large number of other women and children. My captors snatched my two-year-old son, Mayai, from me and threw him harshly on the ground. He still has a scar on his chest from where he was hurt as he was thrown down onto a sharp object.

Our wrists were tied and we were tied to horses. The children were placed on the horses and we were forced to walk for 10 days to the north. We were told that all the people in the village would be killed. We were given very little sustenance, just dura mixed with sand, and water which had been polluted with urine. This was deliberately done to show the raiders' contempt for us. One of the children died on the way from hunger. I and the other women were sexually abused during the trip to the North.

I was taken to Kitep near Goth in Western Sudan where I was kept by the man who had captured me in the raid. His name is Feki and I lived with him and his wife, who both mistreated me. There were five of us who had been taken as slaves who were kept in his household. My children were taken away from me and given to someone else.

I was completely distraught; I did not know what to do; I did not know where my children were and I did not know whether my husband and my five-year-old daughter, Ajak, who had not been taken North, were still alive. I felt overwhelmed and completely helpless.

I was made to work, cooking and cultivating dura. I had to work from dawn for long hours and was given very little food. Only when I became weak would they give me a little food. I had to sleep outside. The children were treated better because it was intended that they would be adopted. I and the other women in slavery with me were sexually abused during our captivity. I was given an Arabic name, Amila, and Mayai was given the name Mohammed.

I am an animist, but I was forced to pray like a Muslim. They told me that since I was their slave I had to do what they said and when I refused to pray they would beat me with sticks. This happened almost daily.

They called us names and told us that Dinkas were worthless and only the Northerners were of value. They said that we deserved only poor food and care and that we were supposed to be killed. I was told that I had been taken as a slave because they were fighting with the Dinkas. I think that the primary motivation of the fighting is that they want the land and the secondary motivation is that they want to force us to adopt Islam.

My brother raised some money to try to buy me back from the owner. However, he was told that it was not enough. He increased the amount and I managed to escape. I had to hide during the day on the way down to the South. It took us fifteen nights to travel back. I arrived about two months ago.

My brother managed to find my youngest son as well and he is now with me. My six-year-old son, Daw, and my three sisters, Abuk, aged eight, Diu, aged seven, and Nyariak, aged six, are all still in the North. I am unable to get them back because we do not have enough money because all our livestock was taken in the raid. I would be able to trace my son; I just do not have enough money to get him when I find him.

I am very happy to be back and to find that there are people still alive after the raid. However, everything that I had was taken in the raid and I am uncertain about the future and do not know how I will live. I am very badly affected by my experiences. I am very afraid for my son who is still in captivity and I cannot sleep at night because I am worrying about him. I also live in fear that the raiders will return.

Here is testimony from Bol Marol, a ten-year-old Dinka child, son of Marol Mai.

I was taken as a slave in 1995 and have been in slavery for three years. I was taken by a slave master. He was tall with a dark beard and he was very aggressive towards me. I was made to look after sheep and goats and to clean dishes. I worked from about 6 a.m. to 6 p.m. and they only gave me a little food. They would beat me with sticks to make me work harder. I have a scar on my face from one of these beatings. My slave master tried to convert me to Islam. He forced me to go to the Mosque with him on Fridays and beat me with sticks to make me go. I did not want to convert to Islam because I am a Christian and do not want to change my religion. What happened to me and is happening to others like me is a very bad thing. I am happy that I can come back to my home and that I have found that someone cares about me and can tell others about what has happened to me.

James Ajing Path, Commissioner for Abyie County, told me in 1998:

> *Everything was destroyed in raids when the area was overrun last year. The SPLM/A have now repopulated the region as far as the River Kiir. The region has abundant natural resources, with water round the year and the Arabs from North like to come in the dry season to graze their cattle. There is also oil and the NIF regime wants to take over the land for both the rich pasture lands and to export the oil.*

> *During the raids last year, Government forces, along with mujahadeen and murahaleem, overran this particular part of Abyie County, taking women and children as slaves, killing seventy-three people, stealing and slaughtering cattle and destroying crops and homes. Such was the extent of the devastation that nothing was left. For example, there are still no chairs to sit on and we sit on the ground in the dust and amongst the ants. The local authority has details of 634 women and children who were abducted as slaves. Peaceable Arab traders have managed to locate and bring back 325 slaves with 309 still remaining in the North. Because the local communities have lost everything during the raids, they have no resources which they can use to buy the freedom of enslaved members of their families. The train which travels from El Obied to Wau, supplying the Government garrison there, is currently stationed at Awiel. Hundreds of militia surround the train fanning out into the countryside, conducting the kind of raids which had been suffered at this village.*

> *Arab traders go to the North to locate children and women; when they find them, they have to pay money to the owners. As many of the local people do not have any possessions left, the contribution of Western organizations which enables families to redeem their loved ones is essential and greatly valued. The Arab traders, who help the Dinka communities by bringing back the women and children, run grave risks of detention and punishment, as they are undermining the NIF's policy and jihad. In my own district seventy-two people were killed last year, including men, women, and children, and hundreds were taken as slaves.*

The following is from a discussion with Arab "slave traders" in 1998 in Bahr-El-Ghazal. The slave redemptions took place under a huge tree in Wunrok where hundreds of children and families were gathered, waiting in hope to be reconciled. The Arab traders had brought about one thousand slaves down from the North. Local families had paid for the release of over two hundred of this number. One hundred ten of the group had escaped from their owners in the North, thus no money was exchanged on their behalf. This left 671 slaves who needed to be redeemed financially.

Here is what several Arab "slave traders," referred to as T1, T2, and T3 to protect their anonymity, told me.

T1 said, "What we are doing here today is a favor ... we often lose money on these deals and if we are discovered by the government we will be killed. We will try our level best to help with the humanitarian needs evident here, using our wealth to help."

T2 said, "My father has more than five thousand head of cattle but no grazing land ... so we now try to improve our relationship with the Dinka by bringing back children so that we can graze our cattle here. ... Many children have been put in camps by the Government so they are difficult to get to."

T3 said, "I was sick for 10 years (*he showed us deep scars on his face and neck*). It is difficult to get treated in Khartoum unless you are a Muslim. You have to join the NIF Islamization program. When the Arabs raid here they take children particularly because they can then train them in Islam and bring them back here to raid and take cattle."

When asked if some children are exported from Khartoum, the traders each responded in the affirmative.

T2 said, "They are taken to Libya, Iraq, and Saudi Arabia mainly. There they are trained in Islam and work in factories or the army. ... They are happy to take those who don't know their father ... then it seems like they are really Iraqi or Libyan."

Northern Uganda

The agonizing poignancy of interviewing those who have been enslaved recurred for me this year in a new context in northern Uganda. I had been aware that the situation there was cause for concern, but it had still been "off my radar screen." Then, I was urged to visit the region by Ugandans in exile. The exiles worried that reports claiming the situation had improved made the international community complacent. My findings exceeded my worst expectations.

For over twenty years, the region has suffered at the hands of rebels fighting in the so-called "Lord's Resistance Army" (LRA). They are supported financially and logistically by the Sudanese NIF regime. One of the LRA's policies is the systematic abduction of children on a massive scale—estimates of the numbers captured range from twenty to forty thousand. They are taken to military training camps, often in Sudan, where they are terrorised, brutalised, and forced to fight against the Ugandan Army and their own people. They are trained to abduct other children and maltreat them in the same way as they themselves have been abused and tortured.

They tell their own stories, each of which is horrific in the barbarities inflicted on them. Here are two testimonies:

Abalo Irene, fifteen years old, from Latwong, was abducted in 2001. She said that the LRA came to the village, near Pajule, and attacked for much of the night. She had fled into one of the huts where the only two occupants were wives of Uganda Peoples Defence Force (UPDF) soldiers. She was abducted, but neither tied nor beaten. She was made to carry the Commander's heavy bag. During nineteen months with the LRA, she was transferred to two different Commanders' units. She didn't receive intensive training, but during captivity she was made to kill, using three methods. Method one called for abductees to be tied up and the neck cut with a panga knife. Method two was to slash open the belly with a panga knife. The third method was to beat the abductees to death. Irene was threatened with a warning that if she failed they would cut her neck so that she would bleed to death. Her captors cut her neck superficially in two places (*scars just visible*).

She knows she killed ten abductees (children and adults) by slashing the belly, scooping up the blood, and placing it in her mouth.

She escaped early one morning when she went to collect water for the Commander's bath. She walked for one mile down the road and left the water container, then ran through the bush and made her way toward home.

Talking about the killing, she explained how she had been indoctrinated to understand that if she did not kill the abductee, then the panga knife would be given over for the other to kill her. She felt it was wrong.

She is now in school, but cannot concentrate and has repeated nightmares about the first killing, which occurred at dawn, and the first time she had to drink blood.

Atim Monica, 18 years old, from Lukole in Pader was abducted in 2003 from her home at night. She said that her brother had already been abducted—she eventually met him a year later in Sudan, before they were separated again.

She was tied up, beaten, and shot in the leg (*scars still clearly visible*) during an ambush. She was not given any treatment.

She was taken to Sudan for military training and was "given" to Commander Palaro. She became pregnant and gave birth with no help at all.

"I was just treated like an animal," Monica said.

She had to fight in Uganda, carrying her baby with her. She fought in Teso and Lango and was ordered to carry out abductions, especially of children. If any resisted, they were immediately killed.

She has had to kill time and again. "In a battle, one has to kill," she said.

During one confrontation not far from her village, she met a woman whom she knew and asked her to take her child, now eighteen months old. She could not continue to carry her gun and the child at the same time. She left her daughter, Apio Consulate, in the area of Lacek Ocot and she has not seen her again.

Monica's father was killed by a helicopter gunship. She desperately wants to go to school, as she was studying at secondary school when she was abducted.

Conclusion

How should we react to such manifestations of slavery in the world today? Applying William Wilberforce's passionate commitment to the fundamental values of human dignity and freedom, we should be shattering the silence and using every means to free the slaves and to end the institutions of slavery. We should:

1. Admit That Modern Slavery Exists

As incredible as it may seem, in a recent debate in the House of Lords, one of the Peers denied the existence of slavery. In a similar fashion there have been those in the press who have challenged the existence of slavery—although they sometimes acknowledge the existence of other forms of violations of freedom such as "abduction."

Denying that modern slavery exists would be similar to denying that the British Empire participated in the transatlantic slave trade. Not only do we have to admit that modern slavery exists, but like Wilberforce, we have to do something about it.

2. Free the Slaves

My colleagues and I have been criticized by some people for engaging in the redemption of slaves. They claim we are "encouraging the slave trade."

I do not accept the criticisms. In the case of Sudan, that slavery was not primarily economic—it was a weapon of war. It will thus continue regardless of whether any slave is redeemed. The only way slaves can be freed is through the process of redemption. Local communities, I have found, have lost not only their loved ones to slavery, but have lost everything else, including their livestock and all forms of property. They are thus prevented from having the resources to enable them to free their family members.

Modern slavery was designed to fulfill the objectives of jihad—the forced Islamization of non-Muslims and the forced Arabization of Africans. That form of slavery would have persisted even if we had never redeemed a single slave. All that would have happened is that tens of hundreds of people would have remained as slaves who could have been freed. I believe we have a moral imperative to liberate those who are held captive unjustly and to free the slaves. I believe that William Wilberforce and the Clapham Circle, who were pragmatic as well as principled, to the extent of offering financial reimbursement to slave-owners for the emancipation of their slaves, would have agreed.

It was also said that we had no guarantee that those whom we freed would not be recaptured on subsequent raids. True. But one does not refuse to help the victim of a war injury because they might be injured again. The proper response is to try to prevent the recurrence by addressing the cause of the injury—in this case, by bringing an end to slavery.

3. Proclaim the Truth

In the early days of our work to expose the reality of slavery in
Sudan and to free those whom we could, the NIF denied the
existence of slavery in Sudan. However, repeated reports detailing
the evidence eventually led to recognition of the practice of
slavery. This led to pressures on the NIF to desist from this
barbaric practice and to participate in initiatives to free those
who have been enslaved.

There is now a cease-fire in southern Sudan and the Nuba
Mountains. Some measures have been taken to identify slaves
and to return them to their homes. But many problems persist:
many have not yet been rescued, some may never be found, and
those who do return often face difficulties of reintegration into
their own communities. For example, it may be very difficult for a
girl who has been enslaved and sexually exploited to find a "good"
husband. Children who were abducted very young may find it
hard to adjust to a culture which they do not remember.

In northern Uganda the problems facing LRA abductees
who have escaped are legion. Often their families have been
killed, siblings abducted, or relatives died from HIV/AIDS.
An estimated ninety-five percent of the population of northern
Uganda has been driven off their lands by the LRA to live in
intensely overcrowded camps where one thousand people a week
die from malnutrition, unsanitary conditions, and disease.

Therefore, contemporary slavery in these parts of Africa
today has far-reaching repercussions that cause suffering and
death on a massive scale. If we are to honor William Wilberforce
and all he stood for, we cannot remain silent or look the other
way. We must use the political arena to expose this human
suffering and to bring all the resources of the international
community to bear on those responsible to end these barbarities.

As Wilberforce noted in one of his speeches on slavery in
Parliament, we cannot use the excuse of ignorance. Nor can we
claim we do not know and therefore have no responsibility to try
to achieve an end to this modern-day slavery. We cannot allow
economic interests or political expediency to require us to condone
or to compromise. International protest, boycott, and prayer
brought an end to apartheid in Africa—an undertaking that surely
seemed as overwhelming as ending modern-day slavery.

The many thousands of people suffering from slavery in
Africa today represent an urgent challenge to us. We have the

privilege of living in free democratic societies and to use our freedoms to strive for their freedom. Like William Wilberforce, we should not rest until our responsibilities to them are fulfilled.

Extended Observation

Reflection & Conversation

Baroness Caroline Cox has dedicated her life to fighting contemporary slavery in Africa. In your reflection, remember the stories she has told, especially those stories that are in the actual words of enslaved people—Akuac Mathiane, Bol Marol, James Ajing Path, Abalo Irene, and Atim Monica. Also share your reactions to the discussion with the Arab "slave traders."

Attend to the Word

Read Isaiah 52:13–53:6. This passage is part of the fourth Servant Song. It dramatizes the suffering of the one who was to come. That suffering is still seen clearly in the slavery stories you have read. Spend some time in silence to let the words of Isaiah inform the rest of your study.

Engage

Baroness Cox has been tireless in her campaign to love others, particularly those who are enslaved. She provides Parliament with first hand knowledge and evidence that the business of human bondage is thriving in Africa.

1. What is your reaction to the testimonies that this chapter reported? Describe both your emotional and your intellectual reactions.
2. How is African slavery reported in the media? As a result, how aware is the average citizen of these atrocities?
3. Baroness Cox and organizations she supports often ransom slaves. Other groups oppose ransom because they feel it does nothing to end the institution of human trafficking. What do you think are good strategies for freeing those in bondage and for ending slavery in Africa?

Move Forward

The chapter gives an overall strategy toward ending African slavery that shatters the silence surrounding it, that uses every means to free those in slavery, and that works to end the various institutions of slavery.

1. How can you tell the truth to the people in your sphere of influence about the existence of slavery? What reactions will you get when you share this truth?
2. How can you and your friends and family work to free the slaves? Remember that this work is best done through groups that are knowledgeable and have the wherewithal to do it.
3. What long-term commitment can you and your friends make to continue the Wilberforce legacy by pressing for the elimination of those organizations worldwide that support or otherwise institutionalize human bondage?

Pray

Use the words of the Psalm to pray in the person of all those who suffer at the hands of oppressors—for those in slavery and for those who are persecuted.

> *O Lord, what are human beings that you regard them,*
> *or mortals that you think of them?*
>
> *They are like a breath;*
> *their days are like a passing shadow.*
>
> *Bow your heavens, O Lord, and come down;*
> *touch the mountains so that they smoke.*
>
> *Make the lightning flash and scatter them;*
> *send out your arrows and rout them.*
>
> *Stretch out your hand from on high;*
> *set me free and rescue me from the mighty waters,*
> *from the hands of aliens,*
>
> *whose mouths speak lies,*
> *and whose right hands are false.*
>
> *Happy are the people to whom such blessings fall;*
> *happy are the people whose God is the Lord.*

Psalm 144:3–8, 15a (NRSV)

sixteen

Fighting Persecution & Human Trafficking

By Michael Horowitz

Michael J. Horowitz is a prominent Jewish human-rights attorney and a director of Hudson Institute's Project for Civil Justice Reform and Project for International Religious Liberty. He served as general counsel for the Office of Management and Budget (OMB) from 1981 to 1985, and as an associate professor of law at the University of Mississippi from 1965 to 1967. Horowitz has maintained a private law practice since 1967.

Horowitz has been an adjunct professor at Georgetown Law School, special counsel for the Committee on the Judicial Branch of the Judicial Conference of the United States, and special counsel to the National Council of Young Israel. He served as chairman of President Reagan's Domestic Policy Council on Federalism and was co-chairman of the Cabinet Council's Working Group on Legal/Tort Policy.

In addition to his domestic credentials, Horowitz also served as an advisor to the Czech, Slovak, and Bulgarian Academies of Science; was vice president of the Bulgarian American Friendship Society; Counsel and Trustee of Save Cambodia, Inc.; and a National Advisory Board Member of the Institute for Democracy in Vietnam. He earned his LL.B. from Yale Law School in 1964.

I place on my desk, always in my sight, the things that remind me of who I am and what I aspire to be. There are, of course, the pictures of my family. And then, these four items: a biography of William Wilberforce, a stone from Auschwitz, the Army Jewish prayer book from my uncle's World War II service with Patton, and a copy of the U.S. Constitution.

From childhood, the high points of my year have been Thanksgiving and Passover—they are the days that give meaning to the symbols on my desk. Both days teach and celebrate the blessings of freedom, and both teach the moral obligation owed by those of us who are free to those who are not.

Both celebrations also teach that, for all the failings of those who profess their truths, Judaism and Christianity have been history's great engines of freedom.

The Fight for Human Rights

In almost ten years of intimate association with Christians engaged in human-rights causes, I've watched Christians as both an outsider and a sympathetic ally. I know pastors who have risked all to go into the forests of China to feed and rescue North Korean refugees. I know of some now being tortured in Chinese jails for their "underground railroad" efforts. I know Christians throughout the world who have been tormented, tortured, and martyred for their faith. I'm fortunate beyond measure to count as friends such great figures as Korean underground leaders Chun Ki-Won, Tim Peters, and Kim Hang Soon; Shahbaz Bhatti of the All Pakistan Minorities Alliance; Bob Fu of the China Aid Association; and comparably heroic Christian leaders from Cuba, Saudi Arabia, Indonesia, Sudan, and elsewhere throughout the world.

In the United States, I've seen Christian leaders asked to uproot their lives and families in order to take up causes on behalf of the vulnerable and persecuted. I've seen them unashamedly drop to their knees in quiet prayer and then get up to say that, as Christians, they have no alternative but to take those risks. I've also regularly seen the faith-based courage and determination of such leaders of the American Evangelical community as Chuck Colson, Richard Land, Rich Cizik, and Barrett Duke, and have seen the near-miracles wrought by such grassroots Christian leaders as Debbie Fikes and her colleagues of the Ministerial Alliance of Midland, Texas.

I've been awed in the presence of such faith; its example has helped make me a better and more observant practitioner of my own—for which I will forever be grateful.

Extraordinary Decade

The Christian community, led by Evangelicals, has become an extraordinary force for human rights during the last decade, a process that began with the release of the January 1996 "Statement of Conscience Concerning Worldwide Religious Persecution" by the National Association of Evangelicals (NAE). The statement's concluding sentence summarized its purpose:

> *Therefore, before God, and because we are our brother's keeper, we solemnly pledge: to end our own silence in the face of the suffering of all those persecuted for their religious faith . . . [and] to do what is within our power to the end that the government of the United States will take appropriate action to combat the intolerable religious persecution victimizing fellow believers and those of other faiths.* (1)

That statement—and comparable declarations from such key groups as Prison Fellowship and the Southern Baptist Convention—sparked a movement that engaged groups of every sort, from Tibetan Buddhists to Catholics, from Iranian Baha'is to Reform Jews, that followed Evangelical leadership, lit prairie fires of action across the country, and caused the passage of the International Religious Freedom Act of 1998.

Has the law solved all the problems of religious persecution? Of course not—no act of legislation ever does. Has it made an extraordinary difference to persecuted believers around the world? It is beginning to—and then some—as America's national commitment to fight against religious persecution has grown by orders of magnitude. Today, the rights of believers have become to the United States government, and to most Americans, a central and basic entitlement whose protection is a core American obligation.

Against the opposition of presidential administrations, against all sorts of interest groups, with no money, with no teams of lobbyists, with little but passion, leadership, and faith, Evangelicals have subsequently championed many other great human-rights causes. Initiatives they have mounted on behalf of trafficked women, abused prison inmates, North Korean refugees, and other vulnerable victims had the further advantage of not being discounted as "mere" parochial efforts to protect their own. By such leadership, Evangelicals have demonstrated how deeply they are moved, and often driven, by deep compassion for the vulnerable victims of injustice. By so doing, they have helped shatter "us versus them" caricatures drawn by those opposed to Christian witness in the public square. They have made it far less possible for those who disagree with their views on given issues to discredit their animating spirit or decency.

For example, Christians have played an essential role in advancing the great slavery *and* women's issue of our time: sex trafficking. The trafficking by international mafias and corrupt government officials of at least 1 million girls and women per year into sexual bondage and slavery had been the world's fastest growing area of international crime. The campaign to end this epidemic scourge was made in the spirit of nineteenth-century antislavery abolitionist William Wilberforce and the Clapham Circle and the anti-trafficking efforts of Salvation Army founders William and Catherine Booth.

The historic anti-trafficking initiative in which America is now engaged first began when former Salvation Army national commander Bob Watson convened a major session of Evangelicals, Jewish leaders, and pro-abortion feminist groups to discuss the issue. The meeting triggered broad coalition action that ultimately led to passage of the Trafficking Victims Protection Act. This historic legislation was fittingly sponsored by Senator Sam Brownback and Congressman Chris Smith (rooted Christians for whom prayer and faith are central elements of their lives), the late Paul Wellstone (a good man, a secularist, and the most liberal Democrat then in the Senate), and former Congressman Sam Gejdenson (the son of Nazi Holocaust survivors).

Anti-trafficking efforts continue to be spurred by Evangelical Christians and feminists under the banner of the Josephine Butler Forum, named after the great Victorian Evangelical who led the 19th-century battle to end the abuse of women through state-protected prostitution.

Working with both Ted Kennedy and the great congressional human-rights leader Frank Wolf, a model of Christian decency, Evangelicals were prime supporters of the Prison Rape Elimination Act of 2003—legislation now putting to an end a form of widespread brutality that has destroyed ten to fifteen percent of all American prisoners at the hands of previously uncontrolled inmate gangs and predators.

Evangelicals also played the central role in mediating the genocidal north-south war in Sudan that had claimed more than 2 million lives and made refugees of at least 5 million more.

Guided by the NAE's "2002 Second Statement of Conscience Concerning Worldwide Religious Persecution with Special Examination of Sudan and North Korea" of May 2002, Evangelicals are playing a key role in protecting the tragic victims of mass starvation, concentration camps, gas chambers, and ceaseless persecutions of the lunatic regime of North Korea's Kim Jong Il—an effort that I am supremely confident will receive, and will require, the very best of their prayers and labors.

Working with Jewish and feminist groups, Christian Evangelicals recently played a central role in passing legislation that will protect runaway girls caught at American bus stations and the hundreds of thousands of girls and women trapped on the streets of America into lives of prostitution, routinely savage beatings, aids, and drug addiction. Thanks to such Christian leaders as Lisa Thompson of the Salvation Army and Janice Crouse of Concerned Women for America, the law of the land is now committed to ensuring that the men who patronize and abuse the battered girls who walk our mean streets, and the pimps who assault and enslave them, will become targets of a justice system that until now has only focused its attentions on arresting the victims.

Christian Evangelicals are also playing an instrumental role in helping to pass a broadly supported Advance Democracy Act that will make the peaceful elimination of dictatorships and the promotion of democracy a central strategic objective of American foreign policy. This is as it should be, if only because the blessings of democracy are a gift to mankind that our faiths have been centrally instrumental in broadly spreading.

In fighting for human rights, Christians have shown their ability not to overload the circuits and, critically, not to tilt at windmills. They have picked targets that few cared about and have seared the consciences of their fellow Americans in order to offer hope and protection to people who desperately needed it. As rightly described by Allen Hertzke, the great scholar of the Christian Evangelical movement and author of FREEING GOD'S CHILDREN, they have become, beneath the radar screens of the national press, America's most powerful force for human-rights progress. And they have done it as Christians whose biblical commands have made silence impossible in the face of slavery and genocide.

The New Scapegoats

Now a word about why Christianity is—secularists gasp at
the mention of this reality—the great force for *modernity* in
those parts of the world poised between freedom and dark-age
totalitarianism.

To tell this truth best, a word about my people is in order. A
hundred or so years ago, oppressive thugs who ruled countries had
ideal scapegoats whom they used to terrorize entire populations
in order to remain in power. In Europe, if you wanted to know
whether the people of a country were free, you didn't need to
conduct a fancy human-rights survey. All you needed was to visit
a few local synagogues. If the Jews who worshiped there were
free, others in the country were almost certain to be free. On the
other hand, if synagogue visits revealed fear and persecution, it
was a safe bet that few others in the country were free.

Thugs need vulnerable scapegoats and find particular value
in scapegoats who share our faiths—this because Judaism and
Christianity send out the most powerful, radical political message
of all time: the equality of all in the eyes of God. This message
makes tyrants vulnerable—a fact they always realize. As Jews
and Christians, we don't always live up to our teachings and
obligations, but we do a better job at it than we generally give
ourselves credit for. Tyrants know—almost always better than we
do—that if they can silence the scapegoats whose faith calls for
love "unbought by price or fear" and whose kingdom is not of this
earth, they can silence and tyrannize all.

Back in the 1970s and 1980s, the world discovered, thanks
in part to the efforts of America's Christian community, that the
seemingly powerful Soviet regime couldn't even turn its back on
a mere synagogue burning. The "Free Soviet Jewry" movement,
which culminated in the Jackson-Vanik amendment that barred
U.S. trade with the Soviet Union unless Jews were free to migrate
from its borders, actually gave freedom to more than Soviet Jews.
Just as importantly, it placed large cracks in the hitherto solid
walls the regime had built around the Soviet Union and thus
offered hope and, ultimately, freedom to Pentecostals, artists,
political dissidents, and all others.

As the battle for the soul of the twenty-first century is
fought, too many of my people have been killed for us to be fully
useful scapegoats. Thus, my Evangelical friends have become
the Jews of the twenty-first century. This is of course not true of

Christians blessed to live in America and other free countries. It is, however, very much true of their brothers and sisters in the developing world—in the Sudan, in China, in India, in Sri Lanka, in Indonesia, in Saudi Arabia, in country after country where dictatorships reign.

To America's Christians, I therefore say: Take pride in *and responsibility for* the fact that religious and secular tyrants realize that their very survival obliges them to persecute and intimidate their Christian communities.

And when you do, please realize this: *In protecting persecuted Christians, you protect everyone else.*

The most moving calls I've received while engaged in the battle against international religious persecution have come from moderate leaders of Muslim countries who, at risk of life, have said to me, "You must keep up this fight against the radical Muslims who are persecuting Christians." They then add: "I may have to publicly denounce you as a Zionist agent, but here is information about what these radicals are doing in my country. Stop them, please, because if the West is silent when Christians are persecuted, we're all going to have to start saluting the radicals."

The battle over worldwide Christian persecution is a battle for the freedom of all—all the more so because the explosive global spread of Christianity has made the paradigmatic Christian a poor and brown third-world female rather than the white middle-class Western male that your patronizing detractors paint you to be.

When the NAE was first getting started on the Christian persecution issue, I spoke with one of its board members. He asked, "You are a Jew. Why are you so involved?"

My response: "That's a good question. When I was a young boy coming home from yeshiva (Jewish parochial school), I got beat up by kids who said, 'You killed our Christ.'"

His response: "Oh, how I apologize. Oh, please forgive me." He was just so bereft, contrite, and ridden with guilt.

I listened and then said, "Okay, I accept your apology. Now may I say something? If it weren't for the rooted Christian decency of this country, I'd be a lampshade. I'd be a bar of soap."

Whatever sins may have been committed in the name of the Christian faith, please know that Rabbi Joshua Haberman got it right when he called America's Bible Belt his "safety belt." (2) Christians should apologize for the sins of Christians as they must, but it is right and important for you to glory in what your faith has done—not only for your fellow believers but for others as well.

The lesson: Christians count for more than themselves. You're better than you often think you are. Your brothers and sisters around the world are canaries in the coalmine whose well-being secures the well-being of all.

Effectiveness

As praiseworthy and effective as Christians have often been, I believe that you can be far more effective. I believe that America's faith communities need to be mobilized as they and others were in the late eighteenth and early nineteenth century under the leadership of William Wilberforce in battles that abolished slavery, achieved prison reform, and reformed a culture that had begun to lose its moorings as the Industrial Age dawned.

The key is to build support for initiatives and require a shift in tone that reflects confidence in one's capacity to persuade others and shows the respect and civility that your faith commands to be given to all.

My personal situation has helped me here. My wife believes that abortions are tragic but that women should have the right to have them whenever they so decide. Yet far from being morally insensitive, she's a physician who stays up until 1 a.m. reading The New England Journal of Medicine to better take care of her patients, and she earns half of what she could in order to be a better physician. She's an extraordinarily loving mother, deeply rooted in family—indeed, she is the most morally rooted person I know. Being blessed by having her as my spouse, and being a conservative, I've learned that when I talk to her about subjects like gay marriage, I must do it in ways that generate respect if not agreement. And I know for sure that it's no more accurate than it is decent to open a dialogue with her on the subject of abortion by calling her a murderer and someone indifferent to family values. Nor, based on all I have learned over the years, do I believe it is the Christian thing to do.

When you're seeking my wife's soul, when you want her to accept Christ (I wouldn't hold my breath here), do you begin by calling her a heathen and a sinner and then give up on trying to reach her when she understandably tunes you out? Of course you don't. You communicate, you reach out. You find out what's in her and search for common ground and common bonds. You don't do this in a manipulative way, but in a loving, caring fashion. And you gain souls in the process.

Why then, wrong as they think she may be, do some Christians call my wife a murderer rather than trying to find ways to reach her on the issue of abortion? By treating people like her respectfully, you will reach many others more often than you may think you can.

Further, by showing one's love for trafficked women, brutalized prisoners, and enslaved North Korean gulag victims, you will earn my wife's gratitude and trust. By following in the footsteps of your nineteenth-century counterparts who successfully reformed prisons, ended African chattel slavery, and protected and empowered women, you will shatter caricatures of who you are. By seeking common ground on issues of disagreement and by leading battles on commonly shared issues where others have not spoken, you will cause my wife, and others like her, to be more open to who you are and to what you have to say, even when you fail to persuade them.

As you enter the public arena in the name of your faith, please be conscious of your power to lead and persuade, even though the prevailing culture may appear daunting and hostile. Make it your solemn responsibility to reject the "us versus them" counsel of the pessimists and separatists among you. And, above all else, remember that you are morally and, to the extent that I understand it, biblically obligated to demonstrate the love and decency that animates your efforts to seek the rescue of vulnerable victims and cultures.

What gives me most hope for the century in which my children and grandchildren will live is that Christians have shown, in important and growing ways, that you have the wisdom and ability to live up to the Wilberforce model and to make your faith a great engine of freedom for all.

Extended Observation

Reflection & Conversation

Michael Horowitz's chapter is a both a tribute and a challenge. As a tribute, this Jewish lawyer and professor recognizes how many Christians have heeded the Gospel and worked for the poor, the hungry, the imprisoned, and the oppressed. As a challenge, the author encourages Christians around the world to get involved to stop all forms of human bondage. Reflect on and share what you have gathered from reading this chapter—especially any new information on persecution and ways to be more effective in working for justice, peace, and an end to human trafficking.

Attend to the Word

Read Isaiah 61:1–4. This ancient text, like the chapter you have just read, is both a tribute and a challenge. The tribute is to those who suffer injustice. The challenge is in the form of a mission to lift the yoke of oppression and to set captives free. Spend some time in silence letting the powerful and poetic words give rise to images of hope and a sense of mission.

Engage

This chapter cites an "extraordinary decade" and lists some of the initiatives Christian people have taken to work for human rights and social justice. Review the accounts of these initiatives.

> 1. What are some of the acts of oppression that Christians around the world have campaigned against? How visible are these incidents of oppression in your world?

2. In your opinion, why have Christians undertaken such specific initiatives?
3. In reading this chapter, what elements could urge you to craft your own "statement of conscience?" Why?

Move Forward

In the last part of Horowitz's article, he sets out some "rules of engagement" for people of faith who try to enlist broad support for their work, who wish to change minds and hearts, and who wish to influence and improve society. Review his suggestions and use the following to help you form your own rules:

1. Draft your own "statement of conscience" concerning your involvement in defeating human trafficking and persecution. Try to form a consensus statement in your group.
2. Choose one violation of human rights that you and your group would like to adopt as an initiative for change. Choose something that has relevance for your community as well as something that you can truly address by your groups actions.
3. Create a brief action plan of what you and your group are going to do about this violation. Who are you going to work with? How will you measure progress? What strategies will you use? What will be your rules of engagement?

Pray

One of the most powerful human rights prayers of all time is singularly appropriate for this chapter. It is attributed to Saint Francis of Assisi, and it describes his personal mission and his "rules of engagement" for making the world a better place.

> *Lord, make me an instrument of your peace.*
>
> *Where there is hatred, let me sow love;*
> *where there is injury, pardon;*
> *where there is doubt, faith;*
> *where there is despair, hope;*
> *where there is darkness, light;*
> *and where there is sadness, joy.*
>
> *O Divine Master, grant that I may not so much seek*
> *to be consoled as to console;*
> *to be understood as to understand;*
> *to be loved as to love.*
>
> *For it is in giving that we receive;*
> *it is in pardoning that we are pardoned;*
> *and it is in dying that we are born to eternal life.*
> *Amen.*

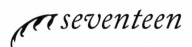

seventeen

Positive Engagement with Islam

By David Blankenhorn & Alex Roberts

David Blankenhorn, president of the Institute for American Values, a leading U.S. think tank, became concerned about Muslim–U.S. relations after the attacks of September 11, 2001. He decided to do something about it and began a dialogue between leading American and Muslim intellectuals. Blankenhorn believes that this dialogue is one of the most important projects the Institute has initiated. The following essay offers some lessons learned from that project.

The Institute for American Values is a non-partisan organization dedicated to strengthening families and civil society worldwide. It works to better society by bringing together scholars and stakeholders from across the political spectrum for joint deliberation and consensus building.

Blankenhorn is the author of FATHERLESS AMERICA: CONFRONTING OUR MOST URGENT PROBLEMS (1995) *and has co-edited seven other books.*

Alex Roberts is a researcher and writer at the Institute, and also serves as managing editor of IJTIHAD/REASONING, *a forthcoming academic journal devoted to dialogue between American and Muslim scholars.*

The following is based on THE ISLAM/WEST DEBATE, *a book published last year by the Institute for American Values.*

In the late eighteenth century, William Wilberforce took on the seemingly impossible challenge of abolishing the slave trade, a practice that was deeply entrenched in the economies of several European nations. Wilberforce first developed broad public support for abolition by engaging the other side—those supporting the slave trade—in a broad national debate in Parliament so that the facts could be made known. This occurred when the Privy Council held hearings and took testimony on the slave trade in 1791. Wilberforce's colleagues were able to take this debate to the people through a series of meetings around the country, particularly in the seaports whose economies depended on the slave trade. It was a slow and painstaking process, but it eventually helped to bring about the end of the slave trade in Britain.

Today, after the September 11, 2001, attacks, we in the United States are also grappling with an immensely challenging issue—the ideology known as Islamism and its violent elements in particular. If we are to respond to this challenge effectively, we must, as Wilberforce did, engage others in a public dialogue that brings universal human values to bear on our situation. Only in this way can we build a bridge across our different cultures and interests and establish a strong moral consensus against extremism.

The Birth of a Muslim-U.S. Dialogue

In February 2002, the international support that the United States had enjoyed immediately after September 11 was falling victim to global discord. Anti-American sentiment was on the rise in Europe, and, in the wake of the war in Afghanistan, support for bin Laden had reached disturbing levels in the Middle East. Early whispers of a stepped-up campaign to effect regime change in Iraq only aggravated this global polarization. Collectively, these developments threatened to convert the war against al-Qaeda into a broader "clash of civilizations."

It was in this context that the Institute for American Values organized sixty prominent American intellectuals to write an open letter entitled "What We're Fighting For" that sought to redefine the struggle against terrorism in terms of universal human values. (1) Our basic argument was that jihadist groups, such as al-Qaeda, pose an implacable threat to the United States and the universal values it embodies. In accordance with the stipulations of "just war" doctrine, the United States has the right to defend itself and its values with military force when other methods will not suffice.

Upon its release, "What We're Fighting For" received little attention from American news outlets, but it drew powerful responses in the Middle East and Europe. Impassioned replies to the letter appeared in newspapers and academic journals and on Islamist websites. Al-Jazeera and other Middle Eastern news networks devoted significant airtime to coverage of the letter. What was especially remarkable about the responses to "What We're Fighting For" is that they came from important figures across the political and ideological spectrums. We heard from liberal and moderate Muslims; the prominent Wahhabi cleric Sheikh Safar al-Hawali; Germany's Coalition for Life and Peace; the Movement for Islamic Reform in Arabia, a leading Saudi dissident Islamist group with ties to Osama bin Laden; and al-Qaeda itself. Throughout the remainder of 2002, these exchanges gave rise to a truly open, substantive, and international debate on terrorism, values, and U.S. policy—a debate unlike any other in which Americans, jihadists, clerics, and progressives all had the opportunity to engage one another's arguments and views directly.

The "What We're Fighting For" Letter

"What We're Fighting For" opens by arguing that there are certain principles, such as equal human dignity and freedom of conscience, that are universally valid and apply to all people without distinction. America's core values and political system, the authors write, reflect and embody these universal principles. After making this argument, the authors go on to characterize al-Qaeda as an implacable enemy that hates the United States not just for what it *does*, but also for what it *is*—that is, for its values. Al-Qaeda wants nothing more than to destroy individual Americans and the universal values they hold dear—and has shown a clear willingness to do so. Thus, in accordance with just war doctrine, the United States has the right to use military force against al-Qaeda in order to defend its citizens and values when other methods will not suffice. The arguments about values, terrorism, and just war ultimately flow together in the letter because America's right to use force is portrayed, in part, as deriving from its adherence to universal values and al-Qaeda's violation of them.

It could be argued that "What We're Fighting For" was an important document for two reasons. First, it provided a moral-philosophical justification for war against al-Qaeda. Second, in making this case, the letter expressed the sentiments of a large segment of the American public.

The Middle Eastern Response

One of the early major responses to "What We're Fighting For" was "How We Can Coexist," an open letter signed by 153 prominent Saudi intellectuals. We considered this document to be quite important because its large and diverse body of signatories suggested that it spoke for mainstream Saudi opinion.

The letter itself begins by agreeing with a basic presupposition of "What We're Fighting For": that Islam and the West share common values that are capable of supporting a just and peaceful coexistence. But the Saudi authors aver that it is not al-Qaeda that poses the greatest threat to peace, but rather U.S. foreign policy, which is unjust and conflicts with universal values. Referring to September 11, the authors write that American foreign policy is largely to blame for "what happened." Accordingly, the United States should modify its aggressive policies and pursue a just world order through international institutions. These arguments about universal values and U.S. policy constitute the letter's basic thesis.

"How We Can Coexist" disagrees significantly with "What We're Fighting For" over what "freedom of religion" means. The authors of "What We're Fighting For" argue that freedom of religion is achieved through the secular state, which guarantees that all citizens can follow whatever religion they choose. For the authors of "How We Can Coexist," however, "religious freedom" means that Muslims should be allowed to fulfill their religious obligations by establishing Islamic states. They argue that the American letter's advocacy of secular government actually transforms "freedoms and rights into tools for conflict" and presents "a limited cultural vision as if it is a universal law that must be generally applied to all, forcibly if need be." In other words, "What We're Fighting For" uses "values" for narrow political ends.

Despite its largely critical view of the United States, "How We Can Coexist" drew vehement opposition from some jihadists (Islamists who believe that violence can be used to establish Islamic states). One such jihadist, Abul Bara, released a lengthy refutation of the Saudi letter entitled "Please Prostrate Yourselves Privately." The letter argues that, contrary to the opinion of the Saudi intellectuals, Islam and Western civilization have nothing meaningful in common. Muslims must avoid infidel ideas and culture and struggle against unbelievers until Islam triumphs:

"Antagonism, fighting and hatred between Muslims and infidels are the basics of our religion." Making frequent reference to Qur'anic passages, Bara maintains that the Saudi intellectuals have obscured the fundamental messages of Islam by taking its values—such as "justice" and "tolerance"—out of their proper context.

The underlying analytical framework of "Please Prostrate Yourselves Privately" is the ideology known as "salafism." Salafists maintain that society, including the Islamic religious establishment, has deviated from the "pure" Islamic community that they think existed during the early years of the religion. They believe that two intertwined courses of action need to be taken to rectify this problem. First, Muslims must jettison accrued religious traditions and directly interpret the primary texts of Islam themselves. Second, Muslims must establish Islamic "states." In such enterprises, *all affairs* will be carried out in accordance with the shari'a (Islamic religious law). These ideas undergird the criticism of the Saudi letter present in "Please Prostrate Yourselves Privately."

Salafists also wrote two direct responses to "What We're Fighting For." The first was "Options are Limited" by the Movement for Islamic Reform in Arabia (MIRA). The second was "Letter to the American People," which was tacitly endorsed, if not penned, by an al-Qaeda member. Both letters echo arguments made in "Please Prostate Yourselves Privately."

MIRA writes that Islam's revealed truth "really calls on its followers to overcome opponents and reach the whole world with its universal message." The "Letter to the American People" states that Muslims have the right and will attack America if it refuses Islam. However, unlike "Please Prostrate Yourselves Privately," these two letters focus on U.S. policies. They attack the United States for supporting Israel, stymieing Arab national liberation movements, suppressing democracy in Algeria, and refusing to sign the Kyoto Protocol. The two letters conclude with conditions for a rapprochement between America and the Islamic world. The reader therefore faces some difficulty in understanding what message these letters intend to convey because they seemingly pursue two distinct lines of logic. While there can be different interpretations of the letters, it seems to us that "Options Are Limited" and "Letter to the American People" may be understood as objecting not only to U.S. policy per se, but U.S. policy insofar as it is an impediment to the goals of salafism. Indeed, in the letters, complaints about U.S. policy are woven into a larger argument for the global hegemony of Islam; the eventual "rapprochement" between the West and Islam is contingent upon the adopting of the latter's beliefs and system of government by the former.

Other articles by several liberal Arab and Muslims reacting to "What We're Fighting For" affirm the need to defeat jihadism, but object to the vision of a just war against al-Qaeda presented by it. Part of this objection has a prima facie basis: war is evil and cannot be associated with "justice." But beyond this point, these articles contend that between its notion of a "just war against terrorism" and its praise of American values, "What We're Fighting For" paves the way for an excessive use of military force by the United States. Woven into these criticisms is a recommendation: the United States should pursue terrorists through international criminal courts, not through extra-legal means. It is argued that such an approach would allow the United States to defend itself while discouraging militarism.

The German Response

A group of 103 German intellectuals called the Coalition for Life and Peace and another group of seventy German intellectuals each wrote responses to "What We're Fighting For." The letters, entitled "A World of Peace and Justice Would Be Different" and "In the Twenty-first Century There is No Longer Any Justification for War," shared a basic thesis: That after the Cold War the United States "concentrated its imagination and its scientific, technical, and economic capacities on strengthening its position as the sole remaining superpower in the world, and establishing a unipolar world order." As a result, there are major imbalances in the global distribution of power. This inequity combined with a lack of local development on many levels— political, economic, and legal among others—creates "structural violence" against the "have-nots" which humiliates them and hinders their "dull human development." This situation engenders a "loss of inhibitions" leading to terrorism in an attempt to improve their situation. September 11, therefore, is construed as a protest or rebellion against the powerlessness experienced by some Muslims. Reflecting the etiology of terrorism, the Coalition argues that the United States should focus its attention on building institutions such as international criminal courts that might moderate power imbalances and therefore help eradicate the roots of terrorism. Military responses to terrorism, they continue, should be prohibited, because war only perpetuates the conditions that create terrorism.

Clear Lessons

What can we learn from the responses to "What We're Fighting For"?

1. The "Letter to America" clearly aims to expand al-Qaeda's potential base of support by defining the "us" as Islamic civilization and the "them" as the United States, the source of contemporary infidelity. The conflict that al-Qaeda urgently seeks is not a clash of governments, but an armed clash of civilizations with the Muslim world as a whole opposed to the American infidels and their allies.

2. It is only a small number of Muslims who typically call themselves jihadis, who believe that the goal of establishing this timeless Islamic order is justifiably pursued by violence. Their appropriation and misuse of the term jihad is tragic, since jihad is a classical Islamic term with multiple meanings. And even among jihadis, only a handful are also takfiris who believe that violence is justified against all persons, even Muslims, who are not jihadis. Osama bin Laden and his comrades, at least in practice, are takfiris—one fringe of a small fraction of a minority of a sub-group called Islamists, who are probably a minority of Muslims.

3. The persons who have declared war against civilization itself are the self-described jihadis and those who assist them. They have not only launched an external war against the United States and its allies, but are also waging—at times with disturbing degrees of success, despite their minority status—ongoing internal campaigns to influence and intimidate a number of Muslim societies.

4. While the letter from the Saudi intellectuals, "How We Can Coexist," was highly critical, it was respectful and called for further dialogue. The signatories to this statement were furiously and publicly denounced by Saudi militants, less for what they said than for having decided to say

anything at all to their U.S. correspondents. In particular, in their Internet communications and elsewhere, al-Qaeda insisted not merely that one or another *particular* conversation with U.S. citizens was wrong, but instead that *any* conversation—any exchange at all short of a promise of war was against the interests of Islam. One al-Qaeda–linked statement attacking the Saudi signatories said that instead of engaging in dialogue, "the signatories should have made clear to the West" that "a person has only three options: become a Muslim, live under the rule of Islam or be killed." The jihadis are seeking to prevent non-governmental leaders from the two cultures from talking to one another. Even the Saudi government seemed upset by this citizen-to-citizen exchange. Our letter that we wrote to the Saudis during this time was published in Arabic in *Al-Hayat*, the pan-Arab newspaper based in London. The Saudi authorities censored the letter, preventing that issue of *Al-Hayat* from even entering the country. What does that tell us? Maybe that in a time of war and discussions of war, and in a world facing the grim prospect of a polarization in religion and even civilization, few tasks facing intellectuals from East and West are more important than reasoning together in the hope of finding common ground on the dignity of the human person and the basic conditions for human flourishing.

5. Americans are not going to win a war of ideas against those who have truly embraced al-Qaeda's ideology. We share no common ground and therefore we have no basis on which to persuade them to believe anything else. So, while the U.S. Congressional 9/11 Commission is right to say that we must "prevail in the longer term over the ideology that gives rise to Islamist terrorism," it may be that the war of ideas will have to be fought primarily by Muslims. (2)

6. While there is significant ideological consensus among al-Qaeda and Islamists generally, direct popular support for the group does not necessarily reflect a high level of ideological agreement. Al-Qaeda's propaganda tends to bury the group's core beliefs and motivations by focusing on issues that anger or interest average Muslims, such as America's foreign policy, the Israeli-Palestinian conflict, and the corruption within some Arab regimes.

Responding to the Challenge

For those in the United States and elsewhere who wish to
see this extremist way of thinking defeated, the intellectual and
strategic imperatives are equally clear. As much as possible, we
must seek to shrink the constituency for holy war in Muslim
societies. Because al-Qaeda and similar groups seek to portray
this crisis as a war against Islam, we must deny them this
definition.

We can begin by describing what we oppose more precisely.
There are about 1.2 billion Muslims in the world—about one
of every five inhabitants. Among all Muslims, probably the
minority are Islamists, meaning that they view Islam as the
defining feature of politics and want to ensure that Islam is
the state religion. Among Islamists, a significant minority, who
themselves are hardly unified, can be described as salafists or
revivalists, meaning that they subscribe to a past, unchanging
model of Islamic law and practice based on their interpretation
of the experiences of the Prophet Muhammad and his immediate
successors.

Americans and others should specify this enemy clearly
and act upon that understanding because unlike al-Qaeda, we
want to define this struggle accurately and in light of universal
human values. "Them" is a specific network of radically intolerant
murderers and their sponsors. "Us," at least potentially, is all
people of goodwill everywhere in the world.

Americans need to be careful to not further inflame the
situation. For example, in the aftermath of September 11,
columnist Ann Coulter wrote, "we should invade their countries,
kill their leaders and convert them to 'Christianity.'" (3) Today,
Coulter regularly mocks Islam in her columns. She may imagine
that she is just striking a clever pose and it may be true that
few serious Americans take her seriously, but her comments are
widely reported in the Islamic world as those of a prominent U.S.
opinion leader.

To help thwart the al-Qaeda strategy, intellectuals in the
United States and in the Muslim world must engage with
one another on what they have in common. One important
purpose of the "Letter to America" was to challenge those Arab
intellectuals who had organized formal responses to the original
U.S. letter to participate in such an undertaking.

Conclusion

Wilberforce's formula for engaging the world on issues such as the slave trade provides an excellent model. Just as slavery was a long time in the making, so too are the challenges and problems at the core of the Islam-West debate and they will be with us for a long time to come. Engaging one another in an open and serious dialogue will not completely solve our problems. But it will be an important tool for promoting mutual understanding and, hopefully, for finding common ground. Let us continue this conversation.

Extended Observation

Reflection & Conversation

This chapter focuses on one of the thorniest and most difficult issues in the world today. Whereas Chapter 11 of this book discusses the enslavement of the mind, this chapter seeks to address the serious and, perhaps, most difficult task facing those who would create a "better hour" for the world today. Focus your reflection and your sharing on your own attitudes toward Islam. Address attitudes you need to foster within yourself to be a positive contributor to the discovery of common ground and respectful coexistence in a diverse and often hostile environment.

Attend to the Word

Read Matthew 5:43–48. Among the challenges of the Sermon on the Mount, this is no doubt the most challenging. Listen to the words carefully and with an open heart. Spend some moments in silence. How can this demanding passage form your attitudes and your actions regarding the issues discussed in this chapter?

Engage

As the chapter points out, for William Wilberforce to be successful in stopping the slave trade, he had to engage the "other side." The authors of the "Letter from America" generated a resource for scholars who are striving for East/West dialogue. Their goal is the exploration of ways to live together in a civil and global society and to seek common ground for positive engagement.

1. What is the nature of the dialogue described in the letter? How is it a "respectful dialogue" even though it builds on the premise that the political ideology of Islamism needs firm opposition?
2. In your own words, what is the fundamental argument presented in the letter entitled "What We're Fighting For"?
3. What are your personal reactions to the responses of Germany and the Middle East? Why did this issue receive so little attention in the United States?

Move Forward

The authors of the chapter posit five elements in a strategy to meet the challenges posed by violent Islam. Review those strategies. Then use the chart below to help you articulate how each step affects you, your community, and your future actions and conversations.

Strategy	How It Affects Us
Shrink the constituency.	
Clearly define opposition.	
Use the light of universal human values.	
Do not inflame the situation further.	
Engage the Muslim world on common ground.	

Pray

Use the following words of the Psalm to frame your prayer for this topic.

*The Lord is my light and my salvation
—whom shall I fear?*

*The Lord is the stronghold of my life
—of whom shall I be afraid?*

*When the wicked advance against me to devour me,
it is my enemies and my foes
who will stumble and fall.*

*Though an army besiege me,
my heart will not fear;
though war break out against me,
even then I will be confident.*

*One thing I ask from the Lord,
this only do I seek:
that I may dwell in the house of the Lord
all the days of my life.*

Psalm 27:1–4 (TNIV)

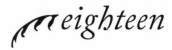

Serving the Least, the Lost, & the Last

By Chuck Colson

Charles W. Colson is a popular and widely known author, speaker, and radio commentator. A former presidential aide to Richard Nixon and founder of the international ministry Prison Fellowship, Colson has written several books—including BORN AGAIN, LOVING GOD, BEING THE BODY *and* HOW NOW SHALL WE LIVE?—*that shaped Christian thinking on many subjects. His radio broadcast,* BREAKPOINT, *airs daily to millions of listeners. In 1993, Colson was awarded the prestigious Templeton Prize for Progress in Religion. The one million dollar prize was donated to the Prison Fellowship, along with all speaking fees and book royalties. He and his wife Patty have three children and five grandchildren.*

I first heard about William Wilberforce during a visit to England in 1977, two years after I founded Prison Fellowship. During a meeting with Michael Alison, a Member of Parliament, I noticed a book on his shelf titled WILBERFORCE, by John Pollock. Curious, I picked it up and thumbed through it. "I have to read this book," I thought. In fact, I read it that week. The life of the great British abolitionist was both an inspiration and a confirmation of the rightness of the work I had just begun in America's prisons.

Wilberforce's decades-long battle to end the British slave trade began on October 25, 1787. That morning, the slight young man sat at his oak desk in the second-floor library of his home in Old Palace Yard, London. As he adjusted the flame of his lamp, the warm light shone on his piercing blue eyes, oversized nose, and high, wrinkled forehead. His eyes fell on the jumble of pamphlets on the cluttered desk. They were all on the same subject: the horrors of the slave trade—grisly accounts of human beings put up for sale, like so much cattle, for the profit of his countrymen.

The young man would begin this day, as was his custom, with a time of personal prayer and scripture reading. But his thoughts kept returning to those pamphlets. Something inside him—an insistent conviction he'd felt before—was telling him that all that had happened in his life had been for a purpose, preparing him to meet this barbaric evil head-on.

After he returned from a tour of Europe with his mother, sister, several cousins, and his old schoolmaster from Hull, Isaac Milner, Wilberforce was no longer the same frivolous young man. He returned to London in early November feeling weary and confused. In need of counsel, he sought advice from John Newton, the former captain of a slave ship who was now a committed Christian.

By the time Wilberforce knew of him, Newton was a clergyman in the Church of England, renowned for his outspokenness on spiritual matters. He counseled Wilberforce to follow Christ but not to abandon public office. "The Lord has raised you up for the good of His church and for the good of the nation," he told the younger man. (1) Wilberforce heeded his advice.

Thus, Wilberforce sat at his desk on that foggy Sunday morning in 1787 thinking about his conversion and his calling. Had God saved him only to rescue his own soul from hell? He could not accept that. If Christianity were true and meaningful, it must not only save, but also serve. It must bring God's compassion to the oppressed as well as oppose the oppressors.

His mind aflame, Wilberforce dipped his pen into the inkwell. "God Almighty has set before me two great objects," he wrote, "the suppression of the slave trade and the reformation of manners." (2)

Wilberforce knew the slavery issue had to be faced head-on in Parliament. Throughout the damp fall of 1787, he labored late into many nights on his investigation of slavery, joined by others who saw in him a champion for their cause.

In February of 1788, Wilberforce suddenly fell gravely ill. Doctors predicted he would not survive more than two weeks, but Wilberforce recovered. Although not yet well enough to return to Parliament, in March he asked Prime Minister Pitt to introduce the abolition issue in the House for him. On the basis of their long-standing friendship, the prime minister agreed.

Pitt moved that a resolution be passed binding the House to discuss the slave trade in the next session. The motion was passed. Then, another of Wilberforce's friends, Sir William Dolben, introduced a one-year experimental bill to regulate the number of slaves that could be transported per ship.

Now sensing a threat, the West Indian bloc rose up in opposition. Tales of cruelty in the slave trade were mere fiction, they claimed. Besides, warned Lord Penrhyn ominously, the proposed measure would abolish the trade upon which "two thirds of the commerce of this country depends." (3) Angered by Penrhyn's hyperbole, Pitt pushed Dolben's regulation through both houses in June of 1788.

By the time a recovered Wilberforce returned to the legislative scene, the slave traders were furious and ready to fight. They were shocked that politicians had the audacity to press for morally based reforms in the political arena. "Humanity is a private feeling, not a public principle to act upon," sniffed the Earl of Abingdon. (4) Lord Melbourne angrily agreed. "Things have come to a pretty pass when religion is allowed to invade public life," he thundered.

But Wilberforce and the band of abolitionists knew that a private faith that did not act in the face of oppression was no faith at all. Nonetheless, despite the passionate advocacy of Wilberforce, Pitt, and others, the House of Commons voted not to decide.

After twenty years of nasty fighting that took a toll on Wilberforce's health, the House of Commons, on February 22, 1807, held a second reading of Wilberforce's Bill to Abolish the Slave Trade. There was a sense that a moment in history had arrived. One by one, members jumped to their feet to decry the evils of the slave trade and praise the men who had worked so hard to end it. The entire House rose, cheering and applauding Wilberforce, who sat bent in his chair, his head in his hands, tears streaming down his face. His long battle had come to an end. The motion carried, 286 to 16.

Later, at Wilberforce's home, the old friends exuberantly crowded into the library, recalling the weary years of battle and rejoicing for their African brothers and sisters. Wilberforce looked into the lined face of his old friend Henry Thornton. "Well, Henry," Wilberforce said with a grin, "what shall we abolish next?" (5)

In the years that followed that night of triumph, a great spiritual movement swept across England, launched in great part by Wilberforce's A Practical View of the Prevailing Religious System of Professed Christians in the Higher and Middle Classes in this Country Contrasted with Real Christianity, first published in 1797. With the outlawing of the slave trade came a twenty-six year battle for the total emancipation of slaves. Social reforms expanded beyond abolition to clean up child labor laws, poorhouses, prisons, and to institute education and health care for the poor. Christianity flourished, and later in the century, missionary movements sent Christians fanning across the globe.

Wilberforce's success is all the more amazing when we consider that in his day, Britain was, spiritually speaking, sinking sand. The church was apostate, and the whole nation wallowed in self-indulgent decadence. But it was there that Wilberforce and his contemporaries took their stand, clinging to biblical truth, resisting barbaric injustice, and striving to change the heart of a nation.

This is the rich heritage of Christian activism in the public square. And it's one we ought to recall whenever Christians are accused of wanting to impose their personal religious view or when the claim is made that Christians involved in politics pose a greater threat to democracy than was presented by communism.

That would be news both to those who suffered under communism and to those whose lives were joyously transformed by Christian activism. In America as in England, it was Christians who led the fight against slavery. It was Christians who enacted child labor laws, opened hospitals, and ran charitable societies to aid widows and orphans, alcoholics, and prostitutes. And it is Christians who are acting as salt and light in our culture today, fighting against modern-day slavery in Africa, international sex trafficking, the killing of unborn children, and tyrannical efforts by judges to impose same-sex "marriage."

A Similar Experience

Like Wilberforce, I had a background in politics. And like him, I had my own "great change" in 1973, during the midst of the Watergate scandal. I was visiting Tom Phillips, president of the Raytheon Company, at his home outside of Boston. I knew Tom had become a Christian, and he seemed different. I wanted to ask him what had happened.

That night he read to me from Mere Christianity by C. S. Lewis, focusing on a chapter about the great sin that is pride. A proud man is always walking through life looking down on other people and other things, Lewis said. As a result, he cannot see something above himself that is immeasurably superior: God.

That night, Tom told me about encountering Christ in his own life. He didn't realize it, but I was in the depths of despair over Watergate, watching the president I had helped for four years flounder in office. I had also heard that I might become a target of the investigation. In short, my world was collapsing.

I listened attentively as Tom told me about Jesus. But when he offered to pray with me, I said no. I told Tom that I would see him sometime after I had read Lewis's book. But when I got into my car that night, I couldn't drive it out of the driveway. This ex-Marine and White House tough guy was crying too hard, calling out to God. I didn't know what to say; I just knew I needed Jesus, and He came into my life.

In 1974, I went to prison to serve out my three-year term for Watergate-related offenses at Maxwell Air Force Base in Montgomery, Alabama. My fellow prisoners ranged from moonshiners and embezzlers to drug dealers, armed robbers, and murderers.

Seven months later, I was released from prison. But one experience toward the end of my term kept haunting me. One night I was sitting in the common room writing a letter to my wife. Other inmates were crowded around the television or playing cards. Without warning, a tall man named Archie stood up and said, "Hey, Colson! What are you going to do for us when you get out of prison?"

I was startled, but responded, "Archie, I won't forget you guys when I leave here."

Archie threw his deck of cards on the floor. "Aw, that's what all you big shots always say, but then you forget little guys like us," he said.

In the months after my release, I was haunted by Archie's challenge. I gradually realized that I had been sent to prison for a purpose. Behind bars, I had encountered people who had no hope. They had no one to care about what happened to them. Many went year after year with no letters, no visits from family. Moreover, once released, some 65 percent of these inmates would commit more crimes and end up back behind bars. And tragically, the children of prisoners are more likely than any other group to follow their parents into the "family business" of crime. Clearly, these men needed a champion—and I was determined to give them one.

In 1976, Prison Fellowship was born in a converted townhouse five miles outside Washington in Arlington, Virginia. For $350 a month, five colleagues and I had two large rooms and one small one, enough to crowd in seven people. My son, Wendell, a proficient carpenter, was commissioned to make desks from flush doors. Within a week—and for only a few hundred dollars—Prison Fellowship was in business.

In 1977, we held our first In-Prison seminar in Oxford, Wisconsin, and began a pen-pal program, linking inmates with Christian volunteers on the outside. We began hiring regional directors to organize grassroots efforts. By the end of 1978, three thousand volunteers had joined forces with Prison Fellowship. Our goal was to form them into ministry teams to help prisoners move through a continuum of discipleship that began on the inside and continued through a successful transition back into society as faithful servants of Christ.

Between 1982 and 1990, we established a Christmas gift-giving program called Angel Tree as a means of helping prisoners keep in touch with their children. We began in-prison marriage seminars to help inmates keep their marriages together under very difficult circumstances.

Working in the prisons gave us a bird's eye view of the unique problems inmates face, and led us to form Justice Fellowship to lobby in Washington on behalf of inmates on issues such as religious freedom and prison rape.

We began printing INSIDE JOURNAL, a newspaper for inmates that now reaches every prison in America. Over the years we have held hundreds of in-prison seminars. We've sent prisoners into the community to serve others, such as winterizing the homes of elderly widows. Over the years we saw our ministry spread to other countries.

In 1986, Justice Fellowship President Dan Van Ness laid the foundation for Justice Fellowship's work for restorative justice. A biblical concept, restorative justice recognizes that we must go beyond punishing wrongdoers and reconcile criminals and victims, make criminals pay restitution, and restore offenders to the community. Restorative justice recognizes that God seeks shalom, which means not just the absence of violence, but also genuine accord and harmony.

In 1988, Prison Fellowship gave the first annual William Wilberforce Award posthumously to assassinated Filipino politician Benigno Aquino. We have since given the award to seventeen others for serving as models of the witness of real Christianity and for making a difference in the face of tough societal problems and injustices. Among the recipients are Baroness Caroline Cox of Queensbury (for her humanitarian work in Kosovo, Russia, and Armenia), Fr. Richard Neuhaus (for his commitment to biblical standards of freedom and justice), and Senator Sam Brownback (for his efforts to end slavery in Sudan and human rights violations in North Korea).

We didn't forget about the victims of crime. In 1990, Prison Fellowship began Neighbors Who Care, a pilot crime-victim assistance program in three cities. Christian volunteers picked up where the police left off, repairing homes that were broken into, buying groceries for victims of theft, and comforting those who'd been victimized by crime.

Two years later, Christian athletes, entertainers, and volunteers began holding evangelistic and follow-up events in prisons through a program called Starting Line. In 2005, 61,589 prisoners attended an Operation Starting Line event; 1,559 reported first-time commitments to Christ, while 5,792 rededicated their lives to Christ.

In 1993, we began an ex-prisoner aftercare program called Transition of Prisoners, Inc. (TOP), and contracted with Evangelistic Association of New England to start MatchPoint, a youth mentoring program.

In April of 1997, Prison Fellowship opened the first "Christian prison" in America, a special wing of a minimum-security prison called Jester II in Sugarland, Texas. The faith-based program is called InnerChange Freedom Initiative, and it is our most ambitious goal to date—nothing less than the total transformation of inmates' hearts. The program is an all-volunteer program whose curriculum is privately funded.

Inmates who volunteer for InnerChange get up at 5 A.M. for devotions, spend the day working at a job or studying for their high school equivalency exam, and attend classes to develop their life skills and spiritual maturity. Evenings are filled with more Christian teaching and discipleship seminars. Inmates must also perform community service, and they're encouraged to apologize and make restitution to their victims. Six months into the program, each inmate is matched with a church volunteer who mentors them during their remaining time in prison. The mentor also spends six months following the inmates' release, helping them adjust back into the community.

InnerChange is now operating in five prisons. Does the intense Christian focus make a difference? A University of Pennsylvania study of the Texas program proved that it did. Inmates who completed the program had an 8 percent recidivism rate compared to 65 percent of other inmates.

Thirty years after the founding of Prison Fellowship, I have come to appreciate the doctrine of providence. Our ministry now reaches more than one hundred countries. We employ more than three hundred people, and have 24,531 in-prison volunteers working in 1,604 prisons. The average monthly attendance at a Prison Fellowship program is 187,026. Over the years more than two million children have received Angel Tree gifts and gospel materials through the efforts of almost 13,000 churches. Ten thousand youngsters have attended Angel Tree summer camps, which allow the children of prisoners to leave often-dangerous urban neighborhoods for Christ-centered camps in the country.

More Change

In the mid-1980s my life took a new direction as I began an intensive study of Dutch theologian and statesman Abraham Kuyper, Francis Schaeffer, and other great Christian thinkers. I began to see that there was no way one could separate Christianity from a view of all of life. In other words, Christianity is not simply a personal experience.

I also realized that we could evangelize the prisons to great effect—and not have any impact on crime rates. We were evangelizing more and more people every year, and yet the prison population continued to rise.

What became clear to me is the same thing that became clear to Wilberforce: We cannot simply deal with a structural problem of society—be it slavery or crime—without also attempting to reverse a society's moral decline—what Wilberforce called "the reformation of manners." If we pass laws without changing hearts, we won't make any difference. People will simply disregard the laws. But if we transform the attitudes of the culture, this transformation will be *reflected* in both changed laws and a willingness to obey them.

I began to address our country's moral breakdown in the 1980s in speeches and in articles. And then, in 1984, I began writing a column in CHRISTIANITY TODAY. Seven years later, in 1991, I began a daily radio program called BREAKPOINT, a commentary on news and trends from a biblical worldview, which now reaches millions of listeners and e-mail subscribers. The worldview message was expanded into a book, HOW NOW SHALL WE LIVE? (with Nancy Pearcey) in 1999.

In 2004, we began an ambitious program to train Christians to identify, articulate, and live out a biblical worldview—and then, teach it to others. The Centurions program pulls together one hundred Christians at a time, from all over America and from all walks of life, into a year-long distance learning program and ongoing web community. We cover everything from politics to education to the arts. Centurions are then taught how to design their own worldview teaching strategy. For example, Centurions graduate Sean Copley, a Maryland graphic designer, developed a worldview curriculum and animation series for Christian television. And Centurions software consultant Rick Hooten hosted a worldview education seminar for some thirty Houston pastors.

Our Centurions have the potential to accomplish the same thing Wilberforce did—to raise up an army of Christians equipped to call the Church to greater faithfulness to God and to change our culture one person at a time by defending biblical truth.

In the first decade of the twenty-first century, Christians are increasingly—and rightfully—taking their place in the political realm, even though others would prefer that we stay quietly at home, reading our Bibles, and leave politics to them. We are often seen as extremists.

But have we really "come to a pretty pass when religion is allowed to invade public life?" as Lord Melbourne complained more than two hundred years ago—and certain critics complain today? Is Christian influence truly "a far greater threat to democracy than was posed by communism"? Nonsense.

William Wilberforce is a special inspiration for today's "extremists" who stride into the public square and stay there, despite debasement, derision, and defeat, as long as we believe that's where God wants us.

As Wilberforce wrote in the conclusion to A PRACTICAL VIEW OF CHRISTIANITY: "I must confess equally boldly that my own solid hopes for the well-being of my country depend, not so much on her navies and armies, nor on the wisdom of her rulers, nor on the spirit of her people, as on the persuasion that she still contains many who love and obey the Gospel of Christ. I believe that their prayers may yet prevail."

The confidence of Wilberforce was not misplaced. May the same hope prevail for Christians today as we, like Wilberforce, cling to biblical truth, resist barbaric injustice, and strive to change the heart of a nation.

A Statistical Epilogue

An independent research study was undertaken in 2001 to review the results of the InnerChange Freedom Initiative (IFI), which was started by Prison Fellowship in 1997 as a joint venture between the Texas Department of Criminal Justice and Prison Fellowship Ministries. Byron Johnson of the University of Pennsylvania conducted this study on the effectiveness of the program, and it was peer reviewed by colleagues at Princeton University and Harvard University. Among the results were the following:

1. Graduates of the IFI program were less than half as likely to be arrested in the two years following release than the control group: 17.3 percent of IFI graduates were arrested versus 35 percent of the control group.
2. The difference in the percentage of those being re-incarcerated was even more pronounced: only 8 percent of IFI graduates were re-incarcerated, as opposed to 20.3 percent of those who never participated.

This program is entirely voluntary and therefore legal, not costing taxpayers any money. The potential savings to society in terms of lower crime and lower prison costs are highly significant. THE WALL STREET JOURNAL, in commenting on this, report noted: "To put it another way, critics of faith-based approach may claim that their only issue is with religion. But if these results are any clue, increasingly the argument against such programs requires turning a blind eye to science." (6)

Extended Observation

Reflection & Conversation

This chapter by Chuck Colson is an intensely personal and
passionate review of the life and work of Wilberforce as
experienced by one man. That one man—a sinner and a criminal
in the eyes of many—took his political skills, his religious
conversion, and the inspiration of Wilberforce and saw in them a
call to care for the least members of society. Focus your reflection
on how this chapter affected you and challenged you personally to
respond to the needs of others.

Attend to the Word

Read Matthew 25:34–40. Many people are very aware of the
judgments of others, and they may live to please those whose
judgment they treasure most. This reading gives quite a different
look at how a person might be judged. The sheep and the goats
are separated by whether they did or did not give drink, food,
clothing, comfort, and personal attention to the very least in
society. Spend some moments in silence as you synthesize the
Gospel words and the personal witness of the chapter into a view
of how to truly have an impact on society.

Engage

There is no doubt that William Wilberforce is a hero and a model
for the author of this chapter. Chuck Colson's story has many
parallels to that of Wilberforce as a result. Through his efforts and
the efforts of his colleagues, Colson has had an impact not only
on the prisoners he has served but also upon thousands of others
he has reached by sharing his worldview. He has urged them to
embrace a worldview that reaches out to others.

1. How was Chuck Colson motivated by Wilberforce's story? What difference did that motivation make in his personal witness and actions?
2. Who are the last, the least, and the lost in your community? How are people of faith addressing their needs?
3. Why would anyone see the activism of those motivated by their Christian faith as a threat? What would be lost should that passionate activism be in any way stymied?

Move Forward

This chapter shows how important it is not to leave all social action to government. It shows how essential it is to bring one's private faith and spiritual motivations into the marketplace and the public square. The chapter also demonstrates that in a world of consumerism, it is possible to make faith into another commodity—something to be acquired and maintained for one's personal benefit. Because caring for the least of one's brothers and sisters is a fundamental principle of faith, it is difficult to see faith as real that does not exhibit this care.

1. What motivates you—drives you to action—when faced with the needs of those lost, last, and least in society?
2. Recognizing the importance of friendships and support, how will you participate with others in the work of caring for others?
3. How will you share the message that "whatever you did for these least ones, you did for me?" (Remember that actions speak louder than words.)

Pray

Gratitude is the parent of generosity. Use the psalm of
thanksgiving as a prayer to nourish your resolve to care for
the least, the last, and the lost.

> *Give thanks to the Lord, for he is good,*
> *for his steadfast love endures forever.*
>
> *It is he who remembered us in our low estate,*
> *for his steadfast love endures forever;*
>
> *and rescued us from our foes,*
> *for his steadfast love endures forever;*
>
> *who gives food to all flesh,*
> *for his steadfast love endures forever.*
>
> *O Give thanks to the God of heaven,*
> *for his steadfast love endures forever.*

Psalm 136:1, 23–26 (NRSV)

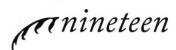

nineteen

Creating a Healthier Society

By Joseph A. Califano, Jr.

*All of Joe Califano's life has been a preparation for his current work
as an advocate for dealing with substance abuse and addictions that
ruin so many lives. In 1993 at the age of sixty, after years of politics
in the highest circles, including Lyndon Johnson's White House, Jimmy
Carter's cabinet as the last Secretary of Health, Education, and Welfare,
and years of being in influential law firms and Fortune 500 Boards,
Califano founded his life mission—the formation of the National Center
on Addiction and Substance Abuse (CASA) at Columbia University. As
Chairman, Califano has formed a top-notch cross-disciplinary team to
provide research on all forms of substance abuse—tobacco, alcohol, and
drug abuse—and programs to deal with them.*

    *Although Califano did not inherit the great wealth that
Wilberforce had, like Wilberforce, Califano believed that he had a
calling from God to serve those in the slavery of addiction and substance
abuse. Building on his success in reducing smoking on a national basis
while he was Secretary of Health, Education, and Welfare, Califano
drew upon his network and contacts to take on all of addiction and
substance abuse. He first researched the problem and then acted on the
research, just as Wilberforce did.*

    This essay is adapted from Mr. Califano's book INSIDE: A PUBLIC
AND PRIVATE LIFE.

After years of working at
the highest levels of government and in the corporate legal
world, I found myself wondering how much better our nation
would be if the monumental concentration of brain power,
energy, and creativity assembled at the law firms that I have
worked at were devoted to revitalizing public schools, fashioning

effective incentives for environmental protection and corporate responsibility, reducing poverty, or reforming cumbersome civil and criminal court systems. I had none of the satisfaction of trying to make the world, or some part of it, a little better. I did not believe that I was putting my experience, good fortune, and the talents God had given me to best use. I was itching to take on another task in life, but I had no idea where I could make a difference. I got a spark of encouragement at a dinner with Lady Bird Johnson at the LBJ Library. As we got up from the table, she put her hand on my arms and looked at me. "Joe," she said, "you were so young when you worked for Lyndon. How old are you now?"

"I am sixty, Mrs. Johnson," I answered.

"Well, let me give you some advice," she said. "Between now and seventy-five, you work very hard and play very hard. Because after that it gets a little difficult."

I began to reflect on my experience in search of clues for the best way to commit my energies. Much of my Navy time in the Office of the Judge Advocate General had been spent defending, on appeal, sailors and marines convicted at courts-martial of illegal drugs charges—usually marijuana and alcohol-related offenses—either for possession or drunkenness, or for assaults and rapes committed while high on such substances.

While on President Johnson's staff, I helped push the Drug Rehabilitation Act of 1966 through Congress, authorizing the first federal funds to treat addicts. We requested $15 million; in our wildest estimates we never thought the annual appropriation would exceed $50 million. By the 1990s, federal spending for treatment topped $2 billion.

In preparing President Johnson's message on crime, we recommended (a first for any national leader) that, in the absence of disorderly conduct or some other offense, states should treat drunkenness—then the nation's number one crime—as a disease requiring detoxification and treatment.

In the 1960s I had tried to consolidate law enforcement responsibilities to deal more effectively with the nation's burgeoning drug problem, but that didn't work. As Secretary of Health, Education, and Welfare (HEW) in 1977, I pressed an anti-smoking campaign and a program to get people interested in fighting alcoholism abuse. In the early 1980s at the request of Hugh Carey, then Governor of New York, I studied substance abuse in New York. On Chrysler's Board of Directors,

I confronted the difficulty in reducing alcohol, marijuana, and cocaine abuse and its impact on productivity and health care costs. In 1982 and 1983, as special counsel to the House Ethics Committee, I had found the widespread pill popping, illegal drug use, and abuse of alcohol among teen pages and Capitol Hill employees.

In the mid-1980s, as legal counsel for Johnson & Johnson, I got to know Jim Burke, Chairman and CEO, who had brilliantly handled the crises in the 1980s when Tylenol capsules were laced with cyanide. Now Burke was planning to retire and chair the Partnership for a Drug-Free America. "You could really do something about this and you ought to," he said. "There's no good public policy research out there. You could make a helluva contribution." Burke confronted me with articles I had written attacking the war on drugs as too narrowly focused on criminal punishment, interdiction, and illegal drugs, and calling for more research and for the creation of a National Institute on Addiction. "Don't just write about this," he challenged. "Do something."

I began discussing the problem of substance abuse with people around the nation—doctors, businessmen, lawyers, film and television artists and producers, editors and reporters, government officials, frontline experts in voluntary agencies, recovering alcoholics and drug addicts. I saw the problem as addiction—regardless whether the substance was alcohol, nicotine, or illegal or prescription drugs. To me, substance abuse was among the most pernicious threats to our society, and our political leaders were not facing up to it. I wasn't sure what I could do about that, but I struggled with what role, if any, I might be able to play. It came together for me as I witnessed the desperate struggle of my father-in-law Bill Paley, the chairman of CBS, to stay alive.

In 1990 his eighty-nine-year-old body was losing its long struggle with emphysema despite an extraordinary life of power and affluence as the founder and dominant force at CBS for half a century, in which he made it the nation's most influential broadcast network, shaping world news and American culture, and making or breaking entertainment stars and corporate executives. He had even conquered emphysema in the 1950s by quitting smoking. This man of enormous charm, energy, intelligence, presence, wealth, and independence was locked in a self-imposed prison of modern medical technology. He was shackled to plastic and stainless steel tubes for oxygen in his

master bedroom to help him breathe, dialysis equipment to do
the work of his failed kidneys, and machines to pump his blood
and keep his heart beating. Tubes fed him intravenously, drained
his waste, and vented blood from his internal bleeding.

As my wife and I saw him draw his final breath, it was
heartbreaking for both of us. All that night I lay awake next to
my wife, reflecting with awe on all that this gargantuan man had
built. All his money and power, I thought, had offered him little
comfort as he lay dying. As I tossed, I thanked God for enriching
much of my own life by His gifts of faith, and I rued the fact that
I had spent so much time and energy on selfish pursuits. By dawn
I had silently determined to live the rest of my life getting to
know, love, and serve God better.

The afternoon of Bill's memorial service, my wife and I
walked uptown along the Central Park side of Fifth Avenue.
We talked about what had happened and what it meant to us.
With instincts as perceptive and a heart as loving as any I've ever
encountered, my wife volunteered before I even had a chance to
tell her what was on my mind: "You know you can do whatever
you want now, what you believe in. I have enough to take care of
the children and myself. You don't have to keep making so much
money."

With God making it this easy, I thought I had better deliver
on the promise I made to him last night.

Forming CASA

Buoyed by the support of family and friends, I decided to put
together a new organization, a think/action tank that would
assemble all the professional skills needed to research and combat
abuse of all substances, in all sectors of society.

As I thought about it, I decided to affiliate with a university.
I talked to several including Harvard, Yale, Columbia, and New
York University. Columbia seemed to be the best fit. On March 5,
1991, Herb Pardes, the brilliant psychiatrist whom I had recruited
to head the National Institute of Mental Health when I was at
HEW and who was now vice president for medical affairs at
Columbia University, urged me to talk with Columbia president
Michael Sovern, with whom I had a passing acquaintance.

A big break occurred before I sat down with Mike Sovern.
I met with Dr. Steven Schroeder, the newly installed president

of the Robert Wood Johnson Foundation. As I made my
presentation, I detected a sense of excitement in this academic
from San Francisco who had been named to vitalize the world's
then-largest foundation devoted to health. I found out why when
he said, "I've just concluded a six-month assessment of where to
take the foundation. I am going to my board soon with a proposal
to concentrate in three areas: health care costs, access to health
care—especially for those with chronic ailments—and substance
abuse." I was overjoyed. Like me, Schroeder saw the problem
as addiction, not as separate problems linked to one or another
substance. He asked me to put together a complete proposal. As
an academic, and for reasons of scientific credibility, he thought it
important to affiliate with a university.

I then met with Mike Sovern and Herb Pardes on April 26.
Sovern and Pardes understood the concept and were prepared
to support the creation of a center within the Columbia family.
Such a center would demonstrate Columbia's determination to
tackle an area of serious concern for New York's Harlem and
Washington Heights communities, where the university and
its medical school were situated. Since the university could not
provide financial support, the center must have its own board and
raise its funds independently. While the center would be closely
aligned with Columbia's schools of medicine and public health,
it would stand alone at the university. That would make it easier
to work with all the graduate schools, such as business, law, and
the renowned Teachers College. This was a key attraction of
Columbia because no one would look at the center as being a part
of another graduate school.

After setting up a team to negotiate the details with
Columbia, I approached David Hamburg of the Carnegie
Corporation, Margaret Mahoney of the Commonwealth Fund,
David Mahoney of the Dana Foundation, Frank Thomas of
the Ford Foundation, and Drew Altman of the Kaiser Family
Foundation. They were willing to commit the necessary core
funding to get the center off the ground, if I were willing to
give it my all. As Steve Schroeder put it, "You commit and we'll
commit." I decided to retire completely from the practice of law
and devote my full time to this new enterprise.

Following a weekend during which my wife and I made that
decision, we had dinner with John and Patty Rosenwald. John,
along with Ace Greenberg, had built Bear Sterns into a Wall
Street powerhouse. He was then the firm's vice chairman. Upon

hearing my idea, John's immediate response was, "If you're going to give your life to this, I'm going to be your first supporter. I'm committing a hundred thousand dollars to help get you started."

Another vote of support came from Sandy Weill, then-chairman of Primerica Corporation, en route to building the financial behemoth Citigroup, on whose corporate board I served. "We'll have a lot of battles with tobacco, alcohol and beer companies," I told Sandy, "so I should resign. I know there'll be financial opportunities in those industries for you."

"Joe," Weill said instantly, "I want you more than ever as a board member. And I'll help you raise money." Weill suggested that I ask for five-year commitments from corporations to show continuing support. "In what amounts?" I asked. "Ask for fifty thousand dollars a year," he said. "Most CEOs can easily do that, and it isn't likely to inhibit their ability to take care of all their pet projects." I decided on the spot to adopt that strategy. Before I could even ask Weill if he would get the ball rolling, he said, "You've got my commitment, now use it to get others."

Twelve Years Later

In my "Message from the Chairman" in 2004, I was able to report that the National Center on Addiction and Substance Abuse (CASA) had released fifty-five reports based on intensive research on the relationship of substance abuse and addiction to a variety of the nation's social problems and conditions. CASA reports have covered topics such as the child welfare system, the dangers of non-medical marijuana, America's underage drinking epidemic, diversion of prescription drugs, and the nation's adult and juvenile justice system. We had developed and tested programs for high-risk eight- to thirteen-year-old children and teens, mothers and children on welfare, families involved in child welfare systems, individuals released from prison, and communities in public housing projects at more than one hundred sites in forty-five cities and counties in twenty-two states. We had surveyed teens and their parents, teachers, and school administrators about smoking, drinking, and drug use in an effort to identify those situations and characteristics that influence teen substance abuse risk. We had held eleven CASACONFERENCES, bringing together top experts to discuss the relationship between substance abuse and addiction to eating disorders, learning disabilities, spirituality, pain management, sexual activity, the American family, and other subjects.

We still had much to learn, but our work during the past twelve years had taught us a great deal about the use and abuse of alcohol, tobacco, and illegal, prescription, and performance-enhancing drugs. Armed with that knowledge and experience in the field, CASA decided to launch a new initiative in 2004 to encourage American institutions to implement policies and practices that we are convinced will reduce Americans' risk of substance abuse, and help abusers and addicts achieve and maintain sobriety. To test our capacity to do this effectively, we had selected three areas that we believed have the greatest potential to influence our nation's children—families, school, and religious institutions. We had chosen to concentrate on children because our research had consistently demonstrated that a child who gets through age twenty-one without smoking, using illegal drugs, or abusing alcohol is virtually certain never to do so.

We have spread the message of our family effort through Family Day—A Day To Eat Dinner With Your Children and CASA's annual NATIONAL SURVEY OF AMERICAN ATTITUDES ON SUBSTANCE ABUSE. Family Day is celebrated on the fourth Monday in September as a reminder of the importance of parental engagement in the lives of children.

To effect change in schools, CASA has been working on a national expansion of CASASTART (Striving Together to Achieve Rewarding Tomorrows), our school-based demonstration program for high-risk eight- to thirteen-year-old children and teens. CASASTART has received numerous awards and is recognized by the federal government as an effective substance abuse and delinquency prevention program. The program has been proven not only to improve academic performance and reduce disciplinary problems for high-risk children, but in many schools to change the entire environment and increase test scores across the board. We believe that CASASTART should be available to every child in America who can benefit from it.

CASA research has found that nine out of ten priests, ministers, and rabbis consider substance abuse an important issue among their congregations, yet only one in ten clergy receives any substance abuse training in their seminaries and rabbinical schools. Building on the findings of the CASA report, CASACONFERENCES, and So HELP ME GOD: SUBSTANCE ABUSE, RELIGION, AND SPIRITUALITY, we are mobilizing an effort to encourage more religious education programs to provide more substance abuse training to clergy, urging clergy to work with medical professionals to combat substance abuse, and recommending discussion of substance abuse and addiction in sermons, newsletters, and other congregational events.

Conclusion

When people ask how would I like to be remembered—as a McNamara whiz kid, an LBJ assistant, an architect of the great Society, the Washington Post lawyer during Watergate, the originator of the anti-smoking campaign, or the founder of The National Center on Addiction and Substance Abuse at Columbia University, I answer the same way Supreme Court Justice Thurgood Marshall wanted to be remembered: "as someone who did the best he could with what God gave him."

And I would add that I want to be remembered as someone who tried to make a few waves to improve the world around them. This is what Wilberforce and the Clapham Circle did with their lives. This is what I am doing with my life.

Extended Observation

Reflection & Conversation

Joe Califano was wealthy and was at the peak of an outstanding career. Yet he chose to change his life and dedicate it to serving people who suffered from addictions. His choice, like the choice William Wilberforce made, was motivated by faith. This chapter is both a testimony and a biographical example of how people can leverage their faith, their talents, their relationships, and their resources to change the world. Let your sharing and reflection focus on how this worked in the life of Joe Califano and how it could work in your life as well.

Attend to the Word

Read Matthew 25:14–30. This is one of the most familiar of all Jesus' parables. It is a dramatic tale of the value of using the "wealth" one has received. In Matthew's Gospel this parable is juxtaposed with the parable of the great judgment you read in the last chapter. That is no accident. Spend some moments in silence looking at the gifts you have received. How are you using them now for the good of others? What return are you getting on your "investment"? What reaction would you receive if you were asked for an accounting of the use of your talents this very day?

Engage

Review the experience of Joe Califano that helped him decide to change his life and work for the health and welfare of the addicted.

1. What effect did the death of his father-in-law have on Califano? Why would anyone want to make the changes he made in his life and career? Does it make sense to you? Why or why not?
2. How did Califano's talents and life experience prepare him for his "great objective"?
3. How is your life experience preparing you—providing you with "talents"—to actively engage in working for the good of your world?

Move Forward

This chapter demonstrates that there are many ways to work for the betterment of society, to engage culture, and to make changes for the better. In short, there are many ways to "create the better hour."

1. What current and important social ill do you have the talent to tackle? What are you doing about that social ill at this time?
2. If you have not already done so, how are you going to use your talents, skills, resources, and personal networks in the service of making the world a better place?

3. What can you do to enlist others into groups of friends and associates who act consistently for the good of others?

Pray

There is a gospel story about Jesus healing the servant of a prominent Roman centurion. Embedded in that story is a prayer that can be a true mantra for those who would work for the "better hour."

The Prayer:

> *"Lord, I am not worthy to have you come under my roof; but only speak the word, and my servant will be healed."*

The Answer:

> *"Go; let it be done for you according to your faith."*

Matthew 8:8, 13 (NRSV)

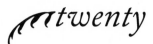

In Memoriam

By Benjamin F. Hughes

This chapter is a eulogy by Benjamin Hughes—a man of color. It demonstrates the significant impact that William Wilberforce had on the United States even though he had never traveled here. Sometime in September of 1833, "the Free People of Color in the United Sates" heard about the death of Wilberforce, which had occurred on July 29, 1833. The officers of the society met at the black Presbyterian Church in New York to draft resolutions expressing regret felt by the people of color for the death of Wilberforce and to request "the most extensive manifestations of feeling be recommended to the people of color throughout the United States, particularly in this State."

Below are first the Resolutions that the officers of the Free People of Color made, followed by the eulogy.

⟶ While we most humbly acquiesce in the providence of God—the all-wise Sovereign Ruler of the Universe—we most deeply regret the demise of our friend, that distinguished patron and benefactor of man, William Wilberforce, Esq.

Therefore be it resolved:

That the colored freemen, throughout the United States, and especially in this city, be requested to wear the usual badge of mourning for thirty days, in testimony of their sympathy and respect for the deceased, to commence with the Sabbath next.

That the Pastors of the colored Churches in this city be requested to deliver discourses in the several Churches, as soon as practicable, descriptive of the life and virtues of the late William Wilberforce.

That a committee of five be appointed to select a suitable person to deliver an Eulogy on the Life and Character of the distinguished Philanthropist whose death we so much lament.

Whereupon, Rev. Samuel E. Cornish, Rev. Theodore S. Wright, James Fraser, Henry Sipkins, and Charles Mortimer were appointed to that Committee; who reported, that they had selected Mr. Benjamin F. Hughes, Principal of the Free School, No. 3., the Orator. (1)

The Eulogy

The praises of departed greatness have ever been said or sung, in the lofty tones of the orator, or in the enchanting strains of the poet.

The statues of heroes and princes and the encomiums of statesmen have proclaimed their worth, as the martial prowess of the one, or the brilliant genius of the other, may have fired the world, or attracted the admiration of men.

The splendid achievements of Napoleon, amid "the bristling points of countless bayonets" and deluged fields of blood, leave him unrivalled in the annals of war. He stood forth a prodigy that overawed the world,

"The King that levell'd haughty Troy." (2)

Napoleon and the band the preceded him in ambition's lawless strife have ceased to breathe—their swords to other hands have passed, their crowns on other heads are placed. A thousand tongues have their praises told—a thousand songs their requiem sung.—The scourge of mankind, the extirpator of his species, the Corsican, is no more; and with him sleep those vast designs, which convulsed the world in bloody contest for empire.—He lives, however, in the hearts of the nation he aggrandized; his cenotaph has been erected in the *Place Vendome*.

There is a charm that attracts the admiration of men to their destroyers; a propensity to applaud those very acts that bring misery on the human race; and on the other hand to pass by unheeded, the placid and even tenor of the real benefactors of their species.

The prodigious in nature and in morals arouse the stupor of the unthinking multitude; they stare and are astonished; while the steady lustre of those heavenly bodies which from age to age maintain their wonted position to cheer the inhabitants of earth—and the moral sublimity of the untiring zeal of philanthropy and virtue, have no allurements, and are of no consideration. But there is a spectacle more glorious and venerable than the transient blaze of a meteor; or the triumphant entry of a conqueror. It is the benign manifestation of those nobler feelings of our nature on behalf of the oppressed; in munificently extending the arms to embrace and succour the unprotected; it is that species of love to man, designated philanthropy; it is not circumscribed within the narrow precincts of country, restricted to religion or party;—it is co-extensive with the world.

Hence, of all men, it is to the Philanthropist that we are chiefly indebted; it is upon his disinterested deeds that we are to stare;—and his is the memory for which we should cherish the fondest recollections. How appropriate then will be our expression this day of the unrivalled worth of a distinguished benefactor of the African Race!

My friends, we have assembled hither under no ordinary circumstances, for no ordinary purpose: it is to announce to you that William Wilberforce is dead! it is to speak his praise.

I present you no bloodstained hero; he has led no slaughtering armies, he has desolated no kingdoms; for him no triumphal arch is reared; his laurels have been won in another and nobler sphere. He was aspirant to popular applause; no time-serving politician; he was the friend of the "robbed and peeled;" (3) he was not one of those, who having fattened on the spoils of the African, turned monitor and moralized the world on the atrocity of the traffic in slaves; he was a perfect character,

"That shot effulgence like the solar ray." (4)

Yes! the earthly career of him, who was emphatically one of the greatest men of the greatest nation of modern times, was terminated on the 29th day of July last; and in him fell the Hercules of Abolition. The frosts of three score and ten had bleached his brow; their snows had whitened his locks; but they did not abate his fervor in his favorite theme.

A distinguished author remarks, that "there is no man who, in a case where he was a calm by-stander, would not look with more satisfaction on acts of kindness than on acts of cruelty. No man after the first excitement of his mind has subsided, ever whispered to himself with self-approbation and secret joy that he had been guilty of cruelty or baseness. Every criminal is strongly impelled to hide these qualities of his actions from himself, as he would do from others, by clothing his conduct in some disguise of duty or necessity."—Now, in the retrospect, if this be fact, in what light are we to consider those persons engaged in promoting the slave trade, despite prohibitory Legislative enactments, backed too by a consciousness of its barbarity? And with whom shall we class those, who on the ground of expediency would rivet faster the chains of the enslaved, and ferret from their homes new victims to supply their place, when they shall have been worn out with toil, or murdered in tortures? It is enough that we know that such fiendlike wretches exist, but that their triumph is visionary.

Mr. Wilberforce was one of the earliest and ablest advocates for the abolition of the slave trade; and in the midst of that assemblage of talent and benevolence which his eloquence and perseverance elicited, he was brightest of the train. He led the valiant band, and pointed onward as to certain conquest.

It is not essential that we enquire by what authority the slave trade originated, or through what instrumentality it was promoted and continued. It is enough to know that it had assumed a shape most odious; a course most demoralizing and devastating to the human species, when the powers of the illustrious Wilberforce were brought into requisition to its overthrow. On Mr. Clarkson's application to him in 1787 to introduce into Parliament its legislative abolition, he at once evidenced the benevolent structure of his mind, in expressing the hearty interest he had felt on the subject, and his readiness to co-operate in the suppression of the greatest evil ever conceived and propagated by man. Nor was he lacking in the redemption of his pledge; for in the year 1788, we find him giving notice in the House of Commons, of a motion for the abolition of the slave trade. And, although he was prevented by indisposition from introducing this measure, still the object was effected at other hands, through the influence he had with Mr. Pitt, his compatriot and friend. (5) The consequence was, the passage of a resolution, to consider the subject at the ensuing session of Parliament.

Commiseration for human suffering and human sacrifice, awakened the capacious mind, and brought into action the enlarged benevolence of this amiable man. He had surveyed this theatre of more than heathenish barbarity; he had contemplated the myriads of inhabiting the vast and interesting regions of Africa; their general character for hospitality; their docility and extensive capacity; and the high estate from which they had fallen. He beheld the extensive coasts of Africa, for thousands of miles depopulated; the wretched victims manacled, driven herds to their floating prisons; encountering all the evils attendant on a voyage peculiar to the trade; the prey of pestilence. Or the voyage terminated—landed in the Colonies; emaciated by disease; examined as beasts of burden; selected by a master; separated, sold and scourged to obedience.—But ah! Avarice thou monster of the soul, thy reign shall not forever last. Awake, philanthropy! And drive the hydra from his throne.

In addition to the brutal usage of the kidnapped African upon the plantations of the Colonies, by the inhuman planter, evidence the most abundant and conclusive had been elicited, to prove a yet more wanton waste of human life. Hundreds of these miserable beings had been thrown alive into the sea, while laboring under the most painful diseases contracted in the corrupt and pestilential atmosphere of a ship's hold, to defraud the underwriters, by claiming indemnity for their loss, as though their death had been ordinary and natural. (6)

In view of all this evil, the soul of Wilberforce shuddered at the thought of Africa's universal ruin; his indignation was aroused; his philanthropy was kindled into flame.

To test the capacity of the African, and to refute the slanderous assertions that he was being of interior origin, and only fitted for servitude, he organized, upon his own resources, a school at Clapham, in which he admitted to instruction several African youths. (7) In these he was enabled triumphantly to hold up to public view, the unqualified likeness of the intellectual structure of Africa's sable sons to that of their fairer brethren.

> *"Fleecy locks, and black, complexion,*
> *Cannot forfeit Nature's claim;*
> *Skins may differ, but affection*
> *Dwells in black and white the same. . . .*
> *Deem our nation brutes no longer,*
> *Till some reason you shall find,*
> *Worthier of regard, and stronger,*
> *Than the color of our kind.*
> *Slaves of gold! Whose sordid dealings*
> *Tarnish all your boasted powers,*
> *Prove that you have human feelings,*
> *Ere you proudly question ours."* (8)

Accordingly in the year 1789, he again directed the attention of Parliament to this momentous subject. But he had almost insuperable difficulties to encounter; specious arguments to over throw; powerful foes to combat. He was opposed on the ground of expediency, of humanity, nay, *even of religion*. It is expedient, said they, that the slave trade should be continued; for in the event of its abolition, the produce of labor must of necessity demand a higher price in market; that the lands must be cultivated; and that the Africans are a race born for slavery; their dispositions narrow, treacherous and wicked; that therefore they are fit subjects for servitude, and that without their labor, ruin must ensue to the Colonist and to the Merchant. On the ground of humanity, it was urged that the African was subject to be immolated in the religious observances of the pagan, and that in his removal from the scene of a rite so horrid, the cause of humanity was subserved. And, to cap the climax, they gravely and piously told, that the easiest and surest method of imparting religion to an African, was, to kidnap and transport him amid the horrors of the middle passage to a foreign land, where nature's sweetest solace all are lost—wife, parent, kindred, home.

Such are the arguments which were sagely devised to retard, if not forever, to suppress the holy cause of abolition. The cry of "down with the fanatic! Down with the incendiary!" was raised, too, against the friend of abolition. But the thunders of Wilberforce silenced and discomfited this array of opposition. On the 12th of May, of the year above named, he entered upon the great work before him with the power of a giant. "In endeavoring," said he, "to explain the great business of the day, he should call the attention of the house only to the leading features of the slave trade. Nor should he dwell long upon these. Every one might imagine for himself, what must be the natural consequences of such a commerce with Africa. Was it not plain that she must suffer from it? That her savage manners must be rendered still more ferocious? And that a trade of this nature carried on round her coasts, must extend violence and desolation to her very center? It was well known that the natives of Africa were sold as goods and that numbers of them were continually conveyed away from their country, by the owners of British vessels. The question then was, which way the later came by them? In answer to this question, the Report of the Privy Council, which was then on the table, afforded evidence the most satisfactory and conclusive."

In continuance of this speech, he proceeded to show the manner in which the slaves were obtained; (9) village instigated against village, kingdom against kingdom, by the slave-trader; truces broken; treaties violated; treachery the most foul;

conflicts the most murderous, resorted to in order to supply the trade with the person of the captives. Hamlets fired, and the peaceable inmates rendered most wretched, by being inhumanly dragged—the husband from wife, the father from his children. He depicted in the most glowing colors, and with the highest indignation the victims' transportation and exposed the duplicity of the witnesses examined on behalf of the trade party. He then examined the contrary evidence and poured upon the subject a flood of light. "Men of the greatest veracity" had given an account widely at variance with that on the other side: the rejoicing of the slaves spoken of, was the most melancholy and heart-rending lamentation at leaving their country; instead of the spacious apartments fitted up for their accommodations, "they were placed in niches and along the decks, in such a manner, that it was impossible for any one to pass among them, however careful he might be, without treading upon them. Instead of the scent of frankincense being perceptible to the nostrils, the stench was intolerable. The allowance of water so deficient, that the slaves were frequently found gasping for life, and almost suffocated. The pulse with which they had been said to be favored, absolutely English horse-beans. Their song and dance forced by the terror and actual use of the lash. Their songs were songs of lamentation for the loss of their country—they sung in tears. The mortality on the passage in the ratio of twelve and a half percent."

Having advanced thus far in the investigation, he felt the wickedness of the slave trade to be so enormous, so dreadful, and irremediable, that he would stop at no alternative short of its abolition. A trade founded on iniquity, and carried on with such circumstances of horror, must be abolished, let the policy of it be what it might: he had from this time determined, whatever were the consequences, that he would never rest till he had effected that abolition.

Thus, in substance, spake the sage—and thus was laid the base of that noble structure which adorns the British name, Abolition. By this speech, an impression was made upon every heart not formed of stone, which no lapse of time could efface. It drew down the applause of Burke, and Pitt, and Fox—no ordinary names in legislation; and secured to its author a fame imperishable as truth, enduring as eternity.

In 1790, Mr. Wilberforce again called the attention of the house to the subject of the Slave Trade. But the struggle was not thus to terminate; the enemy had been on the alert, and that which he could not support on the ground of justice or expediency, he drowned, for a time, in clamor. Philanthropy had therefore to prepare for renewal of the combat; she had to collect her forces, furbish her arms, gird on her armor and again repair to the breach, which she had already made in the old of her adversary.

In 1791, the hero of abolition re-appeared on the field; and in a long and brilliant speech, unsurpassed for fearlessness of manner and purity of thought, he further exposed the evils attendant to the traffic in human beings; the fallacy of the arguments urged for its continuance; and dilated on the advantages and blessings which would inevitably result from abolition. This speech he thus concludes:

> It is the nest of serpents, which would never have existed so long, but for the darkness in which they lay hid. The light of day would now be let in upon them, and they would vanish from the sight. For himself, he declared that he was engaged in a work, which he would never abandon. The consciousness of the justice of his cause, would carry him forward, though he were alone; but he could not but derive encouragement from considering with whom he was associated. Let us not despair. It is a blessed cause; and success, ere long will crown our exertions. Already we have gained one victory. We have obtained for these poor creatures, the recognition of their human nature, which for a while, was most shamefully denied them. This is the first fruits of our efforts. Let us persevere, and our triumph will be complete. Never, never will we desist, till we have wiped away this scandal from the Christian name; till we have released ourselves from the load of guilt under which we at present labor; and till we have extinguished every trace of this bloody traffic, which our posterity, looking back to the history of these enlightened times, will scarcely believe had been suffered to exist so long, a disgrace and a dishonor to our country. (10)

By this speech additional light and strength were elicited, and our champion was prepared, to renew the fight at the session of 1792 with increased vigor. For though the abettors of this nefarious traffic flattered themselves that they had gained a signal victory in the late defeat of the abolition party, to use the language of the historian, "the current ran with such strength and rapidity, that it was impossible to stem it." (11)

The subject of our eulogy brought forth new evidence of the evils attending the commerce in question—"its cruelty, its perfidy; its effects on the Africans as well as on the Europeans," and that the morality consequent upon the crowded state of slave-vessels, in connection with other circumstances, would entirely depopulate the globe, if it were only general for a few months. And after having labored assiduously to convince these countrymen of the injustice and barbarity of what they were willing to term expediency and humanity, he effected the passage of a resolution for the gradual abolition of the Slave-trade; thus effecting that which, although far short of his aim and desire, was infinitely more than could possibly have been accomplished at less able hands, and by a less devoted and persevering agent.

Year after year did the indefatigable Wilberforce urge the immediate abolition of this trade; it was not, however, until the 25th of March 1807, that he was enabled to accomplish this great end, for which he seems to have been created. (12) He had solemnly pledged himself not to lay down his arms, till victory should have declared for him. From his youth he had been engaged in this moral contest; and after almost incessant labor, he achieved the most signal moral triumph the world ever witnessed; and most incontestably proved himself the most distinguished benefactor of the human race.

On what subject was there ever arrayed a brighter train of talents than on this; and where could there have been found a leader, more humane, more accomplished, or more determined? He foresaw and aimed at the ultimate accomplishment of the entire emancipation of the British colonies, which he laid the foundation, by annihilating the commerce in man. The desire of his heart had been met. Not only is the Slave-trade abolished so far as Britain is concerned, but by her treaties with other nations, they too have been led to adopt measures for its final abolition. Not only is this trade prohibited, but the African and his descendant in all the territorial dependence of Great Britain have been admitted to *the rights of freemen*, and millions yet unborn are freed from the curse of slavery.

From this imperfect and brief sketch of the public character of William Wilberforce, Esq., we behold in him a man against whom no political opponent could say more, than that he was misled by the benevolence of his nature. All appreciated his

motives; all admired his talents and revered his patriotism.—
With whom shall we compare him? Shall we seek a parallel in
the warrior, the philosopher, or the patriot of antiquity—for
surely none of modern times, however eminent, can compete with
him for excellence? Shall we call from among the ancient dead,
the Fabii, and Cato, and Pompey, and Alexander, and Caesar?
In these we frequently see traits of courage and fortitude which
emblazon their names on the page of history. But their path to
fame was stained with blood; ambition's lustful fire moved them
to deeds, the renown of which dazzled their contemporaries. And
whatever degree of honor, or glory, or profit, may have accrued to
their respective nations, it was purchased with human blood and
human life. But our hero was invulnerable to ambition; and yet in
his career, *he shone a cloudless sun*.

With respect to his philosophy—it was of noble cast. It was,
that all men are by nature equal; that they are wisely and justly
endowed by the creator with certain rights, which are irrefragable;
and that however human pride and human avarice may depress and
debase, still, God is the author of good to man—and of evil, man is
the artificer himself and to his species. Unlike Plato and Socrates,
his mind was free from the gloom that surrounded theirs.

His philosophy was founded in the school of Christianity;
for be it known that Mr. Wilberforce was a Christian. He was
not only an exemplary and devoted member of the established
church; but at the time when religion was only noticed in
the higher circles to be scoffed at, he became the author
of a work entitled A POPULAR VIEW OF CHRISTIANITY. (13) A
work, pronounced to be "one of the most valuable and useful
publications of this or any age, and which has been rendered the
instrument of religious benefit to multitudes of persons, who
could not be induced to look into any religious books which
came before them less strongly recommended." (14) By his
writings and example in favor of moral reform, it is said that "he
established around him a circle of pious men, which has gradually,
but constantly been extending itself till it has at length included
within it many characters in every class of life, political, literary
and scientific." (15) What a weight of character this individual
must have possessed, if under such circumstances, he could have
influenced polite society to religious reading and meditation. And
how uniformly consistent he must have been to have taken the
stand of "Leader of the religious world."—How very unlike many
sordid professors of the day and their time-serving clergy!

If we consider his patriotism—what are the acts of Epaminondas and Brutus in comparison? Epaminondas the Theban fell with his country and Marcus Brutus the Roman imbued his hands in the blood of his friend to free the commonwealth from tyranny. But the subject of our eulogy devoted his life to remove from his country a stigma more debasing than tyranny, more destructive than the most potent foe. Numa and Lycurgus, the famed Legislators of Rome and Greece—the one called fiction to aid in legislation, and the other stands convicted of inhumanity; but in his legislative capacity, Wilberforce was conspicuous for humanity. His love of country, and love of liberty, and humanity and piety, were the springs which moved his soul to action. In aggrandizing his country, he redressed the grievances of those she oppressed; and in relieving the oppressed he conferred benefits upon many millions of the human race—benefits the most important and inestimable.

I have said that Mr. Wilberforce was a perfect character. Will any dispute the assertion?—Was there ever a man in whom so many virtues blended? In whom there existed such a constellation of splendid qualities? No; he stood alone, without a superior and without a rival.

In private life, Mr. Wilberforce is represented to have been alike free from self-importance or arrogance as he was in the discharge of his public functions. He was cheerful and animated; entertaining in conversation; instructive to youth; the consoler of the poor and afflicted; and it may be assumed, without danger of controversy, that the loss of no individual can be more sensibly felt in the domestic and social circles, as well as in the empire of which he was a subject. As an evidence that he lives in the hearts of his countrymen, the tribute of respect paid to his remains, abundantly attests. His funeral was attended by some of the most distinguished personages of the realm, and his remains lie in peaceful serenity by the side of his co-workers in the stupendous scheme of abolition, Pitt, Fox, and Canning.

Peace to his ashes! He has fought the fight, obtained the victory and wears the crown. But if it were that departed spirits are permitted to note the occurrences of this world, with what a frown of disapprobation would *his* view, the effort being made in this hemisphere to retard the work of emancipation for which he so long and so faithfully labored. In what light would he consider the hypocritical priesthood who give their aid to foster a popular prejudice against a portion of the community to whom they are immeasurably indebted; who enter the lists in a crusade against the imprescriptible rights of man, because in thus acting they obtain countenance and applause from the kidnapper and robber.

And here it will not be amiss to notice that which is perhaps the last public act of Mr. Wilberforce, viz. his "Protest" against the American Colonization Society. (16) Here the language of "the Protest":

> *While we believe its pretext to be delusive, we are convinced that its real effects are of the most dangerous nature. It takes its roots from a cruel prejudice and alienation in the whites of America against the colored people, slave or free. This being its source the effects are what might be expected: that it fosters and increases the spirit of caste, already so unhappily predominant; that it widens the breach between the two races—exposes the colored people to great practical persecution, in order to* force *them to emigrate; and finally, it is calculated to swallow up and divert that feeling which America, as a Christian and a free country, cannot but entertain, that slavery is alike incompatible with the law of God and with the well-being of man, whether the enslaver or the enslaved.*

What a pointed rebuke of Colonizationists and their scheme of delusion! The seal of disapprobation is affixed! And when at some future age, this stain on the page of history shall be pointed at, posterity shall blush at the discrepancy between American profession and American principle.

And could the voice of Wilberforce again be heard, we should hear him declaim in accents of thunder—"The clergy are out of their appropriate sphere—and the church is corrupt that yields them its tolerance".

That religion which seeks to trammel the mind, is but a "gorgeous fabric of self-righteousness," worse than the superstitious rites of the heathen. God will reward the despoiler of His beauteous fabric, the image of Himself!

Friends, we have arrived at a crisis most eventful. The benefactor of Africa—our benefactor—is no more! The structure he began is nigh to its completion; yet much depends upon ourselves. The philanthropists who follow in the path of Wilberforce have much difficulty to encounter, many foes to overcome. They have already passed the Rubicon—nevertheless, our individual assistance is necessary. Union, intelligence, perseverance *must, shall* accomplish the object of pursuit. Then shall the heart of every philanthropist glow with rapture at the scene, and the labors of the immortal chief yield us an abundant harvest in fruition.

Let the name and worth of Wilberforce ever live in our hearts; let his deeds ever be the theme of our praise; and when, our tyrants shall have ceased to press, let us dedicate the trophy to *his worth*, and teach our babes his hallowed name to love and bless.

Extended Observation

Reflection & Conversation

Throughout this book, you have studied the life of William Wilberforce, and an interesting and powerful life it was. But the purpose of your study and reflection is far greater than to become steeped in the lore of this great Parliamentarian. The purpose is to learn how to become an active creator of the "better hour" for this world—how to join with others to make a wonderful difference in your family, your neighborhood, your city, your country, and your world. Focus your reflection and your sharing on the impact for good you and your friends can have.

Attend to the Word

Read Psalm 112:1–10. This is a wisdom psalm that contrasts the fate of the righteous and that of the wicked. It continues the tenor and impact of Benjamin Hughes's eulogy. This psalm should be read aloud. Spend some time in silence pondering its poetic lines.

Engage

It is amazing to realize that a black Presbyterian church in New York would be packed to overflowing on the occasion of a memorial for a diminutive white politician an ocean away. Wilberforce's passionate concern for the sufferings of humankind and his dogged determination to end slavery were the reasons he was memorialized.

1. What words would you most like to hear in a eulogy for your life on earth? How can your eulogy be written by your actions on behalf of others?
2. If you can, distill all you have learned about making goodness fashionable, about creating the "better hour," and about the legacy of William Wilberforce into one phrase or simple sentence.
3. What role does forgiveness and reconciliation play in your work for the good of society?

Move Forward

As you have come to realize, the life's work of William Wilberforce is not complete. With all that he accomplished in his lifetime, his two great objectives remain unmet. There is still slavery and oppression in the world, and there is much in public morality—manners, if you will—that are in need of repair.

1. How will you personally continue the work of these two great objectives?
2. What do you see as the biggest obstacle to your work in creating the better hour?
3. How can you keep yourself motivated to make part of your life story the care, concern, and hope you give to others?

Pray

The Episcopal Church in the United States commemorates the life and work of William Wilberforce on July 30. The collect for that day is a fitting prayer for the final chapter of this book.

Let your continual mercy, O Lord, kindle in your Church the never-failing gift of love, that, following the example of your servant William Wilberforce, we may have grace to defend the poor, and maintain the cause of those who have no helper; for the sake of him who gave his life for us, your Son our Savior Jesus Christ, who lives and reigns with you and the Holy Spirit, one God, now and forever. Amen.

The Proper for Lesser Feasts and Fasts,
Church Publishing Inc., New York, page 309

PART **IV**

A Commitment to Action
on Behalf of Others

Leaven in the Loaf

Throughout this book, you have followed a path that was essential to the life's work of William Wilberforce. For each of the chapters, you have entered into reflection and conversation on what you have learned. You have heeded the Word and have let Scripture guide your reflection. You have engaged the content of the chapters as they relate to your world. You have kept moving forward in that engagement. And finally, you have brought all that to prayer.

William Wilberforce was not in any sense of the term a "lone ranger." Quite the contrary! He was a participant in a community of friends and colleagues that provided mutual support and constant challenge to one another to bring about a better society. Wilberforce experienced a profound religious conversion. Yet, that conversion did not drive him away from the cares and concerns of the world. At the advice of Newton and others, his conversion made him an effective worker for change. He was immersed in the politics of the day, and his whole life was spent to benefit society.

Wilberforce's life and mission was a living example of an extremely brief and simple Gospel parable.

> *The kingdom of heaven is like the yeast that a woman took and mixed in with three measures of flour until all of it was leavened.*
>
> *Matthew 13:33*

This simple parable was quite a radical departure for those who heard it. Yeast was considered a symbol of corruption. In celebrating their liberation the Jewish people would cast away the yeast and eat unleavened bread. Yet the parable said that the very kingdom of heaven is like yeast. Wilberforce and the Clapham circle entered their world—they became the leaven that caused the entire loaf of British society to rise. They changed the world for the better—*from the inside.*

An Attitude

The world you live in is your "three measures of flour." That world is filled with problems: the potential for nuclear proliferation, increased political instability in the Middle East, Islamic jihad, genocide in Africa, active human trafficking, and the sex trade. There are signs of fundamental dishonesty, deception, corruption, meanness of spirit, and personal immorality. There are also business scandals, slanderous political campaigns, the abuse of children, the corruption and over-consumption of natural resources, the collapse of families, and many more. There are signs of a general disregard and disrespect of the rights and feelings of others. Where are the signs of hope?

Almost every culture in the world has some form of the Golden Rule—doing unto others as you would have them do unto you. But even the Golden Rule has fallen into disrepair. The Golden Rule is an attitude, not a law. The Golden Rule seems to be quite straightforward and without any modifying clauses or restrictions. Yet if you carefully observe how it is interpreted in society, you will notice that observance of the Golden Rule falls into one of four categories:

1. ***Exclusive & Passive:*** This category is summed up in one simple sentence: "I will not harm those dear to me." The Golden Rule becomes a boundary outside of which are those beyond my concern. Even inside the boundary, there is no positive action on behalf of others. There is only the attitude of not doing any harm. This interpretation has come to dominate in contemporary society. It provides a sense of self-approval without any significant effort or sacrifice.

2. ***Inclusive & Passive:*** In this category of observance, the boundary is gone but the passivity remains. There are two sentences for this interpretation: "I mean no harm." and "I see no harm in this." The basic attitude in this interpretation centers on intention and not on action. It is an attitude of generic benevolence without test or reflection.

3. ***Exclusive & Active:*** In this category of interpretation the boundary is back. It is best summed up in the sentence: "I take care of my own." In this interpretation, charity begins at home—and it stays at home. There is a limited willingness to help those who are "like me." Outside

the boundary, however, concern vanishes into attitudes that range from casual and disinterested observation to genuine disdain. Actions falling into this category show a certain generosity of spirit, but that generosity is usually in support of family, of friends, or (in its broadest application) of likeminded people.

4. *Inclusive & Active:* The fourth category is outgoing, generous, and knows no boundaries. It is best summed up in the question: "How can I help?" This interpretation is that of the parable of the Good Samaritan. That parable took away all boundaries and defined neighborliness in active terms. Often great tragedies—floods, fires, terrorist attacks, and the like—elicit an active and inclusive response from people of good will. People imbued with the attitude that is the Golden Rule, however, maintain the attitude at all times and in all places.

Few people's actions consistently fall within one or another of the categories of interpretation. Yet it is also true that the fourth interpretation has taken some significant losses in recent years. The losses have been attributed to a "me" generation. Yet the losses are also a result of changes in society. War and strife, information overload, fears for safety and security, great and evident diversity, all often cause people—even generous people—to recoil.

The world is so small that anyone can be anywhere with the click of a mouse button. At the same time the world has never been larger and more complex. The explosion of information makes it harder and harder for people to sift through the chaff and discover the wheat. In addition, public figures and demagogues, in order to perpetuate power and influence, use all possible means to keep people divided, worried, angry, and afraid.

That is not the Wilberforce way. For him a prime motivator was his constant realization of the grace he had received. He understood that of one who has received so much, much would be required. True religion needed an *external* manifestation. It needed to be reflected in personal morality and in a thirst for the good of others—a thirst for justice.

A Benefit

One of the keen benefits of reading and sharing this book ought be a personal commitment to work on behalf of others. Wilberforce both understood and believed in such a commitment. Writing in A Practical View of Christianity, he explains how he came at his commitment from a Christian perspective:

> *True Christians consider themselves not as satisfying some rigorous creditor, but as discharging a debt of gratitude. Theirs is accordingly not the stinted return of constrained obedience, but the large and liberal measure of voluntary service. This principle, therefore, as was formerly remarked and as has been recently observed of true Christian humility, prevents a thousand practical embarrassments by which they are continually harassed, who act from a less generous motive and who require it to be clearly ascertained to them, that any gratification or worldly compliance which may be in question is beyond the allowed boundary line of Christian practice. This principle regulates the true Christian's choice of companions and friends, where he is at liberty to make an option; this fills him with the desire of promoting the temporal well-being of all around him and, still more, with pity and love and anxious solicitude for their spiritual welfare. Indifference indeed in this respect is one of the surest signs of low or declining state in Religion. This animating principle it is, which in the true Christian's happier hour inspires his devotions and causes him to delight in the worship of God; which fills him with consolation and peace and gladness and sometimes even enables him "to rejoice with joy unspeakable and full of glory" (1 Peter 1:8).*

It is important to remember that although this commitment to work on behalf of others is indeed a hallmark of Christianity, it is not exclusively Christian territory. An example of such a commitment from Jewish life is the mitzvah (a term that means "blessing," "commandment," and "covenant") known as *tikkun olam*. Literally translated this obligation is "repairing the earth." It is used to describe the divine command to work personally, corporately, and consistently for social justice in the world.

Better Hour Gatherings

If you have profited from the experience you are having with this book, one way to spread the word of this kind of commitment is to form and foster gatherings of people who are willing to share this commitment. These gatherings can be the source for discovering community issues that need to be addressed. They can provide mutual inspiration and fellowship in the task of working for a better world. They can also magnify the concerns and passions of the individual participants. There is no need for these groups to be exclusively made up of committed Christians. Anyone should be welcome.

Readers of this book who want to maintain and sustain their commitment to work on behalf of others will find help and guidance in forming and participating in Better Hour Gatherings at www.thebetterhour.com/tbh/Gatherings.

Challenging Young People

A most important element of a commitment to work on behalf of others is to engage and involve young people in the process. Younger children will observe the commitment of their parents and other family members. They can participate along with their parents or older siblings. Teenagers and young adults, however, need to be engaged and challenged to use their own creativity and their own friendships in an effort to make their world a better place.

A good spinoff from your own engagement as a gathering or group would be to invite some young people to gather as well. The young people in your families, in church youth groups, or in other young people's organizations are a great starting point. It is even more helpful if the young people are good friends. Invite the young people to join you in one of your gatherings. Then challenge them to do the following:

1. To get together on their own in a Clapham-like circle of friends.
2. As a group they can investigate their communities— schools, neighborhoods, towns, cities, and so forth—to find a pressing social need they can address.

3. Then they can define the problem and assess what resources it will take to make a change for the better. They will soon develop a passion for addressing the problem.
4. Next, they can agree to work together for a specific amount of time to actually address the problem.
5. Urge the young people to work thoughtfully and generously.
6. Finally, encourage the young people to document in some way the effect they had on the problem.

You and your circle of friends can provide help, supervision, and resources, but the young people can and should do the work themselves. Such challenging activity will set young people on a path where they can see that part of the meaning of their life on earth is connected to the work they do for others. Be sure to celebrate their efforts and provide community reinforcement to the young people who undertake your challenge. Let them experience the joy of living an attitude of service and selflessness.

For stories of young people who have been challenged to make a difference in their world, see www.thebetterhour.com/tbh/Contest.

Conclusion

The world needs the Wilberforce spirit. Around the world and right on your doorstep are the little ones that Jesus mentioned in his parable of the great judgment. When William Wilberforce asked the question, "Lord, when was it that I saw you?" he no doubt got the warm response: "Just as you did to the least of these, you did it to me." The recipe is simple and yet profoundly challenging. Give food to the hungry. Give drink to the thirsty. Clothe the naked. Free the captives. Visit the imprisoned and the sick. Your combined actions will make a difference. You will have helped create the better hour!

THREE

1. *Robert Isaac Wilberforce & Samuel Wilberforce*, THE LIFE OF WILLIAM WILBERFORCE (London, John Murray, 1838), 4. See the endpapers for the precise wording of Wilberforce's mission statement. There, a facsimile of Wilberforce's diary entry, in his own handwriting, is presented.

2. *Robert Isaac Wilberforce & Samuel Wilberforce*, THE LIFE OF WILLIAM WILBERFORCE (London, John Murray, 1838), 142.

3. Ibid.

4. Ibid, 319.

5. *Robert Isaac Wilberforce & Samuel Wilberforce*, "Letter from Wilberforce to President Thomas Jefferson," 3:374.

6. See *William Wilberforce*, A PRACTICAL VIEW OF CHRISTIANITY, ed. *Kevin Belmonte* (Peabody, Massachusetts: Hendrickson Publishers, 1996).

7. *Sir James Stephen*, ESSAYS IN ECCLESIASTICAL BIOGRAPHY (London: Longman, Brown, Green & Longmans, 1849), 2:216.

8. Ibid.

9. *Robert Wilberforce & Samuel Wilberforce*, 5:298–99.

10. *Robert Wilberforce & Samuel Wilberforce*, 1:252.

11. Ibid.

12. *Robert Wilberforce & Samuel Wilberforce*, 5:315.

13. *Robert Wilberforce & Samuel Wilberforce*, 1:79.

14. *William Wilberforce*, A PRACTICAL VIEW OF CHRISTIANITY, 183–84.

15. *Robert Wilberforce & Samuel Wilberforce*, 5:229.

16. *Sir James Stephen*, 2:272–73.

17. Ibid, 73.

18. *William Wilberforce*, A PRACTICAL VIEW OF CHRISTIANITY, 120.

19. *Robert Wilberforce & Samuel Wilberforce*, 1:349.

20. *G.M. Trevelyan*, ILLUSTRATED ENGLISH SOCIAL HISTORY (London Longmans, Green & Co., 1952), 4:32.

21. *William Jay*, THE AUTOBIOGRAPHY OF THE REV. WILLIAM JAY, ed. *John Angell James & George Redford* (London: Hamilton, Adams and Co., 1855), 311–12.

22. Ibid, 307–308.

23. *Robert Wilberforce & Samuel Wilberforce*, 1:171–72.

24. *Robert Wilberforce & Samuel Wilberforce*, 4:314.

25. *William Wilberforce*, "Retrospect of the Year 1801," CHRISTIAN OBSERVER (January 1802): 59–60. William Wilberforce was identified as the author of this article by a reference to it in THE LIFE OF WILLIAM WILBERFORCE (3:24).

26. Ibid, 49.

27. *Robert Wilberforce & Samuel Wilberforce*, 1:128.

28. Ibid, 297.

29. See *Frederick Douglass*, THE LIFE AND TIMES OF FREDERICK DOUGLASS: HIS EARLY LIFE AS A SLAVE, HIS ESCAPE FROM BONDAGE, AND HIS COMPLETE HISTORY TO THE PRESENT TIME.

30. See *John Pollock*, WILLIAM WILBERFORCE: A MAN WHO CHANGED HIS TIMES (Burke, VA: Trinity Forum, 1996).

31. *Sir James Stephen*, 2:225.

32. *Robert Wilberforce & Samuel Wilberforce*, 1:119.

33. *William Wilberforce*, AN APPEAL TO THE RELIGION, JUSTICE AND HUMANITY OF THE INHABITANTS OF THE BRITISH EMPIRE, IN BEHALF OF NEGRO SLAVES IN THE WEST INDIES (London: J. Hatchard, 1823), 54.

34. *William Wilberforce*, A PRACTICAL VIEW OF CHRISTIANITY, 5.

35. *Robert Wilberforce & Samuel Wilberforce*, 1:111.

36. *William Wilberforce*, A PRACTICAL VIEW OF CHRISTIANITY, 86.

37. Ibid, 37.

38. Ibid, 167.

39. *Ernest Marshall Howse*, SAINTS IN POLITICS, THE "CLAPHAM SECT" AND THE GROWTH OF FREEDOM (London: George Allen & Unwin Ltd., 1952), 38.

40. Ibid, 39.

41. *Kevin Belmonte*, HERO FOR HUMANITY: A BIOGRAPHY OF WILLIAM WILBERFORCE (Colorado Springs, Colorado: NavPress, 2002), 248.

42. *A Christian [William Wilberforce]*, "The Duty of Great Britain to Dissemble Christianity in India," CHRISTIAN OBSERVER 125 (1812): 261–72. In 1812, Wilberforce wrote this open letter under the pen name of "A Christian." Wilberforce's citation of the golden rule appears in this letter.

43. *Belmonte*, 195.

44. Ibid, 318.

45. *Robert Wilberforce & Samuel Wilberforce*, 5:184.

46. *American Rhetoric: Online Speech Bank*, "John F. Kennedy: Address to a Joint Convention of the General Court of The Commonwealth of Massachusetts," http://www. americanrhetoric.com/speeches/jfkcommonwealthmass.htm.

47. *Belmonte*, 248.

FOUR

1. See *Henry Thompson*, THE LIFE OF HANNAH MORE: WITH NOTICES OF HER SISTERS (London: T. Cadell, 1838).

2. See *William Roberts*, MEMOIRS OF THE LIFE AND CORRESPONDENCE OF MRS. HANNAH MORE (New York: Harper & Brothers, 1834).

3. *Hannah More*, THE WORKS OF HANNAH MORE (New York: Harper & Brothers, 1852), 323.

4. *William Roberts*, MEMOIRS OF THE LIFE AND CORRESPONDENCE OF MRS. HANNAH MORE (New York: Harper & Bros., 1835), 2:82.

5. See *Mary Alden Hopkins*, HANNAH MORE AND HER CIRCLE (London: Longmans, 1947).

6. *Hannah More*, THE WORKS OF HANNAH MORE (New York: Harper and Bros., 1852), 190.

7. See *Mary Alden Hopkins*, HANNAH MORE AND HER CIRCLE (New York, Toronto: Longmans, Green and Co., 1947).

8. See *Frank Prochaska*, THE VOLUNTARY IMPULSE: PHILANTHROPY IN MODERN BRITAIN (London: Faber and Faber, 1988).

9. See *Ray Strachey*, THE CAUSE: A SHORT HISTORY OF THE WOMEN'S MOVEMENT IN BRITAIN (London: Bell & Sons, 1928).

10. *Charlotte Mary Yonge*, HANNAH MORE (London: W.H. Allen & Co., 1888), 196.

11. See *Charles Howard Ford*, HANNAH MORE: A CRITICAL BIOGRAPHY (New York: Peter Lang, 1996).

FIVE

1. See *Al Gore*, COMMON SENSE GOVERNMENT (New York: Random House, 1995).

2. *David S. Broder*, "Cure for Nation's Cynicism Eludes Its Leaders," WASHINGTON POST, 4 February, 1996, p. A1.

3. *Boris Pasternak*, "After the Storm" (1958).

4. Deuteronomy 32:30 (New Revised Standard Version).

5. See *John Pollock*, WILLIAM WILBERFORCE (Eastbourne, England: Kingsway Publications, 2007).

6. *Robert Isaac Wilberforce & Samuel Wilberforce*, THE LIFE OF WILLIAM WILBERFORCE (London: John Murray, 1837), 315.

7. See Wilberforce's letter to Speaker Addington.

8. See *John Pollock*, WILBERFORCE (London: Constable and Company, 1977).

SIX

1. Clarkson & Wilberforce did not create the first so-called "pressure group." They were, however, pioneers in organizing such groups and in developing techniques to mobilize public opinion. One must be careful not to claim too much for Clarkson and Wilberforce.

2. The term "co-belligerence" is one coined by cultural scholar Dr. Os Guinness with reference to the collaborative work of Wilberforce and the members of the Clapham circle.

3. "A point kindred to one made." See *Kevin Belmonte*, TRAVEL WITH WILBERFORCE: THE FRIEND OF HUMANITY (Leominster, England: Day One Publications, 2006): "Thornton and Wilberforce were, by themselves, something less than what they were together. Over time, they both began to see how they complemented each other."

4. A thematic emphasis of *E.M. Howse's* SAINTS IN POLITICS, (Toronto: University of Toronto Press, 1952).

5. *Robert Isaac Wilberforce and Samuel Wilberforce*, THE LIFE OF WILLIAM WILBERFORCE (London: John Murray, 1838), 1:230.

6. *Robert & Samuel Wilberforce*, 3:268.

7. *Robert & Samuel Wilberforce*, 1:171–172.

8. *Adam Hochschild*, BURY THE CHAINS: PROPHETS AND REBELS IN THE FIGHT TO FREE AN EMPIRE'S SLAVES (Boston: Houghton Mifflin, 2005), 155.

10. *Hochschild*, 129.

SEVEN

1. *Anti-Slavery International,* "Directors Report for the year ended 31 March 2005," http://www.antislavery.org/homepage/resources/PDF/accounts%202005.pdf, 2.

2. A GLOBAL ALLIANCE AGAINST FORCED LABOR: GLOBAL REPORT UNDER THE FOLLOW-UP TO THE ILO DECLARATION ON FUNDAMENTAL PRINCIPLES AND RIGHTS AT WORK (Geneva, Switzerland: International Labor Office, 2005), 10.

3. *Centre for Human Rights,* A COMPILATION OF INTERNATIONAL INSTRUMENTS (New York and Geneva: United Nations, 1988), 160.

4. Article 4 of the Universal Declaration of Human Rights states: "No one shall be held in slavery or servitude; slavery and the slave trade shall be prohibited in all their forms."

5. A GLOBAL ALLIANCE AGAINST FORCED LABOR, 46.

6. *Coalition to Abolish Slavery & Trafficking (CAST),* News release (Los Angeles, CA: Bahan & Associates, 27 April 2006). In 2004, Mimin Mintarsih was helped by a Good Samaritan who put her in contact with the Los Angeles-based non-governmental organization CAST. CAST has provided Mimin with case management services and safe accommodation in their shelter for trafficked people. On 27 April 2006, Mimin's former employer, Dennis Lam, President of Guaranty Bank of California, and his wife Dina, were found guilty of bringing her to the United States illegally and forcing her to work without pay. She was awarded $832,000.

7. *United States Department of State,* TRAFFICKING IN PERSONS REPORT (Washington, DC, 14 June 2004), 23.

8. Anti–Slavery International interview, Cacchioli, Romana, Niger, 2004.

9. *India,* BONDED LABOR (ABOLITION) ACT, 1976.

10. *Pakistan,* BONDED LABOR SYSTEM (ABOLITION) ACT, 1992.

11. *Nepal,* KAMAIYA LABOR (PROHIBITION) ACT, 2002.

12. Anti-Slavery International interview, Upadhyaya, Krishna Prasad, India, 2004.

13. A GLOBAL ALLIANCE AGAINST FORCED LABOR, 15.

14. Children's rights, including the right to education, rest, and recreation, are protected under the United Nations Convention on the Rights of the Child (1989). All countries have signed this convention, with the exception of Somalia and the United States.

15. Visayan Forum, "Child domestic workers," www.visayanforum.org.

16. Anti-Slavery International interview, Williams, Sarah, Philippines, 20.

NINE

1. *H.H. McFarland*, "How American Women are Helping Their Sisters," THE NEW ENGLANDER 32 (New Haven: W.L. Kingsley, 1873), 659.

2. *Thomas Babington Macaulay*, Baron Macaulay, THE MISCELLANEOUS WRITINGS AND SPEECHES OF LORD MACAULAY (Whitefish, MT: Kessinger Publishing, 2004), 4:119.

3. Ibid.

ELEVEN

1. *Freedom House*, FREEDOM IN THE WORLD 2006: THE ANNUAL SURVEY OF POLITICAL RIGHTS AND CIVIL LIBERTIES (Lanham, MD: Rowman & Littlefield Publishers, 2006), www.freedomhouse.org.

2. *George Pratt Shultz*, "A More Accountable World?" MEDITERRANEAN QUARTERLY 13, no. 3, 2002.

3. Adel Al-Jubeir, interview by Tony Snow, FOX NEWS SUNDAY, FOX, May 18, 2003.

4. *Elaine Sciolino*, "Don't Weaken Arafat, Saudi Warns Bush," NEW YORK TIMES, 27 January 2002.

5. *Alex Alexiev*, "Wahhabism: State-Sponsored Extremism Worldwide." Testimony before U.S. Senate Subcommittee on Terrorism, Technology and Homeland Security, 26 June 2003.

6. *Steven Stalinsky*, "Inside the Saudi Classroom," NATIONAL REVIEW ONLINE, 7 February 2003, www.nationalreview.com/comment/comment-stalinsky020703.asp.

7. *U.S. Department of State*, INTERNATIONAL RELIGIOUS FREEDOM REPORT 2005 (Washington, DC, 2005, www.state.gov/g/drl/rls/irf/2005/51609.htm.

8. *Nina Shea*, "Saudi Arabia: Friend or Foe in the War on Terror." Testimony before the Committee on the Judiciary. U.S. Senate, 8 November 2005.

9. *Abdurrahman Wahid*, "Right Islam vs. Wrong Islam," THE WALL STREET JOURNAL, 30 December 2005.

TWELVE

1. *John Silber*, "The Media and Our Children: Who is Responsible," WINGSPREAD JOURNAL (Winter 1996), 11–13.

2. *Roger Kimball*, "You are Not Excused," THE WALL STREET JOURNAL, 13 July 1999.

3. *Judith Martin & Gunther S. Stent*, "I Think; Therefore I Thank: A Philosophy of Etiquette," AMERICAN SCHOLAR 59 (Spring 1990), 245.

4. *Thomas Hobbes*, DE CIVE (London: J.C. for R. Royston, 1651), 9.

5. *Judith Martin*, "The Oldest Virtue," in SEEDBEDS OF VIRTUE: SOURCE OF COMPETENCE, CHARACTER AND CITIZENSHIP IN AMERICAN SOCIETY, Mary Ann Glendon and David Blankenhorn, eds. (Lanham, MD: Madison Books, 1995), 67.

6. See *Richard Brookhiser*, RULES OF CIVILITY: THE 110 PRECEPTS THAT GUIDED OUR FIRST PRESIDENT IN WAR AND PEACE (New York: Free Press, 1997).

7. See *Aristotle*, "The Ethics of Aristotle: The Nicomachean Ethics," (Allen & Unwin, 1953).

8. See *Edmund Burke*, REFLECTIONS ON THE REVOLUTION IN FRANCE (New Haven: Yale University Press, 2003).

9. *Lee Bockhorn*, "Do Manners Matter?" THE WEEKLY STANDARD, 16 August 1999, 36.

10. *J. Budziszewski*, "The Moral Case for Manners," NATIONAL REVIEW 47, no. 3 (20 February 1995), 64.

11. *Budziszewski*, 62.

12. *Alexis de Tocqueville*, DEMOCRACY IN AMERICA, trans. Henry Reeve (New York: D. Appleton & Company, 1899), 2:809.

13. *Michael J. Sandel*, "Making Nice is Not the Same as Doing Good," NEW YORK TIMES, 29 December 1996.

14. *Kenneth L. Woodward*, "What is Virtue?" NEWSWEEK, 13 June 1994, 38.

15. *Allen Ehrenhalt*, "Learning from the Fifties," Wilson Quarterly, (Summer 1995), 19.

16. *Ehrenhalt*, 8.

17. From "Images of Ourselves: Washington and Hollywood," a speech by *Bill Bennett* to The Center for the Study of Popular Culture, 24 February 1996.

18. *James Morris*, "Democracy Beguiled," Wilson Quarterly, (August–September 1996), 24.

19. *James Wolcott*, "Dating Your Dad," The New Republic, 31 March 1997, 32.

20. *Jonathan Alter*, "The Name of the Game is Shame," Newsweek, 12 December 1994, 41.

21. *Mark Caldwell*, "A Short History of Rudeness: Manners, Morals and Misbehavior in Modern America" (Picador, 2000), 4.

22. *Ted Anthony*, "Speed," Lancaster Sunday News, Lancaster, PA.

23. *David Masci*, "A Lesson in Civility," Washington Times, 25 September 1995.

24. *Caldwell*, 4.

25. *John Marks*, "The American Uncivil Wars," U.S. News and World Report, 22 April 1996, 67–68.

26. *Marks*.

27. *Don E. Eberly*, "Civil Society: The Paradox of American Progress," Essays on Civil Society 1, no. 2 (January 1996), 2.

28. *Michael Kelly*, "The Age of No Class," Washington Post, 11 August 1999, A19.

29. *Associated Press*, "Man Dies After Road Rage Attack," 23 November 1999.

30. *Associated Press*, "Loudmouth Parents Must Take Ethics Course for Kids' Games," 18 November 1999.

31. *Gil Smart*, "Bumper Sticker Shock," Lancaster Sunday News, Lancaster, PA, 11 November 1999.

32. *Elizabeth Austin*, "A Small Plea to Delete a Ubiquitous Expletive," U.S. News and World Report, 6 April 1988, 58.

33. *Morris*, 24.

34. *Martin & Stent*, 245.

35. *Bockhorn*, 36.

THIRTEEN

1. *Richard R. Follett*, Evangelicalism, Penal Theory and Criminal Law Reform in England, 1808–30, (New York: Palgrave Macmillan, 2001), 94.

2. *William Wilberforce*, Practical View of the Prevailing Religious Systems of Professed Christians, in the Higher and Middle Classes, Contrasted with Real Christianity, (New York: Leavitt, Lord & Co., 1835), 319.

3. *Hannah More*, The Works of Hannah More (New York: Harper & Brothers, 1852), 274.

4. *Mark Caldwell*, A Short History of Rudeness: Manners, Morals, and Misbehavior in Modern America (New York: Picador, 2000), 23.

5. "Washington's Farewell Address 1796" (The Avalon Project at Yale Law School, 1996), http://www.yale.edu/lawweb/avalon/washing.htm.

6. *Jeffrey H. Morrison*, John Witherspoon and the Founding of the American Republic (University of Notre Dame Press, 2005), 28.

7. See *Kevin Belmonte*, William Wilberforce: A Hero for Humanity (Grand Rapids: Zondewan Publishing Company, 2007).

8. See *Ernest Howse*, Saints in Politics: The "Clapham Sect" and the Growth of Freedom (London: Allen & Unwin, 1971).

9. See *Ernest Howse*, Saints in Politics: The "Clapham Sect" and the Growth of Freedom (London: Allen & Unwin, 1971).

10. *Michael S. Malone*, "The Indie Movie Mogul," Wired, February 2006.

FOURTEEN

1. Universal Declaration of Human Rights, G.A. res. 217A (III), U.N. Doc. A/810, Preamble (1948).

2. U.S. Declaration of Independence, National Archives, http://www.archives.gov/national-archives-experience/charters/declaration_transcript.html

3. *Eleanor Roosevelt*, "The Promise of Human Rights," Foreign Affairs 26 (April 1948): 470–477.

4. *Charles Malik*, "1948—The Drafting of the Universal Declaration of Human Rights," U.N. Bull. Hum. Rts. 97 (1986).

5. *Eleanor Roosevelt*, "Making Human Rights Come Alive" (speech, Pi Lambda Theta at Columbia University, New York, March 30, 1949).

6. *Harry Truman*, Closing the United Nations Conference (1945), reprinted in Truman Speaks 56 (Cyril Clemens, ed., 1969).

7. See *O. Frederick Nolde*, Free & Equal: Human Rights in Ecumenical Perspective, with an Introduction by Charles Malik (Geneva: World Council of Churches, 1968).

8. U.N. Human Rights Commission, Second Session, Drafting Committee, 10, U.N. Doc. E/CN.4/AC.1/SR.11.

9. See *Joseph P. Lash*, Eleanor: The Years Alone, (New York: W.W. Norton Company, 1972).

FIFTEEN

1. Encyclopaedia Britannica Online, "Slavery in the 21st Century," (by *Charles A. Jacobs*), http://search.eb.com.ezp. lndlibrary.org/eb/article-9344443.

2. *Hugh Thomas*, The Slave Trade: The History of the Atlantic Slave Trade 1440–1870 (New York: Simon & Schuster, 1997), 805–6.

3. *Bernard Lewis*, Race and Slavery in the Middle East: An Historical Enquiry (New York: Oxford University Press, 1990), 79.

SIXTEEN

1. National Association of Evangelicals website, www.nae.net/index.cfm?FUSEACTION=editor.page&pageID=48&IDCategory=9.

2. *James Davison Hunter*, Culture Wars: The Struggle to Define America (New York: Basic Books, 1992), 104.

SEVENTEEN

1. For this letter and all others discussed, see *David Blankenhorn*, The Islam/West Debate: Documents from a Global Debate on Terrorism, U.S. Policy and the Middle East (Lanham, Md: Rowman & Littlefield, 2005), http://www.americanvalues.org/contentsforweb.pdf.

2. National Commission on Terrorist Attacks Upon the United States, http://www.9-11commission.gov/report/911Report_Ch12.htm

3. *Ann Coulter*, "This is War," 13 September 2001, NATIONAL REVIEW ONLINE, http://www.nationalreview.com/coulter/coulter.shtml.

EIGHTEEN

1. *John Piper*, AMAZING GRACE IN THE LIFE OF WILLIAM WILBERFORCE (Crossway Books, 2007), 13.

2. *Robert Isaac Wilberforce & Samuel Wilberforce*, THE LIFE OF WILLIAM WILBERFORCE, (London: John Murray, 1838), 1:149.

3. *Charles Colson*, KINGDOMS IN CONFLICT (Grand Rapids: Zondervan Publishing, 1989), 101.

4. Ibid.

5. *John Piper*, AMAZING GRACE IN THE LIFE OF WILLIAM WILBERFORCE (Crossway Books, 2007), 38.

6. Taste—Review and Outlook, "Jesus Saves," WALL STREET JOURNAL, 20 June 2003, Eastern edition.

TWENTY

1. The original bibliographic information for this document is: "Eulogium on the life and Character of William Wilberforce. Esq. Delivered and Published at the request of the People of Color of the City of New York, Twenty-Second of October, 1833, by Benjamin F. Hughes, (A Man of Color)" (New York: Printed at the Office of the Emancipator, 1833).

2. A citation from Book 18 of *Alexander Pope's* translation of *Homer's* ODYSSEY.

3. Cross-reference the Old Testament book of Isaiah 42:22. The phrase "robbed and peeled" also occurs in several other early African-American sources, including a book entitled SERMONS, SPEECHES AND LETTERS ON SLAVERY..., by *Gilbert Haven*, (Boston: Lee and Shepard, 1869). Thus, the phrase "robbed and peeled" appears to have been a recurring one in early African-American literature.

4. Again, a citation from Book 18 of *Alexander Pope's* translation of *Homer's* ODYSSEY.

5. In 1788 Wilberforce nearly died from a severe case of what appears to have been ulcerative colitis.

6. A reference to the atrocities committed by the captain and crew of the slave ship *Zong*, who in 1783 had thrown 132 slaves overboard alive during a severe epidemic when

the ship's water supply had run low. The great abolitionist pioneer Granville Sharp sought to have the captain and those complicit with him tried for murder, but when this case came to trial, the Lord Chief Justice Mansfield ruled against Sharp saying: "it was as if horses had been thrown overboard." See page 68 of *Robin Furneaux's* WILLIAM WILBERFORCE, (London: Hamish Hamilton, 1974).

7. For a detailed description of the Clapham circle's philanthropic sponsorship of the education of African children in England, see pages 241–2 of *Michael Hennell's* JOHN VENN AND THE CLAPHAM SECT (London: Lutterworth Press, 1958).

8. Hughes is here quoting lines 13–16 and 49–56 of Englishman *William Cowper's* anti-slavery poem THE NEGRO'S COMPLAINT, first published in 1793.

9. Wilberforce's celebrated speech of 12 May 1789 was published as THE SPEECH OF WILLIAM WILBERFORCE, ESQ., REPRESENTATIVE FOR THE COUNTY OF YORK, ON THE QUESTION OF THE ABOLITION OF THE SLAVE TRADE, (London: The Logographic, 1789). In a 2006 BBC documentary series and book, Lord Melvyn Bragg listed Wilberforce's speech as one of 12 BOOKS THAT CHANGED THE WORLD. Other books so listed include *Charles Darwin's* ON THE ORIGIN OF SPECIES, *Isaac Newton's* PRINCIPIA MATHEMATICA, *Mary Wollstonecraft's* A VINDICATION OF THE RIGHTS OF WOMAN, and *William Shakespeare's* FIRST FOLIO.

10. For the entire text of this speech, see *Hansard's* PARLIAMENTARY DEBATES. Wilberforce gave this speech on 18 April 1791.

11. These words were written by *Thomas Clarkson* in his two-volume HISTORY OF THE RISE, PROGRESS, AND ACCOMPLISHMENT OF THE ABOLITION OF THE AFRICAN SLAVE-TRADE BY THE BRITISH PARLIAMENT (London: Longman, Hurst, Rees and Orme, 1808).

12. The vote in the House of Commons to end the British slave trade took place on 23 February 1807. This bill received the royal assent—that is, it became law on 25 March 1807.

13. Hughes is referring to *Wilberforce's* book A PRACTICAL VIEW OF THE PREVAILING RELIGIOUS SYSTEM OF PROFESSED CHRISTIANS, IN THE HIGHER AND MIDDLE CLASSES IN THIS COUNTRY, CONTRASTED WITH REAL CHRISTIANITY (London: Thomas Cadell, 1797). An apologia for his faith as well as a blueprint for fostering the good society, Wilberforce's book had a profound effect upon the late eighteenth and early nineteenth centuries. Edmund Burke and the noted agriculturalist and travel writer Arthur Young were among the tens of thousands deeply influenced by

their reading of it. Burke had it read to him as he was dying and declared: "If I live, I shall thank Wilberforce for having sent such a book into the world."

14. It appears that Hughes is quoting here from a British newspaper's obituary or from a funeral sermon for Wilberforce. Such accounts would have arrived by ship from England, along with the news of Wilberforce's passing.

15. Again, it appears that Hughes is quoting here from a British newspaper's obituary or from a funeral sermon for Wilberforce.

16. For a detailed account of this protest by Wilberforce, conducted in concert with the American abolitionist William Lloyd Garrison, see the final chapter of *Kevin Belmonte's* WILLIAM WILBERFORCE: A HERO FOR HUMANITY (Grand Rapids, Michigan: Zondervan Publishing, 2007).

selected bibliography

The following short list of works will provide further reading on the life and times and the lessons of William Wilberforce.

Belmonte, Kevin Charles. HERO FOR HUMANITY. Colorado Springs: Navpress, 2002.

Deverell, Liz & Gareth Watkins. WILBERFORCE AND HULL. Hull, Kingston Press: 2000.

Furneaux, Robin. WILLIAM WILBERFORCE. London: Hamish Hamilton, 1974.

Hochschild, Adam. BURY THE CHAINS: THE BRITISH STRUGGLE TO ABOLISH SLAVERY. London: Macmillan, 2005.

Hill, Clifford. THE WILBERFORCE CONNECTION. Oxford: Monarch Books, 2004.

Lean, Garth. GOD'S POLITICIAN. London: Darton, Longman, & Todd, 1980.

Metaxas, Eric. AMAZING GRACE. San Francisco: HarperSanFrancisco, 2007.

Pollock, John. WILBERFORCE. London: Constable, 1977.

Scharma, Simon. ROUGH CROSSINGS: BRITAIN, THE SLAVES, AND THE AMERICAN REVOLUTION. London: BBC Books, 2005.

Walvin, James. BLACK IVORY: A HISTORY OF BRITISH SLAVERY. London: HarperCollins, 1992.

Warner, Oliver. WILLIAM WILBERFORCE AND HIS TIMES. London: Batsford, 1962.

Wilberforce, Robert Isaac, & Samuel Wilberforce. THE LIFE OF WILLIAM WILBERFORCE. 5 Vols. London: Murray, 1838.

Wilberforce, William. A PRACTICAL VIEW OF THE PREVAILING RELIGIOUS SYSTEM OF PROFESSED CHRISTIANS IN THE HIGHER AND MIDDLE CLASSES IN THIS COUNTRY, CONTRASTED WITH REAL CHRISTIANITY. London: T. Cadell, 1797.

————. PRACTICAL CHRISTIANITY. Edited by Kevin Charles Belmonte. Peabody, MA: Hendrickson, 1996.